Practical Guide to

Leaders can shape an organisation through their behaviours and their vision. If an organisation lacks a clear vision or there is disengagement by the leadership team, then the results can be disastrous. In such circumstances change is needed. When change is needed, the value of safety can become a change agent. From the disciplines of leadership and safety comes the emerging topic of safety leadership. Through safety leadership, workplace challenges can be rectified and the desired behaviours reinforced.

These challenges can span from a lack of leadership engagement, poor safety performance, complacency or lack of safety ownership. Understanding how safety leadership differs from other leadership theories can give you a competitive edge which is not solely based upon financial quotas, but instead based upon the moral code of ensuring the health and well-being of your employees.

This book goes beyond mere safety slogans or anecdotal stories that relate to safety leadership. Instead an empirical and research-based approach will be shared which can help improve the overall culture of an organisation as well as the safety of employees. Tools, case studies, theories and practical applications will be shared which can help create the blueprint for organisational change that you seek. Even when things are working well, constant innovation and adoption of best practices can help companies go from good to great and leave a lasting legacy for employees and customers alike.

Detailing the mechanics of safety leadership, this book will drive the change and results you want.

Luke Daniel is a registered psychologist with over 15 years' experience consulting, coaching and developing leaders across the globe. His work has included facilitation of workshops across multiple continents as well as analysing workplace culture.

Practical Guide to Safety Leadership

An Evidence-Based Approach

Luke Daniel

Routledge
Taylor & Francis Group

LONDON AND NEW YORK

First published 2018
by Routledge
2 Park Square, Milton Park, Abingdon, Oxon OX14 4RN

and by Routledge
711 Third Avenue, New York, NY 10017

Routledge is an imprint of the Taylor & Francis Group, an informa business

British Library Cataloguing in Publication Data
A catalogue record for this book is available from the British Library

Library of Congress Cataloging in Publication Data
A catalog record for this book has been requested

ISBN: 978-1-138-20929-9 (hbk)
ISBN: 978-1-138-20930-5 (pbk)
ISBN: 978-1-3154-5737-6 (ebk)

Typeset in Times New Roman
by Taylor & Francis Books
Printed and bound by CPI Group (UK) Ltd, Croydon, CR0 4YY

Contents

Figures

Tables

Contributors

Michelle Oberg is Manager of Safety Research and Partnerships at Griffith University, Australia.

Sarah Colley is Managing Director of Pockets of Brilliance at The University of Queensland, Australia.

Jonathan Lincolne is the founder of a multi-national safety company.

Laura Graham is a registered psychologist and Manager of Systems and Implementation of Pockets of Brilliance, Australia.

Sidney Dekker is a Professor in the School of Humanities at Griffith University, Australia.

Introduction

Cutting through the motherhood statements

Imagine the following scenario: You are at an international conference that addresses the link between leadership and associated challenges with safety. The primed clichés are circling around, which include the often-touted 'visible felt leadership' or building a culture of 'commitment as opposed to compliance'.

A noteworthy industry professional bounds the stage and talks about their safety leadership journey, the language is captivating, the message is there but the details and nuances are void. The specifics and foundations of *how* safety leadership was achieved are jettisoned for the glory filled pie charts and graphics that detail reduced injury rates and improved safety statistics. Slowly a wave of frustration starts to build, as the safety leadership spiel happening on stage becomes more about statistics as opposed to the mechanics of safety influence. It becomes apparent that the definition of safety leadership is neglected like a lonely orphan waiting for their scraps of food or the welder who hasn't been shown what pipes to work on. A feeling of frustration sweeps over you, inherently you know that without any clear direction or guidance, the achieving of any safety process or goal may be inherently flawed.

The above conference experience is something I have endured multiple times. After seeing the same wheels turn and the same philosophies being promoted, it was time to contribute to the field and cut through the hyperbole surrounding safety leadership. The scientist in me was waiting to come out and get my 'geek on' through a total immersion of different research methodologies, statistics and data analysis techniques. Such work reached a crescendo through the completion of my doctorate based upon the meaty subject of safety leadership. After writing some journal articles and presenting some conference papers, there was an apparent need to share my research and experiences in a tangible way that can be grasped by organisational executives, leaders, practitioners, consultants, HSE managers or anyone who is looking for a way to implement change and craft influence through the banner of safety.

After spending many years as a consultant across the globe, I have been privy to the amount of money organisations can invest in or seemingly waste with consultants. Many consulting firms are implementing their intellectual property in an attempt to increase an organisation's effectiveness or safety performance. If left unchecked a dependency starts to build, where a company can only achieve results with the aide of outside assistance. When such a relationship is built, the costs will continue to blow out as scheduled courses fail to meet the quorum or leaders depend on outside advice as opposed to internal capabilities. This notion was recently evidenced on a plane trip across the continent where I was sitting next to the CEO of one of the biggest mining companies in the world. When I asked him about his view on consultants, he thoughtfully answered back that 'sometimes the trap with consultants is that they are an easy fix for lazy leaders'. In this response alone lies the need for a paradigm shift in how business is done. We are living in the age of the 'Jetsons' as opposed to the 'Flintstones' and our quest should be focused on building organisational self-sufficiency and sustainability.

I do recall one experience I had in rural Queensland, Australia when I met another consultant on site at an open-cut mine site. I just finished running a workshop and I walked past an interview room with the door open. Being the guy that I am who is always up for a chat, I reached out and introduced myself. It turns out that the gentleman was working for a consulting company and has spent the last three days on site conducting leadership coaching sessions. Ironically, out of 18 people on his list, only three people attended and those three people were the initial leaders that sourced his services to begin with. No doubt that if the company president got word that they were paying $7000 a day for roughly one coaching session within 12 hours, the process would be put to rest relatively quickly. Two months later, I went back to the same site and I saw my familiar comrade, doing what he did last time ... waiting eagerly for people to coach. If you know a consultant, or are a consultant or have employed a consultant, ask them about what has worked and what hasn't worked in a process implementation. No doubt they will have a couple of stories that will either make you laugh, smile, cry or shake your head in disbelief.

Safety leadership as a valid and noteworthy topic can be traced back to the advantages of leading with safety as detailed by Krause (2005) or other notable research by Read et al. (2010) who detailed the benign effects on organisational culture and workplace morale. Preventing injuries within the workplace is a moral cause and can reflect a humane society where individuals look out for each other. Other flow on reasons of why we focus on safety leadership can range from fiscal savings, improved safe production, improved workplace communication, greater organisational support and the development of a culture of care (Reid et al. 2008). For these benefits to be crystallised into common practice, safety leadership needs to be defined and a framework established which can allow others to emulate the cornerstones of safety leadership.

This book is a response to misspent efforts in improving or tackling safety leadership and is a blend of information, research, case studies, experiences and practical guidance notes. Each chapter will end with summary notes, practical suggestions and questions that help guide leaders in developing safety leadership capability within their company. Consider this book as a blueprint for change or a *how to guide* for implementing safety leadership within your organisation.

Chapter 1 will be detailing the core components that define safety leadership as well as how safety leadership is different from other schools of leadership. Through an empirical definition, a common understanding and context can be provided. Chapter 2 will be sharing the research behind specific safety leadership behaviours. Transforming the elusive and ethereal motherhood statements into practical observable behaviours can be the starting point for ensuring safety leadership is not a buzz word or zeitgeist. Chapter 3 will detail a model of safety leadership that can be applied to most organisations. By understanding the RAVE model, leaders can strengthen their safety leadership capability and develop future safety leaders in their own right. Linkages towards safety culture will be shared in Chapter 4 with guidance in analysing a safety culture and using data as a diagnostic tool to compensate the safety leadership paradigm. Passing fads and the importance of innovation and developing a learning organisation through the '5i' process will be discussed in Chapter 5. Through constant innovation, safety can evolve within the current technological revolution we are currently living within. With the foundations of safety leadership laid out, embedding the behaviours, concepts and ideas into the organisation will be discussed in Chapter 6. Without an adequate transfer of learning, all change initiatives made may have an ephemeral life span. Conclusions will be detailed in Chapter 7 as well as reflections and a pathway forward for leaders, practitioners and organisations.

For those individuals looking for the panacea or 'silver bullet' towards their safety leadership challenge, this book will be a well-utilised bible but not the overall answer guide. Empirical research, case studies and hard data will be shared, although nobody will know more about the intricacies and politics of your organisation like the people within your organisation. There will always be technological, fiscal, market and operational influences that may affect overall decision making. Our focus throughout this book will be on safety leadership and transferring the intangible to the tangible through practical means. Safety leadership will be the glue and core driver in setting up a robust culture.

Closing the gap between the elusive and the practical will be the core ethos of this book. Research presented in this book is an addition to the building blocks created by such predecessors as Thomas Krause and Scott Gellar. Lastly, whilst reading the case studies and information presented, please take in your own experiences and stories and through that lens; see how safety leadership can be achieved through the prompting questions provided at the end of each chapter.

References

Krause, TT 2005, *Leading with Safety*, John Wiley & Sons, Hoboken.

Read, BR, Zartl-Klik, A, Veir, C, Samhaber, R & Zepic, H 2010, 'Safety leadership that engages the workforce to create sustainable HSE performance', SPE

International Conference on Health, Safety and Environment in Oil and Gas Exploration and Production, Rio de Janeiro, Brazil, pp. 1–18.

Reid, H, Flin, R, Mearns, K & Bryden, R 2008, 'Influence from the top: Senior managers and safety leadership', SPE International Conference on Health, Safety and Environment in Oil and Gas Exploration and Production, Nice, France, pp. 1–18.

1 Defining safety leadership
Making sure we are talking about the same thing

To help set the scene, the following chapter is broken down into specific sections aimed at answering the following questions:

- What is the empirical foundation of safety leadership?
- How does safety leadership differ from other leadership models?
- Does safety leadership change according to someone's span of influence?
- How can one utilise the theory and science behind safety leadership and integrate this into their organisation?

Key objectives

The following objectives in this chapter are aimed at increasing individual safety leadership capability across an organisation. After reading this chapter an increased understanding and awareness will be made around the following areas:

1 Individuals will have the ability to define safety leadership and describe the key concepts that constitute safety leadership and the nuances across different levels of leadership.
2 Individuals will have the ability to apply some practical tools that allow the definition of safety leadership to be demonstrated by others and to establish the baselines of implementing safety leadership across an organisation.

Setting the scene

The lack of a clear definition of safety leadership was initially voiced by Zanko and Dawson (2012) who found in their research that safety leadership is often lumped under the human resources discipline. Such categorical labelling thwarts growth in the discipline and may lead to leadership myopia. This is when individuals are not given the blueprint to become robust safety leaders due to discipline blindness.

A plethora of companies provide services aimed at building safety leaders within one's company. Few companies detail what safety leadership is and even fewer companies attempt to define it. For the select few organisations that detail a definition towards safety leadership, it is often detailed in obtuse ways or detailed well without any data or evidence to support where the definition comes from. In a globalised world where international borders no longer restrict work boundaries, the challenge lies where one person's approach to safety leadership can be vastly different from somebody else's. When multiple variances exist, the achieving of team goals may become skewed and the proverbial wheel gets reinvented ... over and over again.

Whilst working at an aluminium smelter in South Africa, I came across a very dedicated and diligent individual who was working on the site's fatal risks. The documents and articles of research were expertly scattered across his desk as the beads of sweat were forming on his brow, as the enviable first draft of the fatal risks were due that afternoon. After just coming off a similar site in Australia for the same company, I knew that the same work was already completed on the other side of the world, for the same company in the same industry. This is a prime example of efficiencies being forsaken, as silo work structures become reinforced and embedded into a company. As a result, inconsistencies start to occur, coupled with a duplication of work. Without a clearly defined and well-communicated process, the evolution of any change or development initiative will slowly crash and burn.

Consistency and certainty is something that most humans crave from a neuropsychological perspective (Rock 2008). Without consistency, people become unsure of themselves and may become restless and fleeting which then limits their capability to focus. Having a clear universal definition towards safety leadership can be the benchmark of consistency across multiple industries. Similar to many workplaces I have been exposed to, if variances exist in internal processes, then variances will exist in the output and overall quality may be jeopardised. It will be challenging to build safety leadership capability, if one does not know what safety leadership means or how it differs from other forms of leadership.

Empirical definition of safety leadership

Through grounding research that was undertaken within a multifaceted business that spans multiple regions and countries, the core elements of safety leadership were explored. As part of this research, I conducted a multitude of in-depth interviews which were conducted with general managers and other senior leaders within the organisation. The common mantra of 'walking the walk' and 'leading by example' were often spoken of as the staple definition of safety leadership. After many hours of further probing, questioning and clarification, the breadth and detail of the definition was eventually brought to fruition. Prior to describing this definition, it is worthwhile sharing some other musings and thoughts voiced by the research participants.

The articulation of an overall definition was proven to be challenging as many individuals spouted the common catch phrases or mantras of leadership. Examples of this included that safety leadership is about demonstrating

your values or was defined by having an internal compass ⁺
When probed further, the common themes of values, honestⱼ
engagement started to emerge. These elements were shared via sₜ
direct experiences from many leaders. Through such experiences, the
spoken started to create added meaning and minimise the risk of clichés
buzz words being used to define safety leadership.

It is interesting to note that many individuals were quick to share what safety
leadership is not about, which links into the work of Sobh and Martin (2011)
where humans are naturally predicated towards the negative in order to avoid a
feared-self. Such a preference may have its roots within evolutionary theory as a
mode of overall survival to avoid the negative. Individuals shared some raw
concepts of safety leadership which included 'it's not about smashing your guys
when they make a mistake' or 'trying not to focus on statistics to drive change'.
Quite a few individuals shared that when tasked with defining safety leadership,
it was a hard concept to place into words, given that safety leadership is often
demonstrated through the behaviours of the individual.

One dividing factor was whether safety leadership differed from other
leadership models, and if so in what way did it differ. Results detailed that
there are many synergies between safety leadership and general leadership,
although differences do exist which will be explained a bit later on. After
compiling and analysing a plethora of data, the following safety leadership
definition was birthed:

> The demonstration of safety values through the creation of a vision and
> the promotion of well-being through the art of engagement, honesty and
> discipline.

Through the above definition, the importance of safety leadership behaviours
is amplified through the importance of demonstrating safety leadership as
well as communicating and promoting well-being. The applicability of this
definition can be shown through an experience I had with a site manager I
was working with on a resources project.

Whilst working in northern Western Australia a number of years back, I
was coaching the site manager in terms of safety leadership. In an environment
dictated by dry heat and temperatures that consistently exceed 40 degrees
Celsius, maintaining the focus on safety and keeping the workers motivated
was of essence. Like many organisational traps, communication was lacking
and there were no regular meetings detailing the schedule for the day. Upon
talking with the site supervisors and superintendents, nobody was aware of
what was happening on site in terms of progress, safety or what the other
crews were doing. When approaching the site manager and exploring their
values and thoughts, I received an insight into their safety leadership ethos.
The markers of the safety leadership definition were void. The site manager
stated that 'the guys know what is going on' despite a lack of formalised
meetings. In addition, safety was promoted when an incident occurred, such

as dust in the eye due to insufficient foam back safety glasses. In terms of a vision of safety on that site, it was often characterised by the guys knowing that everyone should 'not fuck up' which was often spoken by the site manager and therefore echoed by their subordinates. It was apparent that safety engagement and leadership were often dictated by individuals being dressed down when an incident occurred and safety being spoken as an aftermath in preference to production targets.

As mentioned by Carrillo and Samuels (2015) effective safety leadership may be dictated by leaders talking about safety prior to any work requests and ensuring the art of conversation is the key tool for influence. The detailed definition towards safety leadership can therefore act as a blueprint for behaviour and serve as an in-built accountability marker for leaders. Without accountability being present, the core leaders within a company may taint the perceptions and behaviours of others. In the site example above, it was further revealed that there were instances of physical assault between line managers and their team members, and other leaders jeopardised their own safety by being carried across trenches in a bulldozer in order to save time. This can be the corporate equivalent of fabricating tax receipts in order to balance the books or sacking someone instead of managing their performance.

Safety leadership is not a concept that belongs merely in the resources sector. With globalisation taking hold, work is now done quicker and across greater international borders than ever before. Virtual teams across multiple time zones can now be the norm as technology can allow individuals to meet deadlines across variant borders. With added pressures, free reign of information and competing demands, safety outside of the resources sector may be based upon burn-out, stress, anxiety or other work-related psychological illnesses. In a study by Leung, Chan and Yu (2012) it was shown that stress is the number one marker of psychological safety within the workplace, and measures need to be taken to create a resilient workforce in order to cope with variant work pressures.

These pressures can extend beyond the balanced scorecard measurements of finance, customers, people and internal capability and be homed in on the micro elements of managing workloads, interpersonal conflict or feeling valued. The importance of the psychological safety contract and personal inclusion at work was voiced by the work of Walker (2010). Honesty, well-being, discipline and engagement are the cornerstones of safety leadership which are applicable across all industries and disciplines. Well-being can be synonymous with both physical and psychological health whilst honesty is a sure way of enhancing engagement and drawing upon the benefits of authentic leadership (Kernis & Goldman 2006). Further relevance of the markers of safety leadership have been catalogued in Table 1.1 through the direct comments of the leaders who participated in the research such as construction managers, health and safety managers, project managers and general managers.

The comments in Table 1.1 represent a small sample of the core themes that have been used to help define safety leadership. It is from these comments

Table 1.1 Comments defining safety leadership

Discipline	Vision	Honesty	Values	Promotion	Demonstration	Engagement
'When I say fairness, fairness in your levels of discipline, you don't want to be seen as a pushover.'	'So unless they're told, unless they understand what they are there for and believe in it, how will it be effective?'	'We would try and build up a trust conscript; every time an issue was raised we would have 14 days to close it.'	'For me you have to believe that people have the right to come to work and not go home any different.'	'Key thing in safety leadership is teaching your fellow workers what the paper-work means so they understand it.'	'Have to make sure I comment on the incident reporting, I'm actively involved, participate in the closure.'	'Engaging in some deeper sort of discussion with things related to the job.'
'Holding their people accountable for delivering on things.'	'Get them involved when you do share your vision.'	'Transparency in our reporting, I think we have indoctrinated in our people that we report everything.'	'Safety is a value that underpins the core key chunk of something you do.'	'Lead by example, this is not an HSE thing, just living the culture.'	'I can influence through my own behaviour, going out into the field and talking.'	'Tell stories, it's real, not just written on a piece of paper.'
'One bad egg can change it; about stopping that.'	'Bigger vision can cross multiple borders and countries.'	'If I make a mistake, let me have it.'	'It's a personal thing, it's your ethics, it's your morals.'	'Paramount that you set the benchmark and set the baseline.'	'Talking safety with my PMs very regularly.'	'It's all about building rapport first.'
'Raise the points or raise the issues of where they have failed and see whether you get that discussion going.'	'It's all about the goal you want to achieve and that's obviously the vision or main aim.'	'Honesty, integrity, openness and a passion and a belief that of going home safely every day.'	'I think safety is intertwined with personal values and I think it's intertwined with ethics, whereas maybe org lea-dership less so.'	'About believing and preaching ... well not preaching, may not be the right word, it's about living the safety values we have in place.'	'Simplistic view would be wearing PPE, following general policies and providing resources and stuff.'	'Seriously just talk to them, give them the courtesy of talking to them; when we have a staff briefing, hang around afterwards.'

Discipline	Vision	Honesty	Values	Promotion	Demonstration	Engagement
'If you hurt someone, you deserve it, you face the consequences.'	'Need to make sure they see the whole picture.'	'About being yourself, not trying to be something that you are not.'	'Comes down to personality and who has got the values, regardless of money.'	'Eighty per cent of workforce will follow you based on what you do.'	'It's not walking past something, otherwise you condone it.'	'Communication is my best practice.'
'Setting a standard of expectation, as an individual, ethically and morally yourself.'	'You've got to understand why you are doing this stuff or no one's going to take time to do it.'	'I believe integrity is really important here; people need to believe in what you're trying to do.'	'If people fundamentally don't believe safety is a value of theirs as it is for the company, then you are wasting your time.'	'Monthly safety awards to communicate the number of safe days ... how we went last month.'	'Do a walk around on site; don't go to a project and go to the office for eight hours.'	'Really be engaging with the guys rather than forcing it upon them; get them to engage with themselves.'
'Safety culture defines the accountability; it defines actions.'	'I like to use charters; I like to have it published.'	'It's about honesty, belief you know, that authenticity.'	'Bring a bit of humanity into society.'	'The education process is critical.'	'Even if it's 8 o'clock at night, I will always get back to someone.'	'Need to be able to talk and relate to the guys in the field.'

(Source: Developed for this research)

and other similar comments that safety leadership has been defined. Each element has its roots based upon the phenomenological experiences of leaders who have had to influence others in terms of safety. The beacon of safety influence can therefore be prefaced on the specific nuances of the definition provided. By breaking down each element of the definition, further context and applicability can be galvanised into an overall account of safety leadership.

Discipline

Behavioural psychologists are well known for detailing that all explanations can be accounted for by different triggers and the consequences that follow those triggers (Weiten 2004). The adage that consequences can control behaviour may have its proverbial tentacles wrapped around the element of discipline and its application towards safety leadership. As leaders of an organisation, your actions will speak volumes to the people who casually or intently observe you. Integrity and trust can take a long time to build and can be jettisoned at a drop of a hat if your actions contrast what you say. I have seen leaders walk out of a project office without wearing the correct eye protection and when quizzed about their lack of eye protection, they have flippantly responded by saying 'I'm the boss and that shit doesn't apply to me'. Or perhaps the leader who champions vocational training but then openly moans and begrudgingly attends a training course and lets his frustrations be known to all. These frustrations are further amplified by the lack of punctuality or the sly checking of text messages whilst the presenter does their spiel. Through all of the above behaviours, the lack of personal discipline impacts upon their relationship with colleagues and subordinates.

A leader who shows up to a live gas plant in running shoes as opposed to steel cap boots shows their intention of staying within the office and not talking to the craft workers by the mere fact that they are not kitted up to talk to the employees who are the lifeline of the organisation. Discipline in terms of safety leadership is sometimes doing what is needed, even though it may be uncomfortable or there is an internal nagging dialogue that may disagree with an established site/office-based rule. As soon as a leader compromises a lifesaving rule or has a breach in safety, the word will get out quicker than wildfire and the reputation of that leader starts to crumble. Alternatively, the expectation is inadvertently set and others start to follow suit with a disregard to safety. When approached about their unsafe behaviour, an individual may respond that their boss does the same behaviour, so why would it be wrong if they do it the same way. Ways to strengthen personal discipline in terms of safety can include the following:

- familiarisation of site rules and demonstration of compliance
- active support and interest in safety efforts
- wearing required personal protective equipment (PPE), even when sometimes it may not be needed in certain areas

- awareness of any hindering self-talk which may contrast site safety regulations, and reframing as necessary
- matching safe work behaviours with out-of-work behaviours
- voicing to team members that you want to be approached if you are not doing something safely. In turn, if you are approached about your safety, responding with a thank you.
- creating benign habits, where what you do automatically becomes part of your ethos.

All of the above points are common staples to personal discipline. You may start to understand why some larger blue chip companies require the wearing of hard hats in all areas, despite the presence of risk being void. This is to ensure a habit of safe behaviours where it becomes part of your genetic make-up. Many years ago, I was walking around a coal mine where it was company policy to place your hard hat on, as soon as you leave your car in the car park. Objections and protests to this rule were often simmering away and only made public through backhanded comments ... the true staple of passive aggressiveness was present. Protests included, 'what is going to kill me walking 100 metres from the carpark to the office ... space junk, a meteorite, a bird shitting on me?' Of course the mechanics behind such a rule was to generate a habit of behaviour and to enhance self-discipline. If one cannot be disciplined with the mundane tasks, then they may have trouble with the bigger ticket items.

Discipline can also be demonstrated by following through with planned safety meetings or toolbox talks. As soon as the meetings get pushed out, postponed or cancelled it starts to send an unwritten message that safety may not be that important. A prime example of this was with an organisation I was consulting to where employees informed me that the monthly office toolbox talk occurred biannually. Reasons behind such irregular meetings were based around the notion that there are more important things to focus on, or other competing work demands take over. If discipline cannot be applied with staple safety meetings, then the bastion of safety may be demoted to an unwanted add-on and may not be seen as an integral part of the business.

The activities that a person does outside of work can vary greatly to what they do at work. A well-measured and well-spoken leader in a work environment may unravel to be a loose cannon and egotistical maniac outside of work. The matching of safe behaviours at work and at home is key to eliciting a consistency of disciplined safe behaviours. Exceptions to this rule could centre on variances in personality, adrenaline-seeking activities, questionable hobbies, insalubrious pastimes or anything else that may fall into such a category. The cognitive dissidence would be insurmountable if one always wore a seatbelt whilst driving around on a mine site, and then chose not to wear a seatbelt outside the gates of the mine site. Similar would be the individual who is a stickler to ensuring their PPE is up to date, and then contrasts this by walking up an unstable ladder without assistance or not testing for dead before carrying out home electrical work. A perfect illustration of this was with an electrician whom I was speaking with who mentioned at work everything is by the book, although at home it may differ. Upon further probing he mentioned that the best way he checks if the electricity is live is by quickly tapping the wires with his fingers and if he gets a slight shock then it is time to pull up tools.

The discipline to follow through with safety outside of the constraints of work may be influenced by the lack of discipline being applied if something went wrong at home or the absence of guiding paperwork and safety guidelines. The choice to follow through with what is right and what is needed is going to vary across each individual. The discipline to do what is right when no one is watching is the true testament of personal discipline and demonstrated safety leadership.

One of the old staples of leadership that I sometimes share in workshops is that you get what you tolerate. This applies to safety leadership even more so. If there is a blatant disregard to safety or someone is thumbing their nose at the system and nothing is done, then it is pretty much a free licence for others to do the same. Effective safety leadership is ensuring discipline is applied for such breaches and ensuring there is a consistent approach to such discipline. Without discipline, the same unwanted results, or worse, the same disregard for safety will continue. My partner shared with me once that she was working in an office environment where policies and procedures were lacking and that everything was done by trial and error. One day, there was a disagreement between two office workers and one of the workers physically pushed her co-worker and then the perpetrator stormed out of the office. The manager did not address the issue at all, due to an absence of bullying and harassment procedures to fall back on. As a result, a conversation that needed to happen did not occur and discipline in this instance was replaced with ignorance. A big component of leadership is leading with values and having those uncomfortable conversations. For this to occur, policies and procedures don't always have to be in place. With discipline being absent in my wife's workplace, other workers may pick up that you can push others around and not suffer any consequences. This is where discipline is needed, not only in terms of holding yourself accountable but holding other people accountable as well.

Vision

Safety leadership that is void of a vision is leadership without a template for success. From a safety paradigm, the vision can be based upon the absence of injury, reinforcing of safe behaviours or other macro vision that is aimed at minimising harm. Slogans which may mimic a safety vision are plentiful and range from 'zero harm by choice, not by chance' to 'safe every day, all day'. Without constant reinforcement, communication or referencing to the vision, the vision may become redundant and perceived to be a bunch of words without any meaning to them. The benefits of a vision can stem from the ability to communicate to the masses a set goal or management expectations as well as helping to pave the steps necessary to achieve such an outcome (Kouzes & Posner 2007; Long 2013). Each leader may have their own personal vision towards safety which can be shared to harness alignment between different team members. As one leader said to me, a powerful vision can cross geopolitical borders and have a reach beyond your own team.

A clear vision also sets up the expectations of what the desired norms are. Through such expectations the alignment of behaviours can be carried forward. Empathy and concern can be captured in a personal safety leadership vision. Such examples can include the referencing of family, friends and loved ones as a key motivator for individuals to strengthen their safety. A palatable safety leadership vision can be created and promoted by adhering to the following factors:

- utilising language that invokes emotion, which therefore penetrates to the deeper parts of the brain such as the amygdala that acts as the emotional control centre of the brain (Hrybouski et al. 2016)
- allowing other leaders to provide input into the broader vision which therefore provides a pathway of ownership and increases the chances that the vision will be shared and communicated
- contextualising the language that suits the industry and target audience that you are aiming to reach
- referencing the vision through cultural artefacts, environmental cues and embedding the vision through company meetings
- including the safety leadership vision in all go-to-whoa processes within a company. This can include induction processes, performance plans, work plans or performance management processes.

As detailed by Long (2013), a painted vision can be the pathway of what an organisation aims to achieve as well as describing the future state which can assist with strategic planning. Morally a safety leadership vision of not hurting anyone makes sense. Although, to permeate such a message within the business and to ensure a lasting impact, the vision needs to be spoken with the same vigour and earnestness as if someone was ensuring the safety of their newborn baby. In a globalised world, the wording of a vision may change to fit the context of that culture. I have seen American leaders publicly commit in open forums about their company's vision to an international audience, where the Australian leaders scoff and mutter 'what wankers' whilst Japanese leaders sit in obedient solitude, whist others reply in a chorus of agreement. Such past experiences outline the importance of a macro vision that suits the company culture. In those instances where the company vision is in misalignment with your own ethos, your own personal safety leadership vision should come to the foreground. Some questions that can prompt the crafting of your own safety leadership vision include:

- What do you want the future to look like in terms of people's well-being and safety?

- What would workers be doing if they were committed to safety?
- Why do you want people to be working safely?
- How would others describe your safety leadership ethos?
- Is there a way you can transfer your outside passions and link them with your safety leadership vision?
- What kind of language harnesses or commands your attention?

Once personal reflection has been carried out, in terms of what constitutes your own safety leadership vision, then the importance of honesty provides a platform to allow this vision to come to life and further embed safety leadership within the business.

Honesty

Organisations that have a lack of trust are destined to fail due to a lack of organisational commitment from workers (Conchie, Taylor & Charlton 2011). Without trust and honesty coming from leaders, the inevitable 'us versus them' mantra starts to surface and leadership requests may be met with farcical obedience. Building trust within a company can be harnessed from relationships between leaders and employees. The importance of such relationships is often documented in the leader-member exchange relationship, where line manager relationships with staff are pivotal in influencing employee behaviour (Mueller & Lee 2002). Honesty within the scope of safety leadership can be permeated through multiple avenues. This can include the sharing of site wins or challenges, providing data around any recent incidents or regular updates on any expressed employee concerns. As one leader said to me once, 'trust is an interesting thing, it can take years to build and minutes to shatter'. Authentic leadership harnesses the marker of honesty and transparency (Kernis & Goldman 2006) and can be aptly applied within the safety leadership context.

As part of the safety leadership definition, honesty was mentioned. Honesty can have a dual meaning. It can be referenced as honesty from your own moral code or honesty with your interactions with others. Being honest with yourself requires a level of self-awareness which can be confronting and sometimes daunting. From that malaise comes growth. Feedback from others can help guide your own level of awareness as well as asking the internal question of 'what have I done that has contributed to this situation'. Transparency and consistency with one's behaviours can help establish a common expectation of how others will respond to you. How transparent and honest you are may vary the kind of responses you get from others.

I once had a leader who parroted all of the safety mantras and slogans that they viewed as expectant for someone within their role. The ease with which they came out would leave the most gifted thespian in awe. Their colleagues saw through this charade quite quickly and even challenged the leader to demonstrate what he was talking about as this leader was renowned to break safety rules and quietly mock the compliance requirements often needed on a mine site. The social embarrassment would probably sting most individuals, although this individual was not willing to look inwards yet. As leaders, we may have team-members or colleagues who are similar to this, who are not open for self-reflection or they display mixed behaviours, which can therefore translate into a low level of trustworthiness. Self-reflection and personal honesty may be strengthened by the following:

- objective feedback from others or observers of your leadership behaviours
- monitoring your own emotions and that of others when placed under stress
- asking yourself what did I do that contributed to the situation, or what can I do better
- tangible processes such as 360 feedback assessments or coaching
- spending some time throughout the week to reflect upon the footprint of your leadership behaviours.

A marker of how well you are going with being honest and self-aware can be based upon the interactions you have with others and whether or not others are being honest with you. Honesty can breed honesty. Within safety, there is nearly nothing you cannot openly share with the workforce. The more information that gets shared tends to emulate the more information you get back. Even outside of the safety paradigm, transparency of information based upon business outcomes, forecasts and upcoming dilemmas can generate employee involvement (Toor & Ofori 2008) and allow an avenue of ideas to be shared. A workforce that is uninformed starts to confabulate and make up their own stories which can be pieced together from their own fear which then starts to spread like wildfire. With the resources boom entering the third stage of exporting (Colebatch 2013), a lack of information from leaders can be perceived by employees as a potential redundancy being on the horizon. Such perceptions may be completely unfounded, however fuelled by a lack of communication. Without honest communication and trust, leaders of an organisation may spend their valuable time rumour killing as opposed to rallying the workers towards their safety leadership vision.

Values

When empirically crafting the definition towards safety leadership, all parti-cipants made a reference to the importance of having a core value towards safety. An innate drive to ensure the safety of yourself and others can start to permeate the interactions you have with staff members. Cognitive dissidence may start to occur if you preach safety and well-being then your activities outside of work contradicts your voiced values. Examples of this can be shown through such insalubrious activities as drinking then driving or perhaps performing home renovations without the adequate fall protection. Values-based leadership taps into the importance of leading through your internal compass and allowing your behaviours to be driven by your attitudes. If there is an alignment of values between yourself and your team, it will be a lot easier to influence those individuals as a shared understanding would be reached.

If individuals are complying with safety in order to avoid getting a reprimand or the wrath of their boss, then they could be externally motivated which often does not lead to long lasting change in behaviour. An external focus can be linked to increased levels of frustration, stress and feelings of hopelessness as referenced in the locus of control literature (Joseph, Reddy & Sharma 2013). The existential challenge may lie with the individual, as each person has a different upbringing, attitudes and personality factors which can influence their overall values. Over the last decade I have met a range of extremely committed individuals who highly value safety. When I find out their back story, it is often a tale of grief due to an injury they have had themselves or knowing a close friend or family member who was seriously injured. Unfortunately, an injury has had to occur for that cognitive shift to be made. Values can be shaped by life changing events or personal insights precipitated by major challenges. As a safety leader, we can influence others although we have no control over their values. The following are a few ways that we can start to shape the values of the people whom we lead:

- recruiting employees based upon aligned personal values and that of the organisation
- rewarding behaviour that amplifies the value of safety
- finding out what the worker values and linking that with safety
- sharing your commitment to safety and demonstrating such a commitment through tangible actions
- self-examination of what is truly valued to yourself and that of others
- when allocating work tasks, ensuring safety is mentioned first prior to anything else.

Years ago I vividly remember a leader who asked the open question to his fellow peers about who places safety as a priority. A flurry of hands was quickly raised in the air. To their initial confusion the leader said he disagreed with such a notion. Upon clarification he mentioned that safety is not a priority; it should be a value given how priorities change and safety should always remain at the core of everything that we do. These sentiments echo the importance of safety being the underpinning fabric of each person's behaviour. A leader may try and preach that they have a value towards safety; on a long enough timeline the validity of their statements will be unearthed through their actions and treatment towards others.

One thing I have learned after travelling around the world and consulting to many organisations is this: no matter what country you could be in, everybody grieves if someone is killed or severely injured due to a workplace injury. As a human species we are hard wired to ensure the longevity of our genes by making sure our loved ones are safe. As authentic safety leaders we can expand this to our working families to ensure their safety and therefore longevity of our business, morale and culture.

Promotion

Imagine an organisation that is mute and silent towards safety. Alternatively what does get considerable air-time is the driving of deadlines, work goals or other key performance indicators. Cultural artefacts in this organisation are often shown through posters and pictures which are scattered around the office and highlight the values of achievement as opposed to safety. In such an environment, the open discussion of safety is absent, which provides an unwritten cultural clue of where safety sits in the company. The underlying message is that leaders value productivity over safety. A white collar worker who measures their worth by the hours they have worked as opposed to quality of their work becomes the common outcome of such a philosophy. Home life, family life and social life become the back burner for satisfying the unwritten culture that 'around here you work long hours and that is what gets rewarded'. Through a constant dialogue and open discussion about safety, inadvertently a message gets sent about what is deemed important. How that message gets promoted and conveyed can be the marker between a reactive or proactive culture.

With the safety industry being driven by statistics and lag indicators, the conversation around safety is most abundant after someone has been injured. Organisations that focus on safety after an incident are more likely than not going to be the organisations that are chasing their tail when attempting to improve safety. A true learning organisation embraces change, is adaptable and innovative in all aspects of the company (Kontoghiorghes, Awbrey & Feurig 2005). Similarly an organisation that learns from its mistakes and has a favourable appetite for change is more inclined to establish and embed safety innovations within the business. A noticeable shift may start to occur when the leadership focus is on safety conversations that are centred on improvement and innovation. This is juxtaposed to leaders who only talk with the workforce after an incident has already occurred. In those situations it is often too late to reinforce a safety message as someone has already been injured. In adjunct to this is the message being sent to the workforce that the only time safety becomes pivotal is after someone has been injured. As a result a collective trepidation starts to emerge whenever a leader starts to discuss safety, mainly due to all previous safety discussions being held after someone was injured.

Safety leadership which harnesses the beneficial promotion of safety can amplify the core message of safety and establish an environment where safety is embraced and not met with discomfort. As a safety leader this promotion of safety can be broken down to both a macro and micro level. From a strategic point of view, a safety leader who can tout the benefits of any well-being or safety innovations through general work processes is more inclined to keep their employees engaged and motivated. On a micro-level the promotion of safety can be personalised and catered for the individual through previous interpersonal interactions. Such interactions can be linked with personal values and highlighting the importance of safety through the ability to spend time with family and friends. Other tangible ways that safety leaders can promote safety include:

- reinforcing and sharing the safe behaviours that you want to see demonstrated, as opposed to the number of incident free days achieved
- sharing personal stories around safety and the positive effects upon workplace culture and team morale
- displaying innovations around the workplace in regard to safety and well-being
- one-on-one conversations with employees about safety and well-being, with a focus on what is working well and what may need to be improved
- if an incident occurs, being transparent about the details, whilst maintaining confidentiality and outlining the key learnings from the incident
- updating workforce with any resolutions to a safety concern raised and inviting input from others
- showing gratitude and appreciation for safety concerns raised as opposed to dismissal or annoyance.

With constant updates being provided around voiced safety concerns, employees can start to track progress and feel informed. A lack of feedback can breed contempt and disempowerment. Even if small progress is being made, it is better to communicate such small detail as opposed to nothing at all. Lack of information is the fertile ground for unfounded rumours to be generated.

Safety promotion has been around for years and has evolved over time. Track the safety and well-being changes over the last few decades and you can start to see the differences and approaches governments have taken to combat such health issues as AIDS, smoking, responsible drinking or drug use. The war on drugs was a global mantra used by the Reagan administration throughout the 1980s in the USA. Nearly 40 years on and the decriminalisation of drugs and legalisation of cannabis have changed the scope of the environment. This illustrates that any promotion towards safety has to be in line with societal changes and improved information that exists around such topics. Using the example of marijuana reforms across the USA, many organisations still continue stringent drug testing for cannabis with instant dismissal being the result if someone tests positive. Such actions still occur even though it is often argued that marijuana is a lot safer than alcohol based upon fewer road fatalities or alcohol-infused violence. On both fronts, it has been shown that cannabis does impair motor skills that are needed for driving (Bondallaz et al. 2016) and alcohol can be a contributing factor to domestic violence (Leonard 2002). In the current zeitgeist, the alignment of safety and health policies might be on the lower end of the totem pole when referencing societal trends and nuanced research into such areas.

As part of the safety leadership definition, promotion can be inclusive of the education of others towards safety, or communicating updated safety outputs or policies that reflect government reform. A proactive safety leader would be keeping abreast of any political and legal changes and promoting such changes within the organisation, in order to develop a culture of learning and feedback. Folly to the company that only focuses on safety when something goes wrong.

Demonstration

The ethos of being a safety leader is heavily weighted towards demonstrating behaviours that exemplify safety leadership. The proverbial rubber hits the road when any verbiage is matched with visible actions. Leaders are measured by their actions as opposed to their intent. A prime example of this is with a father who has all of the intent to be present at his son's birthday party, although work requires him to be elsewhere. Even though his intent is there, the child can't gauge intent, just the reality that his father is elsewhere on his special day. Safety leadership works in a similar way. All of the leader's intentions may be valid for keeping people safe, although if injuries and incidents are constantly occurring, the workforce neglects intent and instead measures the commitment to safety by what is actually occurring around them. Demonstrating safety leadership can be guided by the values of the individual. From a cognitive psychology paradigm, the thoughts and attitudes you have may drive behaviours and therefore impact upon the results you get (Corey 2001). The catch cry of 'walking the walk and talking the talk' characterises the demonstration of safety leadership. Through visible tangible actions, safety leadership can be modelled and therefore mimicked by other workers within the company. How one demonstrates safety leadership can be personalised to your style, ethos, personality and overall values. Further breakdown of safety leadership behaviours will be provided in the next chapter as it is the hallmark of effective safety leadership.

Engagement

Underpinning safety leadership is the ability to interact and engage with others. In the game of influence, the power of communication holds considerable weight. Engagement from safety leaders does not have to be restricted to one-on-one interactions, as it can also occur within virtual teams and wider masses via the use of technology, social media, blogs, video conferences, printed correspondence or other such methods. In reference to the work of Scott (2004), the conversations we have are the relationships that we have. This also applies to our team members, colleagues and bosses. Building rapport and establishing a robust working relationship would be challenging, if all of your interactions were limited to a transactional greeting of 'hello' and 'goodbye'.

A while back I was coaching a leader who was often labelled as cold and uninviting by his team members. Upon further exploration, it was shared with me that he hates talking to people and gets heavily annoyed by small talk. The amygdala dump you get by socialising with others is backed up by neuroscience and is a physical response to encourage socialisation (Harmon-Jones & Winkielman 2007). A leader who minimises his interactions with others is lacking the reinforcing opiates you get from socialising with others. After setting some small goals of finding out at least two different things about each of his team members, the leader started to get involved with his workers and developed deeper relationships. The change was noticeable and was reflected in the verbatim comments in a 360 feedback assessment that was carried out six months post coaching sessions. This example illustrates the biological impact of engaging with others and also the ability to influence others once you build up a shared experience or bond over common interests.

Maximum influence may be traced back to ancient philosophical times where influence was governed by ethos, pathos and lagos. This in turn equates to engaging and influencing others via logic, emotion and credibility (Higgins & Walker 2012). Under the motivator of safety, the emotion can be easily tapped into via the outcomes of someone being injured and the deleterious outcomes. Credibility can be synonymous with authentic leadership, and the use of logic can be the difference between strategic and operational thinking. As part of the safety leadership definition, engagement is the social glue from transferring your own safety leadership ethos towards others via the art of communication and similarity. Each interaction can add to the social currency. In transactional analysis theory, the total sum of social interactions were called strokes (Stewart & Joines 1999) and that the total sum of strokes will establish the power of the conversation and depth of the relationship. Safety leadership may be dictated by a number of strokes a leader has based upon their interactions at daily or weekly safety forums such as toolbox talks or pre-start meetings. Various ways to deepen engagement with others include the following:

- talking with team members about things outside of work and find out their drivers and motivators which could vary from family, travel, sport or anything else
- being open to feedback by asking for feedback from others and minimising defensiveness when constructive feedback comes your way
- finding out other opportunities to interact with others outside of the routine of work which could be based upon non-work-related celebrations or development days
- fostering autonomy with team members which allows employees to have the personal freedom to grow, learn and adapt, which therefore provides more constructive discussions with team members

- passing on any credit and any recognition to the team which can provide a reciprocity framework and result in increased trust with team members
- spending the majority of your time listening to each word in the conversation and not planning on what you will say next. This is the ethos of listening as opposed to hearing.

The above factors can be the hallmarks of developing robust relationships. Engagement is the vehicle to establish strengthened working relationships. These factors together help establish the model of safety leadership. If there was a lack of safety leadership engagement, the unwanted consequences from team members could range from fear or alternatively a lackadaisical relationship towards all things safety. These unwanted consequences were evident on one site I was consulting to where the leaders very rarely mentioned or promoted safety with their team. The reasoning behind this was based upon the belief that the team do not need to be 'badgered' by safety and are adults. When I spoke with the team members, a lot of individuals mentioned that safety is not talked about because it is not an issue, it is only an issue when someone gets injured. Such statements are riddled with the reactive dilemma of safety. Therefore, the only time leaders engage with work members is when there is an incident. Via the mechanics of classical conditioning, which is a pairing of stimulus for a conditioned response, the leaders are therefore seen talking to team members only when there was bad news to share. Leaders are therefore seen as the constant bearers of bad news. When engagement is based upon such reactive terms, the ethos of safety leadership is neglected and instead replaced by a culture of delayed communication and poor innovation.

How safety leadership differs from other leadership models

With safety leadership now being defined, a construct of what safety leadership entails can be visualised and transferred to actions. A lot of parallels exist between safety leadership and other leadership theories. A discourse can exist between such differences. One school may see safety leadership and general leadership being synonymous based upon the motion that effective safety leaders may also equate to strong general leaders. On the other side of the coin is the argument that safety leadership has some unique elements that are specifically relevant to safety which include the importance of safety values and extraneous factors such as safety statistics. This quagmire can now be clarified through the guiding research that was undertaken which distinguishes the differences between general and safety leadership (Daniel 2015).

Anecdotally, the view that a good safety leader makes up an effective leader in general can be refuted through the leadership actions of the late Steve Jobs, co-creator of Apple computers and arguably one of the best visionaries over the last 100 years. As innovative and creative as Steve Jobs was, there are numerous cited examples of him overworking his team as well as threatening and abusing his team members (Isaacson 2011). These actions do not promote safety and well-being or effective engagement with team members. Despite these actions, Steve Jobs was able to lead Apple into the next stratosphere of success. Safety leadership is not dictated by financial success, but perhaps it could be dictated by the success in ensuring the safety and well-being of the workforce. Within this context, the first differences between leadership and general leadership start to emerge.

Leadership may be defined as the process of influence over others and achieving targets through people (Durban, Dalglish & Miller 2006). The collective term of leadership will be used to describe the schools of leadership that involve transformational, authentic, charismatic and third-generational leadership where the latter specifically focuses on ownership and accountability (Long 2013). The darker models of leadership based upon control, aggression and other Machiavellian processes often leave the employee bruised (Kiazad et al. 2010) and therefore fall outside of the scope of effective leadership. Prior to establishing the unique differences that safety leadership has over other leadership models, it may serve as a robust platform to identify some of the common similarities. Through such similarities, an all-encompassing model of safety leadership can be established which can be the pre-cursor to specific safety leadership behaviours.

Safety leadership and general leadership similarities

With the components of safety leadership being well-detailed, the research underlying the definition has been well-linked to the grounding leadership theory. Effective safety leadership requires a strong internal compass where accountability is demonstrated and encouraged with others. Research into third-generation leadership outlines that leaders should be collaborative, commitment-based and self-directed (Long 2013). This transposes well with the literature surrounding locus of control where events and outcomes of a situation are perceived to be within that person's control (Joseph, Reddy & Sharma 2013). Embedded with safety leadership is the ability to take control of your own actions and responsibility for the things that occur.

Imagine a leader who has been informed by their colleague that an incident has occurred within their workplace. Instead of asking or analysing what they can do to improve the situation, their actions are based upon finding the scapegoat or person to blame for the incident. Immature incident investigations are dictated by this notion of 'who is to blame' as opposed to finding out how we can learn from the incident. Leaders who take responsibility for their actions are cited to have better life satisfaction, lower levels of burn-out and increased organisational commitment (Wang, Bowling & Eschleman 2010). Such actions can foster improved work outcomes and allow employees to take direct action over their circumstances. The parallels with safety leadership can be seen through the reporting of incidents and developing a reporting culture due to taking ownership of one's actions (Hor et al. 2010). Other links between safety leadership and general leadership, from the locus of control paradigm, include:

- taking ownership and responsibility for your actions, whether safety or otherwise
- asking yourself when things do not turn out well, what did you do to contribute to the situation
- recognising what is in your control and what is outside of your control
- understanding that you have a choice no matter what the situation is.

Individuals who have a high locus of control are seen to be natural leaders (Palamar, Le & Friedman 2012). This starts to generate a natural following and transformational leadership style. Transformational leadership can be dictated by meaningful relationships based upon commitment and trust where the leader can motivate others through turbulent times (Simola, Barling & Turner 2012). From a safety leadership point of view, this can translate to leaders steering the ship and taking control in the midst of a safety crisis or gathering commitment from others with simple transactional safety tasks. Transactional leadership can also be tied in with safety leadership through basic safety tasks that are based upon compliance activities without any real dedication to the greater goal. Transactional leaders tend to form surface relationships with staff and tend to be task focused as opposed to relationship focused (Barber & Warn 2005). This may look like a superintendent of a mine site pushing his workers to complete risk assessments or safety interactions because it is part of their own key performance indicators. The Machiavellian leader would jeopardise the safety of their workers if it meant greater rewards for themselves. Machiavellian leadership styles tend to be ego focused and in the most ruthless form cunning and non-supportive (Kiazad et al. 2010). Safety leaders who have a Machiavellian foundation may also have a non-committed workforce which can translate to a poor safety culture.

Authentic leadership is often bounded by transparency, openness and self-awareness of one's own limitations (Kernis & Goldman 2006). When applied from a safety leadership paradigm this could be the realisation of one's own safety shortcomings or areas that need improvement. Safety leaders who are authentic tend to develop trust with their team members which can be reciprocated through improved safety communication and safe behaviours. Linking to robust safety communication can be the actions of the charismatic leader.

Charismatic leadership often details individuals who inspire others through their choice of language, engagement and polished ability to captivate an audience (House & Shamir 1993). When applied to safety leadership, the charismatic leader can influence others towards macro safety goals and motivate the workforce to be committed towards safety. As indicated through the research of Halverson, Murphy and Riggio (2004) charismatic leadership comes to the fore when there is a crisis where leaders use metaphors and stories to penetrate a wall of concern or sorrow. The same can be applied to safety leadership when there is an unwanted event such as a major incident or fatality. Charismatic leadership can be a challenge to execute based upon individual nuances, personality traits and even cultural variations. Imagine a leader full of zest and energy addressing a workforce based in an Asian country where saving face, etiquette and discipline are the social norm. Such environments are labelled high context cultures because the meaning of what is said can sometimes be based on what is not said (Morgan 2015). The charismatic leader in this context may go against the cultural grain of that workplace and inadvertently alienate their workforce.

The similarities with safety leadership and general leadership theories run deep, with the biggest differences being based upon the context of leadership. Differences do exist with leadership and safety leadership although the similarities are just as plentiful when applied to the safety context (Daniel 2015). How one approaches safety leadership can vary based upon their scope of influence and role within their organisation.

Unique elements of safety leadership

With the similarities being plentiful between safety leadership and general leadership, once can easily forget the differences between the two schools. Differences start to occur when you consider the environment of safety within the heavy resources sector and the regulations placed upon organisations to conform to minimum safety standards. After consulting with many leaders through my research, one core aspect that came through was the importance of having a deep personal investment in safety. This was often characterised by leaders who not only speak the gospel of safety at work but take such values home with them which drives their behaviours at home. Leaders who do not have a deep regard for safety are less likely to invest in safety efforts and may even drive their workers to a point of burn-out. Such a contrast in values and behaviours limits the amount of buy-in from team members and therefore tarnishes the overall integrity of the leader. With general leadership studies, the emphasis may not be on health and well-being as it is with safety leadership. The focus on safety leadership may be minimising injury and maximising safety. Another unique element with safety leadership can be seen through the industry focus on statistics.

Leadership can entail the influencing of others to achieve set goals or objectives (Durban, Dalglish & Miller 2006) and these goals could be fiscally orientated or vary to the achievement of business expansion and continued growth. Safety leadership differs due to the industry importance of safety statistics. Within Australia and a lot of other western countries, the performance of an organisation may be whittled down to the injury frequency rate of that site. The depth of statistics can be evident through a variety of acronyms that relate to total injury frequency rate, total recordable injury frequency rate or other related verbiage. After I spoke with many leaders within the construction industry, a common theme emerged, that the securing of work can sometimes be based upon safety performance, and the awarding of work is not always based upon costs or other such efficiencies. As a result, it becomes imperative for leaders to drive safety, in which safety leadership becomes the medium of influence.

Industries outside of the heavy resources sector may not be as heavily driven by statistics, but the impact of an unsafe workplace can lead to increased insurance premiums, decreased work morale, lost productivity and a potential injury to an employee. To minimise such deleterious consequences, leaders may want to track how the company is going in terms of the health and well-being of their employees. The core way of tracking such progress is through safety statistics. An example of ineffective safety leadership could be the leader who is solely focused on statistics and driving the injury frequency rates down without taking into account the tactility and importance of work relationships.

Another unique aspect of safety leadership can be the external fluctuations of the market and subsequent investment into safety processes and safety behaviour. The importance of safety management systems is unequivocal in terms of managing incidents, tracking incident trends and establishing corrective actions (Bottani, Monica & Vignali 2009). How safety leadership links into safety management systems is based upon the promotion and utilisation of such systems. If costs are tight, overheads and variances need to be managed well, otherwise the importance and promotion of safety may vary. When regular safety toolbox talks are forsaken, focus audits are forgotten or money spent on personal protective equipment (PPE) is limited, then the overall impact of safety can be huge. In contrast to general leadership, money spent on safety may be grouped into a general managerial expenditure. In the realms of safety leadership, the cutting of the safety budget may start to unearth the old conundrum of whether production is more important than employee safety.

With the Australian mining boom coming to a close and the resources market now entering the stage of export (Colebatch 2013), some variances in safety have occurred across different projects. As the total number of safety advisors starts to decrease and with possible centralisation of health and safety administration, the direct impact on safety may become evident. A lack of flexibility when responding to safety challenges on a construction/mining project combined with limited safety advice can negatively influence employee safety behaviour. Such changes in the environment can be a tangible example of the impact of the external environment and influence on costs. The variances in safety and the minimum standards required within a workplace can sometimes be guided by legislation.

Safety leadership differs from general leadership because in countries such as Australia, USA and the UK, there is mandated legislation that dictates employer and employee safety responsibilities. Government legislation was birthed through a track history of organisations having loose safety requirements which impacted workplace safety and therefore the social, cultural and economic impact started to influence safety. General leadership and how one needs to conduct oneself is not mandated by legislation and therefore such variances start to exist across different leaders across multiple industries. Illegal activities such as embezzlement or extortion have legal consequences although ineffective leadership styles are not mandated. Safety leadership branches away from general leadership in this sense due to the legal consequences that can occur for employers and employees who do not comply with minimum safety requirements. The influencing factor of legislation can also be impacted by the safety and cultural maturity of an organisation and the operating and legal environment in which that entity works within. Such cultural maturity differences can start to distinguish safety leadership apart from other forms of leadership.

Imagine working in remote areas of Central Asia where the government does not mandate safety requirements and occupational health and safety laws are not even in the vernacular of that culture. Safety leadership starts to take on a brand new meaning where safety is brought down to a true grass roots approach. One of the interesting paradoxes I have been privy to was working for a large Australian-based conglomerate that had a South African leadership team working in a Portuguese speaking country. The company had a wide array of safety requirements and leadership drove the safety message hard. Outside of the workplace, many employees spent many hours a day travelling to work on the back of an overcrowded pick-up truck on roads that are littered with potholes and debris. Safety leadership becomes a unique element because how one approaches safety leadership needs to be contextualised for the safety maturity of the site and with due consideration of the overall culture of that country. General leadership in such environments may exclude such safety considerations and instead focus on the achievement of goals or respond to other business challenges in the true form of situational leadership (Durban, Dalglish & Miller 2006). Safety and well-being in such a setting may become a subset of general leadership due to the nuances of reinforcing safety.

Leaders can be faced with many challenges revolving around the managing of personalities and ensuring the team is firing on all cylinders. Such matters can be sensitive and require confidentiality to be maintained. Imagine the cultural and personal damage done if a leader openly talks to the workforce about a sexual harassment case between two workers with all of the gory uncomfortable details shared with all. Trust in leadership will decrease and inter-team conflict may start to occur. Safety leadership differs due to the importance of transparency in all matters relating to safety. When an incident occurs, the names of the individual are kept confidential but the outcomes and core learnings are shared to minimise the same incident occurring again. Through my qualitative studies, it was outlined that there is nearly nothing that needs to be kept under lock and key when you talk about safety and well-being. Such transparency of information can echo the tenements of authentic leadership (Gardner et al. 2011) and therefore require the safety leader to openly share all safety information as it comes to hand. All of the unique elements of safety leadership have been captured in Figure 1.1.

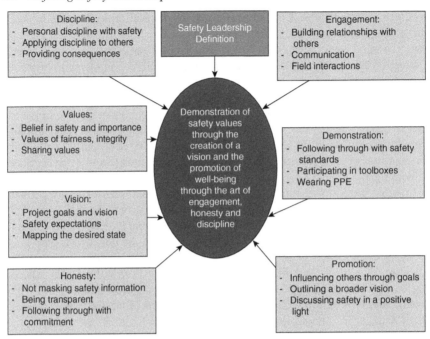

Figure 1.1 Unique elements of safety leadership
(Source: Developed for this research)

Similarities and differences do exist between general leadership theories and safety leadership. The context and environment of a country or organisation can branch safety leadership into a different stream and school of leadership. This is matched with the importance of having a personal value towards safety and the importance of transparency when sharing safety information. Based upon such differences, safety leadership exists as a subset of leadership which can be spoken in the same subset of leadership theories such as transformational, charismatic, transactional or values-based leadership.

Job position and influence on safety leadership

Many years ago, I was commissioned to provide safety leadership coaching to key leaders of a manufacturing company. The context of safety leadership was translatable to front-line leaders who could tangibly see the links between their safety behaviour and the influence on their workers. As the sessions started to expand to office-based leaders, such as accountants and office managers, the transactional safety leadership link was not as clear. One accountant came through and was quite blunt and said 'as a bean counter, what application does safety leadership have for me, given that the majority of my job is about balance sheets and invoices'. The accountant gave me a breakdown of how much my safety leadership efforts were costing his business based upon scheduled workshops, total coached sessions and the impact upon lost productivity time. The cost analysis was so well detailed, that they were able to break down the minutia of overhead costs such as potentially lost work based upon leaders not being able to attend or reposed to customer concerns or issues. This example amplifies the differences that safety leadership has amongst different positions.

With the accountant I worked with, the language that he spoke was in terms of facts and figures, so one way I was able to translate the impact of his own safety leadership behaviour was through the costs of an incident on one of his sites. A breakdown of the associated costs was worked out through associated costs involving insurance premiums going up, impact upon time lost on the incident investigation, lost time due to the injury and increased absenteeism rates. Once we mapped out the potential costs of an injury, I then asked what the flow on impact would be if we did not place safety as a value from a leadership perspective. Over a few sessions, the leader started to increase his awareness that he may not be directly involved with safety related tasks, but what he does have influence over is how he manages his own safety and how he manages the safety of his junior accountants. In this instance, safety was based upon well-being, mental health and the typical workday pushing over 14 hours. Safety does not always have to be based upon physical risks, especially within the office environment where psychological health and mental stress can be the hidden risk that leaders do not consider. Stress, anxiety and depression were the common markers of my case load, back when I was working in the occupational rehabilitation system.

Workers that are operating machines, completing formwork, erecting scaffolding, performing heavy lifts or other such manual tasks are faced with the realities of risk each day. Safety leadership can be brought down to a grass roots approach where the safe choices a person makes dictates if they go home in one piece or not. Each person can therefore act as their own safety leader based upon the choices that they make and how they influence others. As one gets further away from the working interface where risk is apparent, the role of safety leadership may start to vary. Through countless interviews and hundreds of safety leadership conversations, a trend started to emerge based upon how one views safety leadership. This trend has been detailed through the graph shown in Figure 1.2.

As seen in Figure 1.2, the closer one is to the work front, the more distinct safety leadership becomes. As one's span of influence increases, the more safety leadership becomes lumped with general leadership. One general manager mentioned to me that if there is a distinct focus on safety leadership, why don't we also focus on fiscal leadership, environmental leadership or people-based leadership? Such comments can provide a window into the job scope of senior leaders and all the different parts of the business that they manage. As indicated by Long (2013), general managers and senior leaders set the strategy and vision and have a broader scope of responsibility than others. Safety leadership from a governance point of view may be based upon vision setting

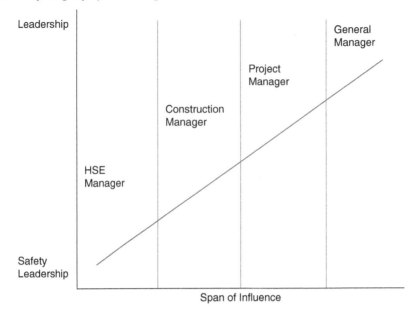

Figure 1.2 Safety leadership between job positions
(Source: Developed for this research)

and embedding safety as a core metric and performance indicator (Ferguson 2015). Executives and board members that do not consider safety leadership as important may create a risk to the longevity of their business due to the well-being of their most valuable asset being jettisoned.

Leaders who are closer to the work front can see the reality of unsafe work practices, where safety can be more tangible and overt based upon risk assessments, safe work practices and hazards. Supervisors and frontline leaders are often responsible for the safety of their workers and ensuring compliance. The importance of the line manager relationship is pivotal in establishing organisational commitment and determining employee satisfaction (Hooper & Martin 2008). This can have a trickle down influence of safe behaviour which can permeate any organisation.

Interestingly enough, safety leadership can be exercised at the top of an organisation or at the bottom of the organisation. If craft workers did not value safety, their livelihoods will be impacted by the reality of an incident. Executives and senior leaders who also do not exercise safety leadership can reinforce negative connotations towards safety and create a reactive safety climate where employee turnover is high and the threat of risk is palpable. If there's a disconnect at both levels of the organisation, then the lifeline of a company will most likely be limited as safety is not valued at both ends of the leadership spectrum. What safety leadership looks like for different leaders can be unearthed in the next chapter, where safety leadership behaviours are broken down in more detail.

Case study

All case studies are based upon real experiences, and the following case study was based upon a large scale international gas company based in Australia.

An international gas company is wanting to initiate a safety leadership programme throughout their business. The structure of the programme is based upon coaching sessions, observation of behaviours and workshops. After a period of 12 months, the majority of the leadership team have not been through the programme although it is mandated that all employees and leaders need to go through the programme. Feedback starts to emerge that the senior leadership team does not value safety and that they view safety leadership as a compliance-based tool that needs to occur within the company to appease shareholders. Further to this, after 12 months the rate of incidents has gone up and a causation relationship is being established that the safety leadership programme is increasing the amount of incidents occurring within the workplace.

Questions

Q1.   What could be some other causes or reasons why safety incidents have gone up since the safety leadership programme commenced?

Q2.   What kind of message will be conveyed to the workforce if the senior leaders are not being involved in the safety leadership programme?

Q3.   How would you address the senior leadership team with some of the problems emerging?

Q4.   What could be the benefits of safety leadership which can be shared with the leadership team?

Epilogue

With the above case study, the issues were stemming from the initial commitment from the executive leadership team and overall communication to senior leaders. The organisation was lacking an overall safety vision and the role of safety leadership was not communicated well. Adding to this problem was the true commitment by leaders towards safety leadership and their own value towards safety. The organisation placed safety as a priority built not a value which therefore gave wriggle room for the leaders to shift their attention on other emerging problems. Such flexibility of values created a sub culture of 'us versus them' which was dictated by senior leaders who are immune to development or training activities compared to those individuals who were committed. Organisational trust with the senior leadership team started to become questioned due to perceptions of inequity and safety commitment.

Incidents started to increase across the company due to changing levels of incident reporting and increased safety conversations that outlined the importance of reporting incidents. The senior leadership team were presented with the data in addition to cultural comments from workers. Employees openly voiced their concerns of a lack of leadership consistency and inequity. An executive decision was made to pause any more workshops until the senior leadership team attend the workshops and coached sessions, and to share their learning with others to keep the information fresh.

Organisational and personal application

Pathways to apply the chapter information into your organisation or into your own leadership ethos can be guided by the following propositions.

Organisational application

- How is safety leadership defined in your company? Are there any differences that exist around the meaning of safety leadership? If differences do exist, sharing a common definition can allow employees to refer to the same concept.
- What are the environmental elements influencing safety leadership within your organisation? Is safety leadership being driven by leaders who do not have a true value towards safety, or perhaps safety is driven by the push for improving safety statistics? Unless there is a true investment into safety leadership, any initiatives may falter due to the superficial investment by leaders.
- Does safety leadership mean different things for different leaders? How one exercises safety leadership may depend upon their scope of influence. An organisation that expects all leaders to demonstrate the same safety leadership qualities will be an organisation that does not embrace diversity. Encouraging unique personality variables with leaders can allow a greater depth of safety leadership behaviours to be exhibited.

Individual application

- Do you have the same understanding of safety leadership as your peers and fellow leaders? If not, what can be some ways to bring them on the same page to minimise confusion and miscommunication?
- With the scope of influence varying, where do you fall in terms of understanding the differences between safety leadership and general leadership? As a senior leader, how do you approach safety leadership compared to frontline managers? Does your strategy reach the core audience and is it permeating the hearts and minds of others?
- If you were to work in an organisation that had a different approach towards safety leadership, how would you adapt your approach? If legislation and statistics were not governing leadership practices, how would you maintain your safety leadership ethos? This could vary from the work conversations you have or approaching safety from a baseline level until the organisation reaches safety maturity.

Chapter summary

Safety leadership has been defined and broken down in further detail. The importance of demonstrating safety leadership is a core ingredient in distinguishing safety leadership from other schools of leadership. The organisational and environmental context can distinguish safety leadership from other forms of leadership. Statistics, legislation and other such variables make safety leadership unique from other leadership theories. Leaders who are closer to the workfront view safety leadership in more transactional terms such as compliance with safety and ensuring risk assessments are carried out. As a leader's span of influence increases, safety leadership may be viewed in more generic terms and may differ in meaning. No matter what the span of influence is, safety leadership can be displayed in different ways. With a common definition to safety leadership being mapped out, consistency across the industry can be detailed and confusion around the topic can be stamped out.

References

Barber, E & Warn, J 2005, 'Leadership in project management: From firefighter to firelighter', *Management Decision*, 43(4), 1032–1039.

Bondallaz, P, Favrat, B, Chtioui, H, Fornari, E, Maeder P & Giroud, C 2016, 'Cannabis and its effects on driving skills', *Forensic Science International*, 268, 92–102.

Bottani, E, Monica, L & Vignali, G 2009, 'Safety management systems: Performance differences between adopters and non-adopters', *Safety Science*, 47(2), 155–162.

Carrillo, RA & Samueks, N 2015, 'Safety conversations: Catching drift and weak signals', *Professional Safety*, 60, 22–32.

Conchie, SM, Taylor, PJ & Charlton, A 2011, 'Trust and distrust in safety leadership: Mirror reflections?', *Safety Science*, 49(8–9), 1208–1214.

Colebatch, T 2013, 'Boom enters export phase', *The Sydney Morning Herald*, May 29, p. 27.

Corey, G 2001, *Theory and Practice of Counselling and Psychotherapy*, Wadsworth/ Thompson Learning, Belmont.

Daniel, L 2015, 'Safety leadership defined within the Australian construction industry', *Journal Construction, Economics and Building*, 15(4), 1–15.

Durban, AJ, Dalglish, C & Miller, P 2006, *Leadership*, John Wiley & Sons Australia, Milton.

Ferguson, KI 2015, *A study of safety leadership and safety governance for board members and senior executives*, PhD Thesis, Queensland University of Technology.

Gardner, WL, Cogliser, CC, Davis, KM & Dickens, MP 2011, 'Authentic leadership: A review of the literature and research agenda', *The Leadership Quarterly*, 22(6), 1120–1145.

Halverson, SK, Murphy, SE & Riggio, RE 2004, 'Charismatic leadership in crisis situations: A laboratory investigation of stress and crisis', *Small Group Research*, 35(5), 495–514.

Harmon-Jones, E & Winkielman, P 2007, *Social Neuroscience: Integrating Biological and Psychological Explanations of Social Behaviour*, The Guildford Press, New York.

Higgins, C & Walker, RW 2012, 'Ethos, logos, pathos: Strategies of persuasion in social/environmental reports', *Accounting Forum*, 36, 194–208.

Hooper, DT & Martin, R 2008, 'Beyond personal leader-member exchange (LMX) quality: The effects of perceived LMX variability on employee reactions', *The Leadership Quarterly*, 19(1), 20–30.

Hor, SY, Iedema, R, Williams, K, White, L, Kennedy, P & Day, AS 2010, 'Multiple accountabilities in incident reporting and management', *Qualitative Health Research*, 20(8), 1091–1100.

House, RJ & Shamir, B 1993, 'Toward the integration of charismatic, transformational, inspirational and visionary theories of leadership', in M Chemmers & R Ayman (eds), *Leadership Theory and Research Perspectives and Directions*, Academic Press, New York.

Hrybouski, S, Aghamohammadi-Sereshki, A, Madan, CR, Shafer, AT, Baron, CA, Seres, P, Beaulieu, C, Olsen, F & Malykhin, NV 2016, 'Amygdala subnuclei response and connectivity during emotional processing', *NeuroImage*, 133, 98–110.

Isaacson, W 2011, *Steve Jobs*, Little Brown, London.

Joseph, C, Reddy, S & Sharma, K 2013, 'Locus of control, safety attitudes and involvement in hazardous events in Indian army aviators', *Aviation Psychology and Applied Human Factors*, 3(1), 9–18.

Kernis, MH & Goldman, BH 2006, 'A multicomponent conceptualization of authenticity: Theory and research', *Advances in Experimental Social Psychology*, 38(1), 283–357.

Kiazad, K, Restubog SLD, Zagenczyk, TJ, Kiewitz, C & Tang, RL 2010, 'In pursuit of power: The role of authoritarian leadership in the relationship between supervisors' Machiavellianism and subordinates' perceptions of abusive supervisory behaviour', *Journal of Research in Personality*, 44(4), 512–519.

Kontoghiorghes, C, Awbrey, SM & Feurig, PL 2005, 'Examining the relationship between learning organisation characteristics and change adaptation, innovation and organisational performance', *Human Resource Development Quarterly*, 16(2), 185–211.

Kouzes, JM & Posner, BZ 2007, *The Leadership Challenge* (4th edn), John Wiley & Sons, San Francisco.

Leonard, KE 2002, 'Alcohol's role in domestic violence: A contributing cause or an excuse?', *Acta Psychiatrica Scandinavica*, 106, 9–14.

Leung, MY, Chan, IY & Yu, J 2012, 'Preventing construction worker injury incidents through the management of personal stress and organisational stressors', *Accident Analysis Prevention*, 48(1), 156–166.

Long, DG 2013, *Delivering High Performance: The Third Generation Organisation*, Gower Publishing Limited, Farnham.

Morgan, S 2015, 'Embracing "high context", "low context" cultures', *Canadian HR Reporter*, 28(17), 11.

Mueller, BH & Lee, J 2002, 'Leader-member exchange and organisational communication satisfaction in multiple contexts', *The Journal of Business Communication*, 39(2), 220–244.

Palamar, M, Le, DT & Friedman, O 2012, 'Acquiring ownership and the attribution of responsibility', *Cognition*, 124(2), 201–208.

Rock, D 2008, 'SCARF: A brain-based model for collaborating with and influencing others', *Neuroleadership Journal*, 1(1), 78–87.

Scott, S 2004, *Fierce Conversations*, Berkley Publishing Group, New York.

Simola, S, Barling, J & Turner, N 2012, 'Transformational leadership and leaders' mode of care reasoning', *Journal of Business Ethics*, 108(2), 229–237.

Sobh, R & Martin, BAS 2011, 'Feedback information and consumer motivation: The moderating role of positive and negative reference values in self-regulation', *European Journal of Marketing*, 45(6), 963–986.

Stewart, I & Joines, V 1999, *TA Today: A New Introduction to Transactional Analysis*, Lifespace Publishing, Nottingham.

Toor, SR & Ofori, G 2008, 'Leadership for future construction industry: Agenda for authentic leadership', *International Journal of Project Management*, 26(6), 620–630.

Walker, A 2010, 'The development and validation of a psychological contract of safety scale', *Journal of Safety Research*, 41(4), 315–321.

Wang, Q, Bowling, NA & Eschleman, KJ 2010, 'Supplemental material for a meta-analytic examination of work and general locus of control', *Journal of Applied Psychology*, 95(4), 761–768.

Weiten, W 2004, *Psychology: Theories and Variations*, Thomson Learning, Southbank.

Zanko, M & Dawson, P 2012, 'Occupational health and safety management in organisations: A review', *International Journal of Management Reviews*, 14(3), 328–344.

2   Safety leadership behaviours
Transforming the intangible to the tangible

The ability to transfer theory into practice is where a lot of leadership efforts fail. This chapter will be broken up into various sections that are aimed at answering the following core questions:

- What are the psychological and cognitive influences on behaviour?
- How does behaviour-based safety link up with safety leadership?
- What are some examples of tangible safety leadership behaviours?
- How can one adopt their style of leadership to develop a specific set of safety leadership behaviours?

Key objectives

After reading this chapter, it is expected that an increased understanding of what influences safety leadership behaviour will be achieved, as well as having an enhanced ability to contextualise safety leadership behaviours into your own workplace. Specific objectives include:

1   Having a holistic understanding of the variables that can influence safety leadership which is rooted within the empirical foundations of psychology, neuro-psychology, cognitive and behavioural safety.
2   Developing one's own suite of safety leadership behaviours through the exploration of some transactional and transformational safety leadership behaviours.

Setting the scene

Leaders are going to be measured by their actions as opposed to their intentions. When people discuss leading with safety, the common transactional behaviours may be mentioned. This can include 'doing a safety walk through' or 'talking about safety with the workers'. The blueprint to safety leadership can be embedded within the behaviours one demonstrates. In the end, any safety leadership behaviours should be observable by others. To ensure clarity, a distinction will first be made with behaviour-based safety and safety leadership behaviours.

Role of behaviour-based safety

It is important to note that behavioural safety has its roots within behavioural psychology which has been around for decades and based upon the fundamentals of such psychologists as Thorndike, Pavolv, Skinner and Bandura (Chance 1999). From this paradigm all behaviours are influenced by triggers, otherwise known as activators or antecedents, and by how the consequences of such behaviour control behaviour. Behaviour in this sense is defined by an observable act. When exploring safety leadership behaviours, a focus will be on the observable.

Organisations that I have consulted with had many variations of behaviour-based safety which are referenced under such acronyms as SBO, SAO, PBS, interactions or other such verbiage. The purpose of a behaviour-based safety (BBS) programme is to identify any at-risk behaviours and to reinforce any observed safe behaviours. Many consulting organisations offer their version of a BBS programme with the caveat that such a programme will be a proactive approach towards safety. The benefits of such a programme can be based upon increased safety interactions within the workforce and the rectifying of any at-risk behaviours prior to those behaviours resulting in an injury. This is conducted through a direct observation of the worker who is then provided feedback based upon what is working well and what could be at risk. Information is then collected and used for data analysis.

How the data is analysed and collected from the BBS process is pivotal as well as supporting quality control systems. I still vividly remember a general manager describing to me that their site has had over 12,000 field interactions, which was accompanied by a beaming smile. When I asked about the quality of the interactions, the smile changed to a grimace which was met with the candid reply 'our quality is shit!' A BBS process that has some kind of coaching or quality control process will gather accurate data which can be used to implement corrective actions.

Notable researchers such as Krause (2005) and Geller (2001) advocate that BBS processes are best utilised with craft workers, where observers are fellow craft workers who give peer-to-peer feedback. Variations of this exist across the globe, where sometimes the leaders of an organisation are the ones who perform the BBS observation. Sometimes the mere observation of the individual and associated interaction may be deemed part of 'visible felt leadership'. In essence, BBS could count towards the exercising of safety leadership behaviour, although it would be on the lower end of the safety leadership maturity scale. Quotas or key performance indicators can drive leadership compliance, although the uniqueness of safety leadership needs to be garnered and demonstrated by the leaders of an organisation through other various means. BBS is beneficial up to a point in addressing smaller ticket items. After this, a possible plateau may occur, and this could be attributed to the absence of values-based leadership or a specific breakdown of safety leadership behaviours and attitudes.

When someone is being observed, the observer effect may come into place where the person may modify their behaviour for the benefit of the person observing them. BBS advocates may mention that if a worker is doing everything they can to work safely, then that is a sustainable outcome as safety is being reinforced. Alternatively, if observations were being made with the worker without them knowing about it, then a climate of mistrust and suspiciousness may start to creep in. Ideally a culture of trust and openness should be the ultimate aim for many organisations. A transparent BBS process can be one of the many vehicles to achieve a culture of trust. Other variables need to be taken into consideration, which can include the role of leadership, fiscal responsibilities, systems and processes. In the end, behavioural safety is not the utopia of guaranteeing well-being but one of the many tools which needs due consideration. An even more influential factor on safety can be the observable behaviours of safety leaders which may be governed by the attitudes of that leader.

Specific safety leadership behaviours

To address the vagueness of leaders defining their own safety leadership behaviour as 'walking the walk', some extensive research was undertaken with many general managers, project managers, HSE professionals and construction managers. From my research, a number of safety leadership behaviours were noted which can be grouped into three categories. These categories fall under the headings of vision, safety and engagement. An example of specific safety leadership behaviours have been detailed in Table 2.1.

The behaviours detailed in Table 2.1 had to be explored and teased out of the leaders I interviewed. Initial safety leadership behaviours described were generic. This is to be expected given that the previous scope of safety leadership has not been adequately explored or defined. For new safety leaders, the behaviours in Table 2.1 can be the starting points of exercising safety leadership. Further demonstration of safety leadership behaviours can be streamlined into the categories of vision, safety and engagement. Gathering and empowering others to a common goal is the ethos of having a strong safety vision. As noted with the safety leadership definition, the importance of a vision is paramount when influencing others. Such an importance can be crystallised on a gas plant I was working at with a major contracting group. As part of a cultural analysis that was undertaken at this plant, it was revealed that the white collar workers which consisted of engineers, health and safety staff, planners, estimators and procurement staff were deeply dissatisfied. Upon further consultation it turned out that the direction of the team was void, even to a point where the leaders were unsure of who they reported to or whether or not they were performing well on their job. This was attributed to a lack of feedback and an absence of a clear vision being communicated by leadership of what the macro goal was. To assist in turning

Table 2.1 Contextualised safety leadership behaviours

Safety behaviours	Engagement behaviours	Vision setting behaviours
Providing positive feedback on safe behaviours observed and the benefits of working safely	Creating a leadership presence at employee inductions to introduce yourself and to share some personal information	Creating a safety charter or safety vision for the project with core leadership team
Abiding by compliance minimum standards in relation to wearing PPE and abiding by policies and procedures	Conversing with employees about non-work-related issues and enquiring about work issues	Talking about the safety vision or charter with all employees and key stakeholders
Providing operational discipline for blatant breaches into safety or disregard for one's safety	Asking questions to seek understanding of tasks and safety related behaviours	Rewarding employees based upon the behaviours that are linked to the safety vision
Actively being involved with safety investigations and client safety meetings	Sharing personal safety stories or experiences from other sites and projects	Detailing leadership expectations for employees at the start of a project
Teaching and mentoring others in safety systems and processes	Utilising humour and other techniques to build rapport	Celebrating success based upon set milestones or goals achieved
Conducting leadership safety walkthroughs where the vision and safety are discussed	Facilitating non-work-related events or presence at reward milestones to converse with employees	Revisiting and modifying the safety vision on an on-going basis
Displaying safe behaviours within the office environment and field environment (housekeeping, etc.)	Talking with people that the leader has yet to approach on a site or project	Using expressive language and rhetoric when communicating the vision
Identifying any at-risk behaviours and addressing them on the spot through personal action	Inviting employee feedback to site leaders or opportunities to provide safety suggestions	Assuring senior leaders of the company are present at major milestones to reiterate core vision and purpose
Participating in and rotating chairing safety forums and realignment safety meetings on the project	Establishing a work and team structure that is conducive to collaboration and job rotation to help build working relationships	Contextualising the vision and including language suited for the client and project

(Source: Developed for this research)

the negativity around, a number of safety leadership suggestions were made and subsequently carried out. Some of the actions included the following:

- Holding a team meeting with the functional leads to discuss broader goals and to create a vision of what the team aims to achieve over the next 12 months.
- Forming an established leadership team and detail what they expect and what they will not tolerate from each other as a leadership group and what behaviours they will foster within their team.
- Leaders providing regular formalised feedback to their team members to help identify their goals, strengths and capabilities.
- Leaders addressing the cultural concerns with team members and addressing such misgivings and provide data with earnest and honesty.

The last action listed above is coming from a place of authenticity and genuineness. Through such transparency, the establishing of trust can be recaptured. Simplistic in nature, the above actions were not easily carried out due to the leader's general malaise in dealing with such matters. A preference or priority was placed upon completing the project schedule and ensuring set productivity was on time. To transition leaders from a place of contemplation to action, the potential fiscal, moral, team and safety costs was shared if no action was taken. Of course, one can bring a horse to water but can't make it drink. In this case the horse was made to drink by a project director who dictated the personal consequences if nothing was done. Such a positional power play is a prime example of how consequences control behaviour. About four months later I revisited the site and noticed a team charter that was created and was referenced regularly as an antecedent of behaviour.

Transactional safety behaviours can create a conditioned response where employees start to associate their leader with safety. This can include the reviewing of safety documentation, enquiring and challenging others during safety meetings or even the low hanging fruit of wearing all personal protective equipment (PPE) within the workplace. Safety behaviours can also be placed on the forefront of someone's mind by engaging with that person and discussing specific safety related matters. The opportunities for engaging with others as a leader are endless.

After traveling to many mine sites around the world, I am privy to the early morning bus routine to get to an isolated site. As a scientist, I always find it interesting observing each person's unique morning routine. Individual routines vary from individuals who mentally switch off and listen to music, others who catch up on missed sleep, parents who look at pictures of their children to remind them of why they are working away from home. A small collective group on the bus often provide a food review or voice any issues with the camp food offered at each meal service. By analysing these behaviours on the bus, an opportunity to exercise safety and engagement behaviours can be put into action. Inadvertently such behaviours are demonstrated by workers performing a covert fatigue check by asking their work colleague 'how did you sleep last night?' Or even the bus driver reminding everyone to wear their seatbelt. Such micro interactions may be subconscious but start to create the ethos of safety leadership behaviours. These early morning conversations are separate from people completing a job hazard analysis or personal risk assessment. Safety leadership can occur prior to one even travelling to work. Similar engagement and safety behaviours can occur within office environments where the exposure to risk may not be as heightened.

A leader who enters the office without greeting others and goes directly to their cubicle or workspace is impairing the work relationship with colleagues and not enhancing the social currency that they possess. Typical morning greetings are often characterised by 'how are you?' Or 'what did you get up to over the weekend?'. Such engagement related questions open the dialogue to increased trust between the individuals as well as a window into their own personal state. A colleague who is going through a hard time by either purchasing a property, separating from their partner or dealing with illness within their family may have a different mindset and impaired cognitive status compared to someone who is not dealing with such challenges. It is important to note that merely asking questions is one aspect, but unless there is a level of sincerity and patience involved the message will be seen as transactionally disingenuous. Safety can therefore extend beyond a resources environment where physical threats are apparent. Safety in office environments could fall under the realm of psychological safety via stress, depression, fatigue and anxiety.

To ensure individuality and genuineness, it is suggested that each person come up with their own set of safety leadership behaviours. Emulating other people's behaviours is not always a ticket to success, especially if the behaviours do not suit your personality style or the way you interact with others. For someone who is quite demure, extending yourself in group settings may cause a challenge and therefore another option many be needed. Even though extraversion is one of the big five personality traits (Mischel 1999), it is not pivotal in exercising safety leadership. The quiet confident leader who does not have to grandstand can be just as effective in demonstrating safety leadership. Some markers and consideration points to help establish your own set of specific safety leadership behaviours include the following:

- How do you currently monitor your own health and well-being?
- How do you broach the subject of safety?
- Are you more suited towards one-on-one conversations or do you like talking in larger groups?
- Are you more of a technical person or someone who likes to engage with others?
- What would extend you beyond your comfort zone?
- How would others describe your safety ethos?
- What are your own internal triggers towards safety that you loathe or love?
- What safety legacy would you like to leave behind as a leader?

By considering the questions above, one may start to realise what they are comfortable doing and how they can use their strengths to further promote safety leadership. Extending yourself past your comfort zone may cause initial malaise, but the benefits include personal learning and growth. An example of this could be with someone who is more of an introvert starting to lead safety moments in team meetings or facilitating safety discussions. If other people are describing your safety ethos as below par then such feedback can create a baseline of how you can measure yourself in the future. In contrast, if your colleagues describe you as the apex and pinnacle of safety leadership, then the challenge could be based upon how you can pass on that enthusiasm and experience to others.

Building a repertoire of safety leadership behaviours around vision setting, safety and engagement factors can amplify your safety leadership profile. Adjusting your style and understanding the environment in which you operate in becomes the key to truly adaptive safety leadership and also mirrors the situational leadership research, where adaptability is the cornerstone of a leader's leadership ethos (Durban, Dalglish & Miller 2006).

Adaptive safety leadership behaviours

Through a rich experience in consulting with multiple industries, I have been able to pick up the smaller points of what makes each company unique, and therefore altered my own consultative style. Working within construction, no rambling double speak is needed and forthright communication goes down well. Alternatively my experience working with various government organisations is quite the opposite, where a unique and complicated tangle of relationships may influence how I share a message to core leaders. Within any industry, risks will be present and how you manage and navigate those risks will influence how you voice your own safety leadership vision and subsequent engagement behaviours.

Where an organisation sits within their own safety journey will help establish what level of safety leadership is needed within such a company. A case in point is with some work I completed in Papua New Guinea. The level of compliance and commitment to safety by the national workforce was beyond many sites I have visited within Australia, South Africa and the USA. A strong sense of pride was rampant across the site and the level of detail to all housekeeping and administrative tasks was phenomenal. When asking the site leader their thoughts upon such a strong level of compliance and commitment, they quickly mentioned that merely having a job was seen by the local workforce as a sense of status, even to a point where someone's PPE would be taken home and freely worn outside of work hours.

In the weeks leading up to my visit to Papua New Guinea, I was working at another site manned by a typical westernised workforce. On this site many gripes were shared and begrudging acceptance was demonstrated by workers in regard to wearing gloves or having to do pre-start vehicle checks each morning. Such a contrast in safety attitudes and behaviours may be linked to the availability of work in industrialised countries compared to Papua New Guinea or other factors such as the evolution of safety across different cultures or varying levels of perspective. How one approaches safety leadership in such environments would vary based upon the safety and cultural maturity of the organisation. One thing is consistent though, no matter what the cultural, social or economic background of a site, each person will experience similar feelings if a severe injury or fatality occurred to one of their close work colleagues.

Any blueprint or action plan aimed at improving safety performance needs to be catered for the individual, site or organisation. Safety leaders who drive lead indicators into an organisation may be better served by checking the level of maturity and understanding of such metrics with their employees. In cases where employees have had no previous exposure or understanding of lead indicators, safety leaders may be better served by starting with some fundamental safety processes, prior to stepping up their efforts with their employees. Going from zero to hero in one large swoop seldom occurs and is rarely implemented well. A more staggered approach that is crafted by the safety leaders on site is often more successful. Large rapid changes without proper consultation or execution may leave others confused, irritated and disempowered. A disempowered workforce equates to a dependent workforce which can then translate to a lack of free thinking or innovation around all elements of work which can extend beyond safety.

Have you ever noticed that general managers or CEOs of large blue chip companies can switch around from different industries, even without having detailed subject matter expertise on the industry that they may be emerged within? The higher up the organisational chart one goes, the more breadth and influence one has. This is where core leadership skills are needed as opposed to unique subject matter knowledge. On a micro scale it may be similar to the uneasy transition that technical experts have when they first move into a leadership or supervisory position. Reliance upon technical ability starts to be shadowed by the ability to harness a team towards group goals and the provision of team support. Safety leadership behaviours from a high-end leadership spectrum may be based upon governance as opposed to more tactile behaviours. This notion is reflected in Long's (2013) work where it was stated that the pointy end of the organisational chart is concerned around overall strategic direction, whereas further down the organisational chain more operational and tactical plans are executed by leaders.

Safety leadership exercised by executive boards may be etched into action via the values and safety vision that is set by the directors, which will then act as the running sheet for the workforce. The tangibility of safety leadership behaviours exercised by executives may be demonstrated by the exercising of corporate social responsibility. Such responsibility expands beyond the legislative requirements of ensuring employees are working in a safe environment and can be expanded to company actions or quotas that are beneficial for the greater community. Examples of this are often demonstrated by profits being siphoned off towards chosen charities or team building events that are focused on giving back to the community. In the end, executives and board members can demonstrate safety leadership and cement their legacy by focusing on the vision and macro goals that are set as part of any strategic planning.

One of the true measurements of integrity may be linked to the adage that how one operates when no one is looking can be an indicator of their values and beliefs. What better way to set this in motion by comparing behaviours within the workplace compared to behaviours outside of work. On a construction/mining/petroleum or any other high-risk site, safety behaviours are often mandated by established safety rules and performance expectations. Compulsory PPE and compulsory safety paperwork are common staples for the craft worker who may be fabricating pipes or the welder working on flanges. Driving to speed limits and exercising hyper caution whilst driving in a work vehicle could be contrasted to how one drives their own personal car and what PPE one wears whilst mowing their lawn or doing home renovations. One may argue that the work environment fosters such compliant behaviours because there are consequences in place if one does not follow the established safety rules. Outside of work, each person is left to their own devices in navigating their lives to a benign safety outcome that allows them to live their lives safely. Such differences in behaviour illustrate that one can adapt to their environment according to such influencing variables. The quintessential safety leader may be seen as the individual who applies as much caution towards their well-being at work as they do to outside of work.

Psychometrics are available which can ascertain an individual's risk propensity and level of situational awareness or attentional blindness. Organisations can use such psychometrics in an attempt to screen out potential risk takers within their organisation. The flaw in this approach can be the subsequent group think that may occur due to staff members having similar personality traits. Using psychometric personality tools for the purposes of safety needs to be astutely considered. Diversity may become jettisoned for the rule-abiding employee who may be too inhibited to question how things are done. As a result, the echo of 'we have always done it this way' can be the marker of an organisation that is unwilling to adapt or change. Consider how adaptive safety leadership needs to be due to the kind of employees one may lead and the outside influences of the work environment. A skilled and multi-talented workforce can generate solutions from multiple angles as opposed to the same solutions being brought to the table by the same individuals. Awareness and insight into risk propensity can be a marker for change, although individual motivations, attitudes, responsibilities and skills can influence overall behaviour. These personal variables not only can influence behaviour, but in turn influence workplace culture.

Personal variables and influences on behaviour

The zeitgeist that followed the behavioural psychology paradigm was a push towards the cognitive functions and abilities of the individual. Cognitive psychologists held a viewpoint that an individual is not the sum of their behaviour, but instead a product of their thinking. In the early 2000s, such thoughts were transitioned to cognitive safety which was a blue ocean strategy at the time, which has now become more common in the lexicon of safety. Prior to considering other external and socio-technical influences on behaviour, it is worth considering the influence that psychology, biology and the environment has had on safety leadership.

Integrated bio-psycho social model

Matching psychology with safety and leadership can help provide an explanation for individual behaviour. Biological factors such as bio-mechanics and genetics can have their foundations placed within biological psychology. Elements of personality, mood, cognition and internal dialogue can also influence leadership behaviour. Outside influences that pertain to the nuances of the work environment and broader political and economic trends have a large influence on both internal company processes but individual behaviour. Early foundations of the bio-psycho social model occurred in the 1970s, where the model was utilised by clinicians as a diagnostic and therapeutic tool to assist in the promotion of an individual's health (Borrell-Carrió, Suchman & Epstein 2004). Even within a different academic stream, safety was being pursued under the banner of psychology. Recent paradigms into safety have started to apply psychological principles within the safety context. A more holistic approach towards safety leadership can be embedded through such an approach. One of the more recent applications of psychology towards safety has been evident through cognitive safety.

Cognitive safety

I am about to reveal what is behind the curtain when avid supporters of cognitive safety tout their cognitive safety efforts over behavioural safety. This inside information was based upon marketing meetings I used to be involved in when describing the advantages that a cognitive approach to safety leadership has in comparison to other competing behavioural-based safety approaches. The core touting tool and example used was explaining that the way someone thinks about safety will influence their behaviour and therefore drive certain results. This is stemming from the foundations of cognitive psychology (Beck 1995). Cognitive safety was positioned over BBS methods by outlining that the decisions made by the individual are made prior to any behaviour occurring. Therefore any unsafe behaviours may be linked to the attitudes or beliefs of the individual. Before discussing the contradictory research into this paradigm, let's look at the psychology of attitudes and beliefs in more detail.

Through an understanding of neuropsychology and advancing studies into neuro-leadership, leaders can start to see and understand that there is a biological link to leadership behaviour and the brain. The pioneering work of Rock (2008) was able to break down leadership influence by appealing to someone's status level, ensuring consistency, expanding autonomy and ensuring the person can relate to others and demonstrate fairness. These elements can be transposed across to the safety leadership spectrum where influence is specific to safety. Contrasting work by Lindebaum and Zundel (2013) warned that neuro-leadership can be a reductionist approach which does not take into account other factors outside of the sum of the person and that tangible application may need further refining. Cognitive safety may be characterised by the exploration into individual thinking patterns or how such frames of thinking can inhibit safety. The neural footprint of thoughts may be influenced by connecting neutrons towards safety which may be formed at the beginning of someone's work career or influenced through role modelled behaviours from a young age.

Whilst I was growing up in a rural area, it was common for individuals not to wear seat belts and in some instances to learn how to drive well before the legal age. Being immersed in this environment and early exposure to such practices started to shape my own behaviour. When moving back to the city, I initially thought that the wearing of seat belts was optional and not so much of a safety requirement. Thoughts started to shift when I had to apply for a driver's licence and knowing that an automatic fail would be handed to me if I failed to wear a seat belt. As a side note, when seat belts were made compulsory to wear by law, I can still hear my mother explaining to a policeman that she chose not to wear a seat belt because her work as a nurse had exposed her to burn victims who were trapped in their car due to wearing a seat belt. Such excuses today would no doubt go down like a lead balloon, similar to how it went down in the 1980s when such seat belt laws were introduced across Australia. Internal commentary does have an influence on behaviour and even in the above example, mirror neurons might have been in place.

Mirror neurons is a term used to describe some of the research that showed the same neural pathways are firing in the brain when people interact with each other. This can be when two individuals are conversing with each other for a prolonged period and therefore have a rapport which makes them more readily susceptible to influence (Carter 2007). Specifically, the mirror neurons are reflected in the frontal mirror neurons and echoed in the parietal mirror neurons. From a safety leadership perspective, the safety behaviours of one person can therefore influence similar safety leadership behaviours of others. The importance that neural activity has in shaping the attitudes and experiences of an individual can be shown through the literature into neuro-plasticity.

Neuro-plasticity

To help understand why people do what they do, or even lead the way they lead, it is worthwhile exploring the role of our brain chemistry. Our brain is made up of billions of brain cells called neurons which are connected to each other through synapses. The more connections you have, the more fluent or competent you would be in a task, based upon these neural connections (Scholl & Priebe 2015). If an individual has a history of leading in a manipulative manner, then what they have are a series of synapses connected in a certain way which allows them to lead in such ways. Changing their behaviour is not impossible; it just requires a rewiring of the brain via the neural connections. The challenge may lie within how many months, years or even decades those neural pathways have been solidified for. New connections are formed each day based upon our activities and learnings. Well-documented research (Harmon-Jones & Winkielman 2007) has often shown how the brain can change itself, even if there is damage to the frontal lobes. Anecdotes about motor vehicle victims who have lost their ability to speak, only later to have regained the ability are well publicised and spoken about. In such cases, new neural pathways are being formed around the damaged neurons and therefore creating new connections. This is a process called neuroplasticity. Even with any damaged brain cells, new brain cells can be formed via a process called neurogenesis which is often triggered by exercise. Via exercise, a certain protein gets released which aids neural development (Price et al. 2011). Such science can help negate the old adage that 'leaders are born, not made' or 'you can't teach an old dog new tricks'. Even with insalubrious leadership practices, people can biologically change the wiring in their brains which therefore can start to change the way they lead others. The challenge though could be based upon how many neurons are linked to unsavoury practices. Awareness and personal levels of insight can be the catalyst for change, although how one reaches that insight can be a unique pathway that differs for each person.

Unless one is living as a hermit, it is almost impossible to not interact with others. As safety leaders it is even more paramount that we interact and engage with team members. As mentioned by Iacoboni (2007) human beings need to have the skill of navigating a complex set of social interactions which we are faced with and we are wired to 'think socially'. Stimulation via social interactions can release neurotransmitters and dopamine neurons which act as a reward mechanism (McBride, Murphy & Ikemoto 1999). A malfunction of this wiring could be based upon the Machiavellian leader who is ego-based and not in the business of developing others. Our social wiring may explain why individuals have a natural push back to such a style. It almost becomes instinctual to act as a safety leader in order to engage and effectively socialise with others.

Psychological considerations

Each individual processes information from both internal and external stimuli. How each person makes sense of this information can help influence current behaviours. With a broad understanding being reached on how the neurons are connected, we can now start to look at the psychological factors that may influence safety leadership behaviour. Specifically a breakdown of the conscious and subconscious brain will be shared, to help present a working model of how we process and make sense of the world.

There is a constant stream of stimuli that enters the human brain. Such information may be based upon environmental cues such as people speaking around you, weather temperatures or background noise. Alternatively, your own self-dialogue can be wreaking havoc and influencing the focus of your attention. As human beings, we do not process every bit of stimuli, as all this information is processed by the reticular activating system of the brain, where relevant information is sent to the conscious brain and other superfluous information is sent to the subconscious brain. What one pays attention to could be a product of previous activities or information that is deemed important. A practical example of this can be demonstrated with a leader I was working with. This particular leader did not value the development of his team members. The mantra that they were running from was based around the notion that if they were in his team, they would already be top performers and they had already participated in leadership courses and therefore did not need any further development. As a result, the development of his staff was seen as a chore and not deemed enriching. Over a period of time, the scope and quality of the workers started to suffer. After working with some of this leader's team members, I noticed an overconfidence bias which was governed by their leader's belief that no further development was needed. After providing objective feedback to these team members, they shared with me how their lens of the world had been polluted. Information they received from others via a 360 feedback process was not fitting with the mantra that was portrayed to them by their boss. In this example, any learning or development opportunities were not in the conscious mind of the leader, and therefore those opportunities were not passed on to their team members. Opportunities for growth, innovation and personal development then became forsaken.

As an overall function, the subconscious brain is the endless storage silo where all of our memories and past experiences are stored (Baars & Franklin 2007). This could range from our earliest experiences to our most recent activities. On top of this, all habits are stored in the subconscious brain. This can provide an explanation for leaders who may act in unsavoury ways, who may in fact be acting out of habit and routine as opposed to exercising conscious leadership. How one makes sense of information will be dependent upon one's personal database of previous knowledge, experiences, personality and motivations. On top of these variables is the individual variability that each person is socialised differently due to differences in their upbringing or through different role models that one has acquired throughout their lives. One of the orbiting elements which may be influencing safety leadership behaviour could be through one's own internal dialogue, in the format of negative self-commentary. Such negative self-commentary is often known as cognitive distortions (Beck

1976). If left unchecked these cognitive distortions can adversely influence not only your leadership style, but also your ability to function in most social situations.

Cognitive distortions can also be colloquially known as automatic negative thoughts or 'ANTs'. These negative thoughts can come unannounced, unplanned for or in some instances triggered by certain situations or individuals. There are a plethora of distortions which are well documented by Beck (1995). Examples of such distortions are as follows:

- Filtering: categorised by an individual paying undue attention to one negative detail without seeing the bigger picture. This distortion may be evident when a leader judges one of their team members by one safety mistake without taking into account all the other elements and activities that have occurred beforehand.
- Overgeneralisation: sweeping negative conclusions that go beyond the current situation. An example of this could be shown through a team member who gets unduly reprimanded for a non-conformance towards safety. Due to such feedback, the individual may start to feel that all leaders are negative and untrustworthy.
- Catastrophising: predicting the future negatively without considering more plausible outcomes. Commonly shown through an individual who has a bad day at work where an argument ensues with a team member which then starts a downward spiral. From that argument, it may kick start general malaise, where the person will never have a civil conversation and therefore it will impact promotion opportunities, decrease job satisfaction and lead to an inevitable demise due to overall unhappiness.
- Emotional reasoning: feelings start to drive thought processes, where logic may be jettisoned due to the way someone feels about something. A safety leader who 'feels' their workplace is safe and therefore does nothing to ensure its safety may find that the reality is vastly different.
- Personalisation: the belief that other people are behaving negatively because of something you did, instead of considering other alternatives. From the safety leadership paradigm, this could be evident through a leader perceiving that people are getting injured on their work site due to something they said.

As a leader, if one is not aware of their cognitive distortions, they may start to fall into the trap of such negative commentary. Through the adherence of such thoughts, one's leadership behaviour may be adversely impacted. Imagine a leader who has the cognitive distortion of 'catastrophising' where they shy aware from challenging safety conversations because of a fear that it may lead to a heated argument, which then cascades to performance management, which then trickles to unemployment, which then concludes in poverty and homelessness. All of this based upon magnifying a problem to the worst case scenario. You might have experienced the common rhetoric that 'all real estate agents are shysters' or that 'all lawyers are untrustworthy'. Such a lens amplifies the cognitive distortion of overgeneralisation. When applied to safety leadership, overgeneralisation may take the negative shape that 'all safety is about ass covering' without realising the importance that leadership has in shaping the safety culture of an organisation. Ensuring the cerebral does not turn into the visceral is the hallmark of managing cognitive distortions.

Having an increased understanding and heightened awareness of our own internal dialogue is the first step in managing the psychology of our behaviours. From a cognitive behaviour paradigm, ways to beat the negative thoughts are governed by helpful questions that are aimed at seeking alternatives to the thought or thinking about the evidence that backs up that thought (Padesky & Greenberger 1995). Applying artful questions to the safety leadership paradigm can help foster stronger safety leadership behaviours in the workplace by focusing on managing our own internal thoughts. Helpful questions can include the following:

- What alternatives are there?
- Am I assuming my view of things is the only view imaginable?
- What are the advantages or disadvantages of thinking this way?
- Am I expecting myself to be perfect?
- Am I over-estimating the chances of disaster?
- Am I asking questions that have no answers?
- What is the evidence? Am I confusing a thought with a fact?
- Am I jumping to conclusions?
- Am I only paying attention to the dark side of the moon?
- Am I assuming I can do nothing about my future?

Psychological factors and related nuances can have an influence on each person's safety leadership behaviour. As part of a holistic approach to safety leadership, the psychological elements need to be considered. The blueprint of how to demonstrate safety leadership through the RAVE model will be further detailed in Chapter 3, which takes into account these psychological factors. An individual's behaviour can also be influenced by external elements.

Environmental considerations

Within the work environment, there is a range of factors that can guide employee behaviour. Internal policies, outside trends, fiscal constraints, organisational culture, workplace relations and the physical structure of the work environment are just a few of the influences on behaviour. As mentioned by Cooke and Rohleder (2006) each person works in a socio-technical work environment. To consider safety leadership in isolation would be similar to judging someone solely on their looks. There is always a lot more going on behind the curtain than what you see. To help understand some of the external influences impacting an organisation and someone's safety leadership mindset, it may be worthwhile to consider the political, environmental, social and technological variables at play as well as other grounding research that can be influencing safety leadership behaviour. As mentioned by Mintzberg (1996), all elements of the external environment should be taken into consideration to ensure effective strategic planning.

Research from Hashim and Chileshe (2012) detailed that the biggest challenges for many organisational projects were issues around 'commitment and responsibility', 'leading projects' and 'conflict and communication'. On top of this, the researchers shared that resource allocation and competencies of project managers is also an area of concern. With these issues in place, the focus on safety leadership by general managers would probably be low on the totem pole. The prioritising of work and the fiscal workings of an organisation would probably trump the importance of leadership development. Toor and Ofori (2008) stated that project managers in large projects are more seen as managers as opposed to leaders due to the focus on short-term goals, budgets, quality and adherence to set schedules. During my many years on different resource projects around the globe, the biggest issue that is still shared with me is the completion of a job on time, ensuring it is completed within the budget and without any safety incidents. Those issues are often shared in that order, which may be a window into the mindset of the leader, where safety is mentioned last as opposed to first, which could reflect the priority of safety.

Political factors that may influence safety leadership behaviour include increased regulation of foreign investment into resource projects or local businesses (Ibarzabal 2011). Regulations around foreign investment may start to influence the broader industry which can therefore impact capital works, compliance requirements and leading others across multinational boundaries. Across the western world, democratic processes and elections may see political changes in governing bodies which can change every three to four years. Changing governments can reflect changes in subsidised businesses, development programmes, public funding, resourcing and regulations. The core example of such changes in policy can best be seen through the global issues of climate change. Work from Wittneben et al. (2012) outlined that climate change is no longer an act of corporate social responsibility, but instead a political issue that involves multilateral organisations, industries and state agencies. USA President Donald Trump's early 2017 withdrawal from the Paris Climate Treaty is an example of the backlash that can face politicians if their choices are not on the right side of popular opinion.

Changes in political policy may influence compliance and safety management systems through increased regulation. How safety leaders adapt, promote and approach such changes may influence the behaviour of others. The common catch cry from many leaders can be the amount of 'paperwork' involved in safety and the threat of consequences. Back in 2010, I was working in South Africa when a leader posed a realistic scenario to me. They mentioned that at the time, people caught speeding on the road do not accrue demerit points which can lead to a loss of their license. In comparison, Australia has a demerit point system which influences driver behaviour, under the threat of losing your licence. The leader asked, if such a system were not in place, would they have a higher number of people speeding on the road? This is a prime example of how political and legal factors can directly influence individual behaviour. It could be argued that a committed safety leader would not be motivated by such extrinsic factors, and instead they are motivated to drive to the speed limits to ensure the safety of themselves and others. Of course such sweeping conclusions do not take into account other variables.

Economic factors which can influence the overall organisational culture, which in turn can influence individual behaviour, includes fiscal costs, feasibility studies, tendering and administration (Li, Arditi & Wang 2012). Industries that are influenced by commodity prices have been economically impacted due to fluctuating resource prices (Garnaut 2013). Changes in economic investment can therefore impact the nature of whether or not organisations can make a profit. Shortened balance sheets can impact upon learning and development budgets, which can therefore inhibit the growth of safety leaders within an organisation. A shortcut to thinking that I have been privy to over the last few years is the slashing of learning and development budgets. Reducing costs in overheads does not always equate to sound business practice, as the impact can cut deep into the organisation. As posited by Delahaye (2011), the best time to develop your employees is during quieter periods as when the market turns around, employees will be better skilled and equipped to meet any challenges that occur.

Social influences on safety leadership behaviour can be evident through changes in social policy, importance of diversification and changing societal attitudes. The days of the typical office environment that required employees to work the regulated office hours of a nine-to-five desk job are starting to change, due to an emphasis on promoting a sustainable work-life balance. Leaders who do not value the work-life balance and drive production can therefore jeopardise employee well-being, which can be just another pseudonym for safety. The shift towards the work-life balance can start to enhance employee morale and provide the flexibility needed for many individuals who are working in the twenty-first century. In a true sense, safety leaders would be promoting the work-life balance to ensure psychological and mental health. A drive towards improving diversity in the workplace can be an antecedent to creativity, innovation and discourse. The quagmire may lie within vastly different industries and the cultural maturity of such environments to employ a diverse workforce. An example of this was shown through the research of Loosemore et al. (2010) that revealed diversity in the Australian construction industry is encouraged. Despite this, negative issues such as racist joke telling is an inevitable outcome of diversity within the construction industry. Safety leaders who accept such behaviour may start to breed a culture where such practices become the unexpected norm. With varying zeitgeists abounding, safety leaders need to stay abreast of such changes, otherwise they may be left behind in the changing stream of social consciousness.

In the knowledge economy, expertise can become the new wanted commodity. Changes in technology have made information more readily available than ever before. Social media applications have resulted in individuals expecting a higher level of interactivity by businesses (Berthon et al. 2012). Safety leaders who are not tapping into the latest trends and information may be operating off old adages which are not suited for the ever-changing workforce. Technology has more of an influence on behaviour than ever before. All one needs to do is go to a local café and spot the number of people interacting with their smartphones or other forms of technology. Information management systems that are used astutely can help share different learnings and experiences across multiple industries. To minimise the safety leader turning into a safety manager, it is imperative to keep in mind that information systems are there to serve humans and not the other way around. Further advances in technology may appeal to futurists in terms of different mediums or options that safety leaders can use in order to interact with their team members. The presence of the virtual network may kick start other more adaptable ways to exercise safety leadership from afar.

Understanding the external factors that are influencing safety leadership behaviours can provide a more measured approach to understanding why people do certain things. Streamlining all behaviours based purely on choice is only half the story. There are surrounding elements that are bigger than the person which can coat their leadership behaviours. A corporate entity that is going through a downsizing may start to elicit avoidance behaviours with their employees which can result in organisational silence. The socio-technical environment that each person works within runs deep and has varying influences on safety leadership behaviour.

Case study

A manufacturing company was having challenges with their site safety record. Individuals were not actively participating in safety activities, leaders were attributing incidents to workers making the wrong choices and the workers were attributing the incidents to external factors. When I met with the leadership team, they wanted to implement a programme that targeted safety leadership behaviour, aimed specifically at line managers. On top of this, they were keen to focus on cognitive safety for the craft workers in order to improve their 'safety attitude'. The budget for improving such efforts was endless, providing that their goal of improved safety performance was being met. A variety of cognitive and line manager development processes were introduced, although the safety performance only slightly improved.

Questions

Q1.   Which segment of the employee group is missing from this leadership engagement programme? What impact could this have on the final outcomes?

Q2.   What other information should be collected and sought out, prior to any leadership engagement programmes being facilitated to the workforce?
Q3.   How would you address the psychological, cognitive, environmental and biological factors of the workgroup, as asked by the senior leadership team?
Q4.   From the information provided, what could be some specific safety leadership behaviours present, which could be driving current results?

Epilogue

A multitude of factors impaired the overall success of the leadership development programme. As described in the case study, a lot of action and support was directed towards craft workers and front-line managers. The senior leadership team did not feel they needed to participate in any developmental training or coaching. Leaders attributing their poor safety record to unwise employee choices as opposed to deeper systematic issues was a scapegoat towards accountability. A cognitive programme was rolled out as well as frontline management training. A constant echo was heard in each training course which was along the lines of 'why don't our senior leaders go through such training?' To further complicate matters, an individual was killed on site, three years prior to the leadership engagement occurring. Suggestions were made that the senior leadership team should be the first pick of the rank to participate in the coaching and developmental workshops. Even though commitment was made by the leaders to participate in the process, when it came time to deliver the workshops, the workshops were often cancelled or postponed due to other issues or more important matters arising.

Further consultation revealed that plant machinery and equipment were well overdue for replacement, and a lack of consistent policies and procedures were in place to guide employee behaviour. Safety performance did slightly increase, but the root issues of what was causing some of the challenges were left unchanged. The estimated costs to repair the hazardous machinery and implement a robust safety management system ran into the millions of dollars. The consulting engagement was the cheaper option that only cost the organisation half a million dollars. This case study illustrates well that safety leadership and associated behaviours cannot always be tackled from a one-pronged approach.

Organisational and personal application

The following commentary can be utilised as a blueprint for applying the chapter content to your organisation or individual leadership profile.

Organisational application

*   When considering specific safety leadership behaviours, what are the outside variables and influences which can affect the overall organisational

culture? Without a PEST (political, economic, social, technological) analysis being undertaken, potential blind spots may start to emerge at a later date.

- How is safety leadership demonstrated in the organisation and are there processes in place where new starters are mentored by other safety leaders or cultural champions? Without outlining or crystallising what is expected from other employees in terms of safety leadership, it would be hard to embed safety leadership into the organisation.
- Ensure all other background challenges or 'noise' have been accounted for prior to engaging or embarking upon a safety leadership process. Embarking upon a new process may hit a stumbling block if there is unresolved energy around other issues. This could stem from impaired interpersonal relationships, lack of equipment or tooling, poor safety management systems or other related challenges.

Individual application

- What is your foundation behind robust safety leadership behaviours and what are you basing your experiences upon? Observing others, being mentored by someone or emulating a well-respected leader could be some pathways in establishing desired leadership behaviours.
- How would you place your own time stamp and flair towards safety leadership? Your own personal background, psychology, biology and experience can shape the safety leader that you want to be.
- Think about a time when you reacted as opposed to responded to a challenge. What were the factors that were outside of your control and what did you have direct influence over? How did these variables influence your behaviour? Considering other factors that may be impacting your current situation provides a broader perspective to the overall problem.
- What could be some common cognitive distortions that you might have experienced? What kind of cognitive distortions will you consciously be mindful of in the future? What could be some questions that you can ask yourself to alleviate such negative self-talk? Looking for the evidence to any cognitive distortion can help address such thoughts and assist us in achieving the goals that we want.

Chapter summary

Picturing safety leadership through the actions of an individual is only part of the equation. Safety leadership behaviours can be based upon engagement, vision or safety related behaviours and also influenced by a myriad of different factors. Specific behaviours can range from the transactional to the transformational, depending upon the position of leadership one has and overall scope of influence. Consideration of the bio-psychosocial model can help increase understanding when choosing to implement specific safety leadership behaviours. Accounting for all things within the realm of possibilities can provide a strong compass for exercising safety leadership. Exercising one's own brand of safety leadership will galvanise authenticity with your team members.

References

Baars, BJ & Franklin, S 2007, 'An architectural model of conscious and unconscious brain functions: Global Workspace Theory and IDA', *Neural Networks*, 20(9), 955–961.

Beck, AT 1976, *Cognitive Therapies and Emotional Disorders*, New American Library, New York.

Beck, J 1995, *Cognitive Therapy Basics and Beyond*, Guildford Press, New York.

Berthon, PR, Pitt, LF, Plangger, K & Shapiro, D 2012, 'Marketing meets web 2.0, social media and creative consumers: Implications for international marketing strategy', *Business Horizons*, 55(3), 261–271.

Borrell-Carrió F, Suchman AL & Epstein, RM 2004, 'The biopsychosocial model 25 years later: Principles, practice, and scientific inquiry', *Annals of Family Medicine*, 2, 576–582.

Carter, SC 2007, 'Neuropeptides and the proactive effects of social bonds', in *Social Neuroscience: Integrating Biological and Psychological Explanations of Social Behaviour*, The Guildford Press, New York.

Chance, P 1999, *Learning and Behaviour*, Brooks/Cole Publishing Company, Pacific Grove.

Cooke, DL & Rohleder, TR 2006, 'Learning from incidents: From normal accidents to high reliability', *System Dynamics Review*, 22(3), 213–239.

Delahaye, B 2011, *Human Resource Development: Managing Learning and Knowledge Capital*, Tilde University Press, Prahran.

Durban, AJ, Dalglish, C & Miller, P 2006, *Leadership*, John Wiley & Sons Australia, Milton.

Garnaut, R 2013, 'The contemporary China resources boom', *The Australian Journal of Agricultural and Resource Economics*, 56(2), 222–243.

Geller, SE 2001, *Keys to Behaviour-based Safety*, Government Institutes, New York.

Harmon-Jones, E & Winkielman, P 2007, *Social Neuroscience: Integrating Biological and Psychological Explanations of Social Behaviour*, The Guildford Press, New York.

Hashim, IN & Chileshe, N 2012, 'Major challenges in managing multiple project environment (MPE) in Australia's construction industry', *Journal of Engineering, Design and Technology*, 10(1), 72–92.

Iacoboni, M 2007, 'The quiet revolution of existential neuroscience', in *Social Neuroscience: Integrating Biological and Psychological Explanations of Social Behaviour*, The Guildford Press, New York.

Ibarzabal, JAH 2011, 'Natural gas infrastructure investment, regulation and ownership: The Australian case', *Policy Studies*, 32(3), 232–242.

Krause, TT 2005, *Leading with Safety*, John Wiley & Sons, Hoboken.

Li, H, Arditi, D & Wang, Z 2012, 'Transaction-related issues and construction project performance', *Construction Management and Economics*, 30(2), 151–164.

Lindebaum, D & Zundel, M 2013, 'Not quite a revolution: Scrutinizing organisational neuroscience in leadership studies', *Human Relations*, 66(6), 857–877.

Long, DG 2013, *Delivering High Performance: The Third Generation Organisation*, Gower Publishing Limited, Farnham.

Loosemore, M, Phua, FTT, Dunn, K & Ozguc, U 2010, 'The politics of sameness in the Australian construction industry', *Engineering Construction and Architectural Management*, 18(4), 363–380.

McBride, WJ, Murphy, JM & Ikemoto, S 1999, 'Localisation of brain reinforcement mechanisms: Intracranial self-administration and intracranial place conditioning studies', *Behavioural Brain Research*, 101, 129–152.

Mintzberg, H 1996, *The Strategy Process: Concepts, Contexts, Cases*, Prentice Hall, New Jersey.

Mischel, W 1999, *Introduction to Personality*, Harcourt Brace College Publishers, Orlando.

Padesky, C & Greenberger, D 1995, *Clinician's Guide to Mind over Mood*, Guildford Press, New York.

Price, D, Jarman, A, Mason, J & Kind, P 2011, *Building Brains: An Introduction to Neural Development*, Wiley-Blackwell, Oxford.

Rock, D 2008, 'SCARF: A brain-based model for collaborating with and influencing others', *Neuroleadership Journal*, 1(1), 78–87.

Scholl, B & Priebe, NJ 2015, 'The cortical connection (neuroscience): Understanding neural connections', *Nature*, 518, 306–307.

Toor, SR & Ofori, G 2008, 'Leadership for future construction industry: Agenda for authentic leadership', *International Journal of Project Management*, 26(6), 620–630.

Wittneben, BBF, Okereke, C, Banerjee, SB & Levy, DL 2012, 'Climate change and the emergence of new organisational landscapes', *Organisation Studies*, 33(11), 1431–1450.

3 Model of safety leadership influence

Golden road to safety leadership

Practical tools and suggestions to help leaders exercise safety leadership will be the core focus of this chapter. Through an empirical framework, safety leadership can be transferable, translatable and applied within the workplace. Over the course of this chapter, some of the following key questions will be answered:

- How can one build safety leadership relationships with others?
- What does authenticity look like within a safety leadership paradigm?
- How can one establish a vision that permeates throughout an organisation and personally resonates for others?
- What are some ways that safety leaders can engage with others?
- How can safety management systems complement safety leadership processes and behaviours?

Key objectives

The bedrock of safety leadership will be mapped out in this chapter through the empirically founded RAVE model. This chapter will help map out the importance of the RAVE model and provide leaders with practical and easy steps to apply safety leadership within their teams and within their organisation. At the conclusion of this chapter, it is forecasted that individuals will be able to have an increased understanding and application of safety leadership, which is guided by the following objectives:

1 Understand the core components of the RAVE model of safety leadership and be able to apply some of these concepts into one's own safety leadership ethos.
2 Have the ability to exercise the nuances of safety leadership into greater safety management systems and to integrate these components well into an overall safety leadership process that is beneficial for both the individual and organisation.

Setting the scene

Leadership models and frameworks are plentiful and can be integrated well if contextualised wisely into an organisation's culture and safety processes. After being caught up in the tertiary system for a number of years, I do remember fellow professors touting research which in one way or another they were directly involved in. Sometimes this myopic stance can lead to similar results being achieved, whilst stifling innovation. Not only does this self-serving bias exist within some university circles, it can exist within the consulting world. Comparisons between one organisation's safety leadership process over another safety leadership process can be like splitting hairs. Any safety leadership implementation should be rooted in research. Programmes that outline the differences between leadership versus management and the principles of behavioural psychology via ABC analysis are probably echoing relics of the past. Off the shelf programmes are most likely going to be broad attempts at addressing the nuances of each organisation's safety leadership challenge. Contextualising any organisational challenge into a chosen framework would be better served at embedding long lasting change.

During my doctorate research, I was able to take a broader perspective and utilise a lot of the existing research into leadership into an integrated safety leadership model. To ensure validity, my integrated model into safety leadership was empirically founded through a range of individuals who were interviewed across multiple geographical areas. The safety leadership model is called RAVE which is centred on the pillars of Relationships, Authenticity, Vision and Engagement. Each section of the RAVE model is further broken down to specifics which can allow all safety leaders to practically implement safety leadership within all settings. As touched upon in the previous chapter, there are a lot of variables that can influence behaviour. The RAVE model will break down core components that safety leaders can morph into their leadership profile, in order to get the results they are looking for.

Introducing the RAVE model of safety leadership

Safety leadership extends beyond transactional behaviours and can penetrate the deeper structures of an organisation. I once met a leader who was well regarded as the living specimen of what safety leadership looked like. Upon doing a site walk around with him, he detailed to me that, no matter how hot it is, he always wears his gloves, even though he is not doing any practical work. This was said on a site where the daily temperature constantly soared well above 40 degrees Celsius, where the only weight loss routine needed was to do a few leadership walk-throughs on site. He also went out of his way to speak to people that he did not know in order to build up relationships and to open up the conversation towards safety. Some of these actions reflect the components of the RAVE model which have been detailed in Figure 3.1.

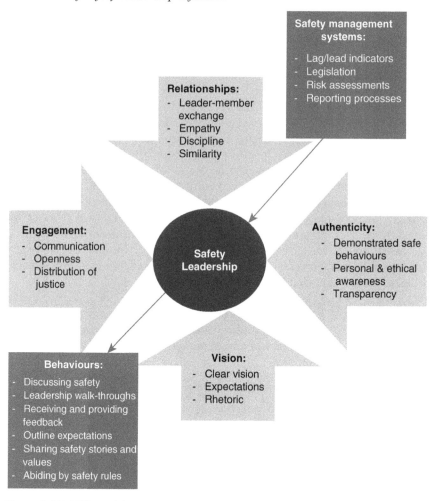

Figure 3.1 RAVE model
(Source: Developed for this research)

The components of the RAVE model are all inter-related in order to achieve the utopian vision of safety leadership. Without due consideration of supporting safety management systems, a proportion of safety leadership behaviours may not be embedded within the company. As a result, opportunities to develop a learning organisation may therefore be forfeited whilst the possibility of sharing any learnings vanish into the atmosphere. The demonstrated outcomes of safety leadership have been captured in the RAVE model under the subsection of 'behaviours'. Measuring effectiveness by leadership intent is only a half measure compared to overt observable leadership behaviours. Leaders who work within organisations or industries where safety is not a pivotal part of business may sometimes struggle with the notion of safety leadership or how to exercise effective leadership. Countless times, I have had project managers who are at the top of their game share with me that one of the biggest challenges is influencing others. This is often quickly backed up by the project managers sharing that they never received any formal training whilst studying or were never 'shown the way'.

On a long domestic flight back home once, I chatted with a CEO of a large conglomerate company who was embedded within their business for over 30 years. Upon asking what his biggest learnings have been, he thoughtfully replied that 'you cannot judge all of humanity based upon the people that come through your office door'. This was attributed to most people appearing at his office to share their gripes, concerns or problems as opposed to sharing any successes or celebrations. How one handles such factors can become the edifice of all leadership, including safety leadership.

Relationships

Imagine trying to influence someone that you have never spoken to before. Or perhaps influencing someone you cannot find any common ground with. If there is no social currency generated between two people, the ability to form solid working relationship may be impacted. From a safety perspective, this could explain the malaise or uneasiness people feel when intervening in the presence of a safety breach or unsafe condition. The worker/manager relationship can become pivotal in allowing the safety relationship to thrive. I still remember sitting in on a leadership meeting on a construction site where the construction manager openly belittled and scolded a supervisor for parking in the wrong area. After this public humiliation, in the next breathe, the leader than asked for any suggestions from others to improve safety on site. In response, the answer he got was deafening silence sprinkled in with large doses of tension. This is a prime example of relationships impairing the free flow of information and adversely impacting the level of openness between the worker and the manager. Without due consideration of the leader/worker relationship, safety leadership efforts may hit a stumbling block. It is for this reason that the backing research and practicalities of leader-member exchange (LMX) have been included in the Relationships part of the RAVE model.

Leader-member exchange

Accessing the social capital of work groups and being able to influence employee satisfaction has been shown to be the cornerstones of leader-member exchange (Koh & Rowlinson 2012; Mueller & Lee 2002). Leader-member exchange can be characterised by how well one works with their leader and how well the leader works with them. Through enhanced working relationships, the ability for employees to voice their concerns starts to increase which is precipitated by a foundation of trust (Hsiung 2012). Prevalence of the LMX relationship has been show to increase perceived organisational support which can mitigate the unwanted elements of bullying and harassment via improved well-being and care (Nelson et al. 2014). Possible pathways to enhance the LMX relationship have included a magnified focus on team development and team effectiveness (Graen & Schiemann 2013). Practical components of embedding LMX can include driving team alignment, development of team capabilities and contextualising rewards to desired behaviours. A leader who develops team capability is also a leader who invests in their staff, whilst upskilling team members to be better equipped to tackle upcoming challenges.

The premise that upward communication between team members and their line managers improves safety communication and therefore limits safety incidents was empirically founded by Hofmann and Morgeson (1999). The simplicity in having good team leader relationships cannot be underestimated. Employees who have a poor relationship with their leaders are going to be less inclined to extend themselves beyond what is needed and may even start to look elsewhere for guidance and support. The LMX relationship can be further enhanced through the following:

- developing mutual trust by sharing information and being transparent in all communication
- reinforcing the desired behaviours, which in turn can increase employee confidence
- identifying common bonds and working towards a shared group goal
- providing autonomy for the team member, where individual decision making is encouraged
- treating team members with respect to allow a relationship of trust to be developed.

The above behaviours can be coated with the broad-brush of safety through specific safety goals, behaviours, information and autonomous decision making. If barriers exist between team members and their line manager, then the loyalty that the person has towards their organisation may be waived and alternative employment options may be sought. If left unaddressed, the infamous 'us versus them' mentality may start to emerge. If investigating the reasons why an employee leaves, the true reason is sometimes glanced over. In such situations, the core ill-advised leadership behaviours are left unaddressed and will continue to occur for the next generation of employees which are recruited to the company. The safety leader who is immune to the emotions and feelings of others may lack the empathy needed in order to operate as an effective safety leader.

Empathy

Many years ago, I was consulting to an organisation that had offices worldwide. When I was talking with one of the general managers, based upon their challenges and concerns, one thing kept coming up: namely, how to approach safety from a global perspective. It was perceived that the value of life in the outskirts of Johannesburg was vastly different to the sun-scorched earth of the Western Australian outback. One thing which can be universal across multiple cultures and geographical boundaries is that everybody grieves when there is a loss of life. If organisations can minimise that grief by leading a strong safety culture, that promotes well-being, then the benefits are going to extend beyond the immediate family unit and favourably impact the bottom line (Krause 2005). My research into safety leadership epitomised the importance of having a personal belief in safety and displaying empathy towards others when promoting safety.

Without compassion and empathy, the emotional intelligence of an individual may be deemed quite low, as shown through the research from Rankin (2013) who looked at emotional intelligence within the nursing environment. In a safety context, if a leader cannot empathise with someone who has been injured or potentially injured, then the level of connection will be void and the working relationship adversely impaired. In the majority of cases, it is often accepted that individuals who call into work sick are given a reprieve to get better prior to coming back to work. Imagine a leader who orders a team member to get back to work straight after a workplace incident. It would be similar to a leader who orders their sick employee who is riddled with mucous and other bacteria gyrating throughout their whole being to get back to work. Both situations are focusing on safety, although in different contexts.

Through multiple interviews that I have conducted with top leaders across multiple industries, many leaders shared the importance of empathy. Such comments included: 'the feeling of having hurt someone on the job for me is the worst thing that can happen' and 'I couldn't think of anything worse than confronting someone's family or the individual themselves and saying that I'm responsible for the actions that have occurred'. During my research, the participants were reflective of how they would feel and how their family would react if an incident or major injury occurred within the family. Such thoughts triggered an emotional response which tapped into the depths of empathy. Self-reflection is a helpful tool to enhance awareness and build emotional intelligence (Goleman 2002). Being able to see outside of your own parameters and to understand the predicament of someone else is not only a great way to build empathy and rapport, but to increase overall understanding. For individuals analysing workplace incidents, it is important to understand the person's choices and the prior situation that led to the incident. Doing so not only minimises the person being unfairly dismissed but also identifies any possible systematic challenges. Empathy within the safety leadership paradigm can be built by abiding by the following principles as adapted from Jones et al. (2014):

- When an incident occurs, try and see the situation from the other person's perspective before responding.

- Minimise stereotypes, labels and other inflammatory language which could diminish the individual's input. Labelling someone as 'accident prone', 'stupid' or using other such language creates a distance between yourself and others.
- Managing your own frustration and annoyance when an incident occurs or any other challenge arises assists with self-regulation of your own emotions.
- Comparing someone with another may create pressures that impact the building of trust and undermine empathy. Comparing how one team is safer than the other team starts to create an external focus which limits self-awareness.

Through the identification of non-verbal cues, the roadblocks of empathy can be established. A safety leader who cannot empathise with their team members will probably be a safety leader who is despised by their team members. Discipline is needed to ensure safety leadership is brought to the foreground.

Discipline

As part of developing robust working relationships, safety leaders need to have a strong moral compass, be disciplined in their approach and in turn apply discipline as needed for anyone who blatantly disregards the safety agenda. It never ceases to amaze me the amount of leaders who shy away from tough conversations and instead go for safer routes such as anonymous 360 feedback assessments. In the past I used to facilitate many 360 feedback sessions with leaders where that leader receives feedback from their subordinates, peers and their own line manager. Prior to commencing any 360 feedback process, I would always reiterate that any 360 feedback assessment should be used for development purposes. On the contrary, by the time I get deep into the feedback sessions it soon becomes apparent that either a line manager has not had a frank and authentic discussion with their team member or discipline has not been applied for previous misdemeanours. Without discipline being applied, the unwanted behaviour becomes the common norm. Employees who are not reprimanded for blatant safety breaches will not learn the error of their ways or understand what is expected of them at work.

Research from Long (2013) described three separate generations of leadership. The first generation is driven by a command conquer style, which would be similar to the authoritarian leader. Evolving from this style of leadership is the 'carrot and stick' approach where rewards and punishment are used to influence behaviour. Third generational leadership was a term coined to describe leadership behaviours where commitment is sought and the leader is self-directed and has strong internal locus of control. Using Long's descriptions of leadership from the safety paradigm, you may start to see the differences between general leadership versus safety leadership emerging. In a life and death situation, where someone's safety is balancing on a tightrope, the authoritarian leader may be needed. If someone continues to disregard safety, a reprimand or other form of discipline is needed. As mentioned to me by a number of leaders in my research, 'in construction you are always going to need that amount of discipline and line of authority' and 'the most disciplined sites tend to be the safest sites'. A distant cousin of discipline could be assertiveness, where it has been shown that assertiveness can be a core element for building effective teams (Epitropaki & Martin 2013). Discipline within safety can be linked to the Just Culture model that aims to ensure fairness and accountability in the safety management process (Dekker 2012). Discipline is a pivotal part of safety leadership because instead of looking at fiscal or group goals, we are looking at the human frailty of life, where the wrong circumstances can lead to death. It is for this reason that safety leaders will need to adapt and flow between the different generations of leadership as posited by Long (2012) when disciplining others.

In terms of personal discipline, third generational leadership is a staple. The safety leader who is quick to blame others for incidents or attributes poor safety performance to external factors is probably the same safety leader who says 'it was just bad luck' when explaining why someone got injured. Being privy to a range of incident analysis techniques and safety management systems, the factor of 'bad luck' is not often shared as the root cause for someone being injured. Imagine telling shareholders at an annual share meeting that the company's safety record is dropping due to 'bad luck' as opposed to other factors at play. Personal discipline is the visceral side of safety leadership. The leader who does not wear the required PPE, blatantly takes shortcuts or does not manage their stress levels will also be the leader who lacks credibility. A pathway to develop personal discipline is to ensure an internal locus of control is present.

Personal discipline can be influenced by whether or not the person believes they are in control of their situation or whether they attribute their situation to external factors. This personal discipline can be linked to locus of control which can be referred to the degree to which the events and outcomes of a situation are perceived to be in that person's control (Joseph, Reddy & Sharma 2013). Human beings were attributed to have a natural default to have an external locus of control, which has been linked to primal instincts or not being cognisant of one's actions (Long 2013). Safety leaders who are quick to blame others or attribute poor safety performance to outside influences are not well positioned to change their current predicament. Seminal research from Jones and Wuebker (1993) showed a statistically significant link of hospital employees who had an external locus of control ending up having more accidents and injuries than those with an internal locus of control. The rate of incident reporting and near miss reporting may be altered if individuals do not exercise ownership and take accountability. Organisations that are burdened by externally focused leaders may find themselves victims to market variables. Creating internal capacity or developing suitable actions to shape the pathway forward may be jettisoned for a quick external attribution.

Many years ago I attended a marketing meeting with a colleague of mine as a subject matter expert in the areas of safety culture and leadership. Upon meeting the executive team, we quickly introduced ourselves and got down to the bones of the meeting. To help establish context for myself, I asked the leadership team what were some of their challenges. A breathless retort was shot back at me by the general manager who hastily said 'every company has challenges, who doesn't have challenges, but we are a lot safer than the company across the road who recently just killed someone'. Whilst listening to this response, I had to mask my dismay as my internal dialogue was racing a hundred miles an hour. This site I was at was comparing their safety performance and how they were tracking by the number of people they had killed. It would be similar to me comparing my health and diet to that of a competitive eater at the hot dog eating contest at the Coney Island 4th of July celebrations. When the general manager shared this point of view, I replied back by saying 'is that how you measure your safety performance, by comparing yourself to sites that have had a fatality' which subsequently went down like a lead balloon. In this instance the leadership team had an external locus of control where the shoe was always on the other foot, and merely looking into the mirror of their own capability was not even on the radar. Exercising personal safety discipline when there is an external focus can adversely impact team members and, if left unchecked, create a culture of blame. Over the years, through counselling and coaching, I have shared a number of foundation principles to help increase someone's internal locus of control. Such considerations include:

- Identify what is in your control and what you have influence over.
- Utilise the power of personal choice, regardless of the situation you are in.
- Ask yourself 'what can I do to contribute to the situation?'
- Recognise all of the events/people/factors outside of your control.

Safety leaders who are quick to blame and deflect responsibility are going to be leaders who form surface relationships with their team members and peers. If you had a leader who constantly 'passed the buck', then subconsciously you may start to limit the number of interactions you have with that person. Opportunities to discuss safety start to become limited and you become educated on how to treat that person based upon their actions. Discipline through personal accountability forms part of effective safety leadership through the development of strong relationships.

Similarity

Have you ever tried to have a conversation with someone who you were not able to connect with? Perhaps they shared their interest in fine art, whilst you shared your interest in MMA fighting. Alternatively perhaps they were a

President Trump staunch supporter whilst your views differed to the contrary. Human social connection allows the richness of meaningful relationships to shine. Individuals who have similar interests or similarities are going to be able to build rapport quickly and form solid working relationships. If personal similarities are absent in the workplace, the common bond could be through shared goals. Research from Vlachoutsicos (2011) detailed that persuasion can be exercised through the identification of shared working goals, which can help establish a relationship of trust. Trust can be exercised through a similarity of interests and goals as well as social identification of common activities. The ultimate safety goal for many leaders is to ensure that their workplace is free of incidents and that the safety of their staff is secured. Having a shared safety goal is one way to help foster relationships, although further shared similarities can create rapport and help the relationship deepen (Kouzes & Posner 2007). Safety influence through similarity enables social identification to transpire which creates common bonds. When there is a crisis or core safety concern, an effective safety leader can tap into the tenets of charismatic leadership and emphasise the collective whilst articulating broader goals (House & Shamir 1993). Reflecting back on past global catastrophes, such as the 9/11 attacks in New York City or the tsunami in Asia in 2004, general populations rallied together to support grief stricken communities. Mass mobilisation of support is concentrated through the similarity of a common goal, regardless of someone's demographics, age or gender. If there is an injury in the workplace, a similar wave of support may also be present. One common staple and similarity that leaders may have with their team members includes the common bond of family and friends. In addition, the general malaise and sorrow one may feel if someone was to be killed in the workplace would most likely be universal. Building similarities and connections with others can also be precipitated by the following:

- Alignment of organisational and personal values. If there is a misalignment between values, it may equate to a short tenure of employment.
- Referencing a broader safety vision and purpose which links into macro goals and creates a greater sense of purpose.
- Identification of shared sporting interests or hobbies. Bonds over your favourite football team, travel interests and other such hobbies can solidify relationships.
- Linkages to family, children or common acquaintances. Social identification through children or certain individuals one may know can act as a reference point during conversations.
- Sharing work-experiences based upon previous companies that one has worked for and how that company has approached safety can provide context to others and allow a discourse into safety.

Establishing similarities is a fast track way to build rapport and create a sense of safety. The importance of safety leadership and relationships can be warranted through the development and validation of a psychological contract towards safety. A psychological safety contract is defined as an individual believing that employer and employee safety obligations are contingent upon each other (Walker 2010). If safety leaders have aligned goals with their team members, they can expect reciprocity of safety practices which can influence the overall safety of a company.

Relationships are pivotal in the art of influence and even more so when influencing others towards benign safety practices. If individuals are demure and shy away from interacting with others, they may inadvertently be impacting the safety relationship they have with their colleagues. One leader I was coaching was very clinical in their approach, did not enjoy making small talk and was annoyed by the nebulous conversations that would happen within the office. Upon asking how he would be perceived by others, he was insightful to realise that he would come across as 'cold' and 'uncaring'. A challenge was set forward for this leader. Over the next three weeks, he was tasked to find out something non-work related about each of his colleagues and team members that he works for. To his surprise and to the surprise of others, he became a chatty Kathy and would sometimes embody the person he used to be frustrated with. On a biological level, neurotransmitters were being released and the conversations were biologically reinforcing and also enriching. Through a conscious effort in building relationships, he found more people approaching him about work-related matters and his general level of approachability increased. A safety leader who refuses to build relationships is also a safety leader who will most likely be out of the communication loop.

Authenticity

Nothing damages credibility more than a leader who says one thing and does something else completely different. When this occurs, cognitive dissidence starts to creep in which creates a sense of unease. I can always remember an HSE manager that I worked with who was about to go outside and do some safety interactions, when he was reminded by his colleague to wear his safety glasses. Without hesitation his reply was 'I don't need to wear them, I am the HSE manager here on site'. The tenure of his position was short lived as he only lasted a few more days before he was terminated from his position. The contrasting of statements between what is said and what is done impacts the level of authenticity that someone displays. There is a spiking presence in research that pertains to authentic leadership. A lot of the early pioneering work identified authentic leadership being characterised by increased self-awareness, unbiased processing and a relational orientation (Kernis & Goldman 2006). When authentic leadership is exercised, the influence on employees can be reduced burn-out, increased empowerment and enhanced job satisfaction (Gardner et al. 2011).

As part of my early research, I explored the notion of authentic leadership from a safety leadership paradigm. Components of authenticity were well referenced as many participants outlined the importance of 'honesty', 'being genuine' and 'admitting your weaknesses and not bullshitting your way through'. This level of candour can set the tone for other people sharing information. Safety information that is shared becomes safety information that is more likely to be actioned. Pathways for developing a learning organisation are strengthened when safety leadership is demonstrated, transparency is present and there's a high level of personal and ethical awareness. Authenticity becomes the next pillar towards safety leadership and the second component of the RAVE model.

Demonstrated safe behaviours

The nebulous term of 'walking the walk' in terms of a leader demonstrating safety leadership can be further broken down to specific behaviours, as explored in Chapter 2. How one demonstrates safety remains an integral component to safety leadership and can be a differentiating factor compared to other leadership styles. It is a lot more tangible to witness a leader being compliant with safety in contrast to leaders who are being compliant with other managerial tasks such as balancing the budget or planning daily duties. The demonstration of safe behaviours is included in the Authenticity component of the RAVE model due to the detriments to credibility and integrity if there was a misalignment between someone's spoken words and visible actions. Sometimes the litmus test could be whether or not a leader displays safe behaviours outside of the workplace. Within a work environment there are supporting rules, procedures and other mechanisms that promote and in some cases enforce safety. Once these elements are removed and the workplace culture is out of the mix, the actioning of safe behaviours may be driven purely by the individual and their own regard to safety.

It is important to note that risk-taking behaviours outside of the workplace do not necessarily mean you have the same risk profile within the workplace. If someone regularly bungee jumps, followed by a serve of sky diving and then rounded up by some free base jumping, it does not correlate to whether or not they will be more inclined to take shortcuts in the workplace. Within the work environment, there are too many variables in place and any risks are often mitigated through the appropriate controls. Sometimes muddy waters do occur in terms of demonstrating safe behaviours at work or at home. When I was working in a remote mining town, individuals shared with me that the 'policing' of safety was encouraged outside of work. Examples of this were based upon employees driving past someone's house and if their light vehicle was not reverse parked (as per requirements on site) or if the wheels of their car were not stabilised through plastic blocks, then that person's name would be shared with the leadership team. Subsequently that person would then be reprimanded. The impact of such a touted philosophy had a detrimental impact on inter-team trust, teamwork and culture. Whether or not such a supported process was ethical or crossed the boundaries could be argued from both sides. What is pivotal is ensuring safety behaviours are present within the workplace where the greatest exposure to risk is present.

Personal and ethical awareness

There are notable companies that have floundered in the past due to poor ethical practices. This can include the well-publicised collapse of Enron or Lehman Brothers, which had their similarities rooted with unethical leaders making questionable decisions. When faced with moral or ethical dilemmas, it has been shown that in the face of contrasting temptations, authentic leadership can be the mediating factor (Cianci et al. 2014). From a safety leadership paradigm, the ethical dilemma could be in the face of taking a safety shortcut in order to save time or to get the job completed on time. Thinking about the consequences of behaviour is a more mature thinking pattern, which can be classified as formal operational thinking, which matures in later years (Corey 2001). The possibilities of physical injury or harm to others may get neglected when someone is behind on a task or getting pressured by others to get the job done as quickly as possible. Not wearing PPE has obvious consequences when things go wrong. There can also be other negative consequences for other tasks such as failing to vet new employees coming into the organisation or 'cooking the books' from a fiscal point of view where liberties are shared with the misappropriation of funds. As safety leaders, it becomes a greater imperative to act in a safe manner to ensure that the health and safety of employees, or in some cases members of the community, are not placed in jeopardy. Consideration of the wider population can also become an organisation's distinct competency through the practising of corporate social responsibility (CSR). A competitive advantage can be achieved by exercising strong CSR as the business world is calling for increased responsibility and greater ethical awareness (Carroll & Shabana, 2010). Personal accountability can be the antecedent towards ethical awareness. Exercising self-leadership through reflection and through the lens of ethics has been shown to increase levels of moral judgement (Steinbauer et al. 2014).

When exploring personal and ethical awareness with leaders across the resources sector, a strong theme came through where leaders were stating that 'you need to be able to sleep at night' and have a 'clear conscience'. To amplify the importance of personal ethics with safety leadership, one leader stated that 'safety is intertwined with personal values and I think it's intertwined with ethics whereas maybe organisational leadership is less so' and that 'I'm doing this because I know it's the right thing and I know it's in the best interest of the business in setting that example'. Safety leaders who are not ethically minded may also be the safety leaders who over-work their employees or engage in practices that are dubious. One organisation that I was consulting with had to take legal action against one of their leaders who was utilising workplace labour and supplies for their own home renovations. When such unethical practices or safety behaviours occur within the workplace, a call to arms is needed to voice such behaviours as unethical. This is where the role of the infamous 'whistle blower' comes into it.

In regard to safety, 'whistle blowing' can be as innocuous as calling attention to the person breaking a life-saving rule within the workplace or as murky as speaking out against nepotism, bribes or misdirection of funds. From an interpersonal perspective, if a strong workplace culture exists, having that one-on-one conversation about an at-risk behaviour becomes easier compared to an organisation that is embedded in mistrust and workplace politics. For the more complicated ethical dilemmas, how one is treated by the leadership team for speaking out against such actions can become a cultural clue of whether or not other people will be willing to speak out against such actions. Individuals who have the courage to speak out against unethical behaviour may be vilified, scrutinised or met with scepticism. During my counselling days, I had a client that I was helping out who had anxiety and depression based upon speaking out against a person who was siphoning funds from the budget. The psychosocial issues that were experienced by this 'whistle blower' were overlooked and overshadowed by the publicised fall out of such unethical actions being made public. Sometimes there is a personal cost for being brave and speaking the moral truth. Safety leadership can also be inclusive of exercising CSR for environmental misdemeanours, violations against governing bodies or known risks to the consumer which are not made public. Different ways to prioritise safety ethics and encourage an environment where people can speak out against unethical behaviour can include the following:

- Training and education. It is hard to hold people accountable if they are unsure what is expected from them, by their leaders and from their company. Sharing ethical conundrums and expected behaviours can be a pathway to educate others. A code of ethics or a team safety charter can assist in such education.
- Rewarding ethical behaviour. Reinforce the behaviour that you want by recognising individuals who act ethically or go above and beyond what is expected from them. This can be in the form of individuals speaking up and preventing an incident or intervening as needed.
- Work-life balance. Employees who are placed under stress may be more inclined to make unethical choices (Menzel 1996). Minimising burn-out and encouraging work-life balance by promoting exercise and managing one's own stress levels through relaxation or other methods can assist one's ethical compass.
- Discipline. If breaches towards the ethical standard are left unchecked, then the questionable behaviour may become the norm. Supporting processes that encourage complaint processes can minimise fear of the non-reporting of unethical behaviour (Mayer et al. 2013).

Sometimes speaking out and intervening with unsafe behaviours may be a challenge due to internal processes or outside cultural influences. Safety leaders who are driven by a strong sense of morality may be more inclined to act ethically. Ethical awareness to actively speak out against the norm requires a strong sense of character. Role modelling such behaviours can create a transparency which can lead to trust and increase the likelihood of further safety information being shared between leaders and employees.

Transparency

Safety leaders can set a safety culture through their actions and behaviours. Research from Toor and Ofori (2008) outlined that transparency and trust are hallmarks to establishing a robust safety culture. Leaders who proverbially lay their cards out on the table can create a sense of transparency with their employees which can minimise the unwanted politics that can plague an organisation. Transparency can come in many different forms, from the sharing of one's own capabilities to the sharing of information pivotal to the work being completed. Individuals who share their own shortcomings can aide transparency whilst modelling authenticity (Shamir & Eilam 2005). Imagine a leader who is quick to vocalise their own mistakes compared to a leader who hastily covers up their own misgivings. Individuals who are not confident in their own ability may mask their mistakes which therefore limits the trust they elicit from others.

Many years ago, I was undertaking a safety culture analysis for a large organisation. During countless interviews and focus groups, a common story emerged about one of the core leaders who was 'covering up their mistakes'. It was alleged that one specific leader underquoted on a multi-million dollar job and was attempting to overcharge the client through additional variations to the initial contract. Being the kind of person who attempts to exercise transparency, I eventually talked to the leader in question to get their take on the situation and shared the story that was being communicated around site. Upon hearing this information, the leader was quick to ask who specifically was sharing this story and that all rumours were untrue. Further details and data was absent from this leader and instead a focus was placed more upon who I was talking to as opposed to the information that was being shared. The level of defensiveness and the bulging vein that was appearing on the person's side of the neck suggested to me that something else could be at play. A month went past and eventually the leader was moved on due to unsavoury practices that were exposed via a human resources investigation. This example outlines the dual importance of ethics but also the absence of maturity in leadership practices. The actions undertaken by this leader flies in the face of the research undertaken from Leary and Tangley (2003), which outlined learning can be maximised when an individual identifies their own personal cognitive biases, strengths and weaknesses. The fear of sharing such biases and weaknesses may dampen the tendency for someone to exercise full candour.

Transparency can be a bridge to developing credibility and trust. The honest sharing of information has been shown to promote trust and increase vocal engagement with employees (Hsiung 2012). Vocal engagement is para-mount when encouraging employees to share safety information. Among the many interviews that were undertaken as part of my research, participants stated that 'I don't think there is any reason not to be transparent, particularly the blue collar workers who are very adept at separating the woods from the trees'. Other comments included 'if you try and play your cards close to your chest, then I think you lose respect and then your integrity is up for question'. Trust and integrity can take months or years to build and can be demolished within minutes. If a leader is not cognisant of their own actions, then inad-vertently they may be adversely judged by others. Just as politicians are easily crucified for social gaffes or brash comments, the tide can also turn for leaders who make similar mistakes.

I once remember providing some 360 leadership feedback to a senior manager. A consistent theme came through that the leader had a penchant towards micro-managing and not being forthcoming with information. Upon exploration it was shared that the main reason why information is not shared with the wider team is because 'it's outside of their pay bracket'. The con-sequences of withholding information were shown in the verbatim comments of this person's 360 report. A lack of transparency created a culture of politics and second meanings. When a message was shared, employees would look for the true message of what was being shared. Communication starts to suffer as a result. To minimise this impact and to relish the benefits of transparency through increased trust, engagement and employee ownership, the following actions can be taken:

- Update the team with your current work load, what is on the horizon and core focal points for the upcoming month or year. Ensuring there is a successor minimises dependency on the safety leader and promotes interdependence.
- Admitting to one's own mistakes or failures is not only humbling but creates the environment where it is ok to make mistakes, providing one learns from such mistakes. Entrepreneurs may fail many times before success is achieved. A learning environment is marked through the acceptance of failure.
- Constant communication is one of the hallmarks to increasing empower-ment and engagement. Sharing core information through different mediums helps crystallise the leader–member exchange relationship. Even in the face of dire news, treating people like adults and being direct with employees is better received than withholding information under the pretence that it may damage someone's self-esteem. As referenced in the work of Stewart and Jones (1987), treat people like adults and they will respond like adults.
- In organisational structures that are complex and bureaucratic, the free flow of information may be stagnated (Hayes 2010). Structures that allow easy access to leaders can minimise the infamous 'us versus them' mentality and allow a direct flow of communication.

Safety leaders who are transparent with safety information and upcoming goals are more inclined to get the same information reciprocated back to them from their team members. Confusion can be minimised if there is a broader goal or vision that has been forged by the leadership team. Such a safety vision can help align employees to a greater purpose.

Vision

A sense of purpose can be the ultimate guide in achieving moral satisfaction and greater meaning. Safety leaders who are authentic probably have an acute awareness of what they are aiming to achieve. This could come in the form of a macro vision or personal vision of what they choose to achieve. The importance of a vision has been linked to achieving main goals and aligning employees (Kouzes & Posner 2007; Long 2013; House & Shamir 1993). I have come across workers who get a sense of purpose by linking up what they do to what the end product is, and other workers who cannot see beyond their finality of their day-to-day tasks. In the latter, a sense of hopelessness occurs. Upon arriving on a remote site, I was disembarking the plane when I heard the person behind me say 'shit, another four weeks in this shit hole'. We had not even stepped off the plane and the worker behind me was already in the mindset of misery. When I hear such comments, I equate those comments to someone wishing away the next month, in order to celebrate their short rest break. If an individual is not able to see how their work links into the greater picture, a sense of futility may become the norm.

The importance of having a clear vision is not unique to safety leadership, as it is also a core ingredient within transformational and third generation leadership (Long 2012). If a safety leader is unclear on what they are aiming to achieve, it will be challenging to empower and engage others to a common cause. It would be similar to a sailor navigating the seas without a compass or clear destination in sight. Via pure serendipity they may reach their destination. Similarly to the sailor, safety leaders who lead without a vision may reach the outcome of zero incidents, but it would be through a process of chance as opposed to choice. Through a clear vision, detailed expectations and rhetoric, safety leaders can maximise the collective to a specific goal.

Clear vision

Have you ever met an individual who is present in the moment, mindful of what they do and non-phased about the challenges that are thrown their way? When coupled with clear direction, such characteristics can be a powerful combination, especially when leading others. The innate ability to achieve goals or attain a vision has been neurologically traced to the medial pre-frontal cortex (Matsumoto & Tanaka 2004). So even from a biological level, we have a predilection for achievement. Within a business environment, the leader who does not achieve their goals will probably be on the bullet train towards demotion or alternatively have a sharp change in their career progression. Safety related visions can be as generic as ensuring no one gets injured or as one leader shared with me 'having a target of continuous improvement'. Visions that are emotive, clear and specific can help enliven others and provide clear direction and sense of purpose.

Safety leaders who are amiable and adaptive can tailor their safety vision to calibrate with changes in the work environment. In the face of adversity and potential incidents or workplace injuries, a change in direction or renewed focus may be warranted. Vision setting has been a staple in the change management literature through the pioneering work of Kotter, which still has plausibility and relevance in today's complex environment (Appelbaum et al. 2012). A sense of urgency that can precipitate change can be governed through any major challenges or incidents which may plague an organisation. With a heightened sense of urgency, a collective vision can set the new goal posts and boundaries of expected behaviours. One of the preambles to such a vision will be based upon the authenticity of the safety leader and how sincere they are in communicating their vision. A previous general manager once said to me that 'we are probably kidding ourselves if we think everybody is going to be buying into this safety vision'. Such comments may reflect one's own reservations towards a safety vision, indicate cultural challenges or possibly reflect previous experiences. Linkages towards safety as a value can be the glue that aligns a greater safety vision to individual employee behaviour. If interpersonal connectedness is absent, then the reluctance to adopt a leader's vision would be valid. A safety leader's values can be reflected in their vision, through the communication of the vision and the language and emotion used.

Aspirations to achieve safety excellence can be approached from a micro or macro perspective. A broader safety vision can help align the masses, whilst a personal vision can contextualise the message directly with team members. As an example, think about a broader slogan that aims at achieving the ultimate goal of safe production. This can take the shape of 'zero harm', 'goal is zero', 'safe choices everyday' or any other such verbiage to describe the greater goal. Sitting underneath these goals and slogans can be the safety leader's own commitment of what they will do to help achieve that safety vision. If a leader detailed to their team that their goal is to innovate, learn and prevent incidents through robust communication and heightened awareness, then the safety vision can become elevated. Team charters, pledges or other such mechanisms can help solidify commitment, although unless referenced and reviewed, such commitments can become background fodder. Reward processes and reinforcement that taps into the broader message or vision can embed the vision further whilst enriching the importance to others. I still remember walking around on a mine site and seeing the edges of a brightly coloured and well-detailed banner. Upon closer inspection, the banner was in fact a team charter, which was hidden by two industrial bins. Such a placement of the team charter spoke volumes to me of how ill-referenced the charter was and what level of importance employees placed on the charter. It appeared that the notices that got the most attention were the employee notices that detailed someone's utility vehicle being for sale, which was strategically placed in the lunch room, for all to see.

Exercising safety leadership through a clear vision can be approached on two fronts. This can be the creation of a personal or organisational safety vision. After assisting many organisations and companies to develop their broader company or personal safety vision, the following factors can help guide safety leaders in crafting a clear vision:

- Imagine what the ideal state or goal would be and articulate the purpose behind such a desired state. The purpose provides the reason why the vision is being crafted.
- Differentiate what is unique about your organisation or leadership style to avoid motherhood statements that may become hyperbole.
- Undertake a stocktake of the company's strategic goals and whether or not your current safety leadership vision matches the broader plan. Amend as necessary and involve core members of the leadership team.
- Communicate the vision through various mediums which go beyond vanilla notices and posters. Options can range from the moniker being included at the bottom of email signatures or use of the intranet, signed charters or pledges.
- Link the work of each person in the organisation to the broader vision. Allowing the bigger picture to be crystallised from the most mundane work to other complex roles can create a sense of purpose, regardless of position.
- Align your personal safety vision with your values to provide a strong moral compass when faced with ethical dilemmas. A heightened self-awareness of what is accepted and not accepted makes moral dilemmas easier to navigate.

A well-established safety leadership vision can be contextualised to your strengths, environment, industry and team. A safety leadership vision within an underground coal mine may differ vastly from a leader who works in an accounting firm based in a major city. The common staple could be the bloodline of safety or maximising well-being within the organisation. Outlining the importance of safety can be exercised through clear employee expectations. A clear vision can outline the grander goal, although individual employee impact may be diluted unless leader expectations are communicated to the safety leader.

Expectations

Trying to discipline an employee who has never been shown what to do or was never told what is expected of them becomes counterproductive. It would be similar to chastising a child for putting their hand in the cookie jar, when they were never told that the cookie jar was off limits. Establishing and communicating personal expectations with employees can promote the leader-member exchange relationship and act as a feed-forward technique. Typically feedback is characterised by the sharing of constructive information, after an event or situation has occurred. Expectation setting through the format of feed-forward techniques can establish the desired behaviour from the start and paint a clear picture of what is expected. Safety leaders who establish and communicate their safety standards and workplace expectations to employees can minimise the rebuke from workers who may say that they were 'never informed' of what was expected of them when their behaviour is called into question.

Sharing employee expectations can be the close cousin of establishing a realistic job preview. Detailing what the task or job is realistically going to be like and what actions and safety choices an individual should make can create certainty. Realistic job previews have been shown to minimise early resignations (Stone 2007) then naturally detailing what is expected from staff can also ensure the longevity of work from employees. As a safety leader, the grounds of performance management become a lot easier to navigate if clear expectations are set with the employee at the start of their employment and reviewed as necessary. Outlining the potential consequences for not abiding by the set expectations can be the antecedent for desired behaviour. If automobile drivers were informed by news outlets and by government officials that there was a zero tolerance for driving cars under the influence of alcohol, then this may curtail many people from having any alcoholic drinks at all, especially if drivers know that their blood alcohol limit has to be at 0.00 when driving their car. As a side note, many Western countries do not require current licensed drivers to re-sit their driver's licence test or go through any periodic theoretical assessment, even if laws and road rules change.

One of the mature safety leaders I was working with on a construction site recognised the importance of clear expectations early in his career. Any new starters who reported directly to him would sit through an alignment session where he shared his expectations and detail what he would expect from that person on the job. These alignment sessions were not just privy to his direct reports as he would also address the broader workforce at the start of their tenure and again one week into the project. Safety expectations were well detailed which focused on the importance of health and safety compliance tools (Take 5s) but also company expectations of having hard barricading around at-risk work and ensuring employees exercise personal discipline by having all sleeves rolled down. The follow-up session, one week into the new starter's employment, was an opportunity for the workers to share their feedback on the site culture, what was working and what was not working or what needed some fine tweaking. On a construction project that had up to 400 people, these alignment sessions were a way to enhance communication and reinforce the messages from the core safety leaders on site. Alignment sessions that detail personal safety expectations from employees can also feed into the larger safety vision of the organisation or work group. In the resources sector, the focus on safety can be palpable where the consequences for blatant safety breaches can often mean termination. Alternatively, an absence of clear expectations within other environments can inadvertently cause stress to employees.

In a previous life as a treating psychologist, I was able to witness first-hand the drawbacks of not establishing clear expectations to employees. Whilst working at a rehabilitation company, the hours would be long and the work quite draining. As with most new employees, you try and establish yourself within the fold and try and work out the lay of the land. Upon my quick orientation, I was introduced to my colleagues and shown the computer management systems for documenting client notes. Being naturally curious and fresh faced, I noticed all my colleagues working well back into the evening hours of the day. As self-imposed group pressure came into, I would also stay back and work the hours, even though my own workload was well and truly finished. About two months into my job, a senior psychologist shared with me that I didn't have to stay back and work longer hours, just because everyone else was doing it. Then he explained the nugget of gold to me, the crucial bit of information that was missing at the start of my commencement. It was shared that as long as I meet my minimum billable hours each day, then I am doing what is expected from the company. If I wanted to earn a bonus, then that's where the additional hours come into. Savouring my personal time over the proverbial carrot hanging over my head, I started to finish work at a reasonable time, as my own personal expectations came to the fore. Outside priorities were deemed more important than living to work as opposed to working to live.

A few rules of thumb when detailing expectations to employees can include the following:

- Understand the employee's skill set and how their work is going to fit in with what you expect from them. For example, if an employee is an electrician, then greater safety diligence would be placed around isolating prior to performing any electrical work compared to talking about job set-up.
- Share what the consequences will be if your expectations are not met. Blatant breaches of any lifesaving rules on a mine site or construction project may result in termination, depending on the outcomes of an incident investigation.
- Provide the reason *why* any expectations are being shared. When individuals understand the reason behind any expectations or goals, then they are more likely to oblige and meet those expectations.
- Utilise different forms of feedback on whether or not the expectations are plausible, current and reasonable. Alignment sessions, regular reviews and other mediums can help establish such feedback channels.

The dual combo of a clear vision and well-established employee-site expectations are core components of establishing safe employee behaviour.

The extra juice to drive the message home can be in the form of specific language used or rhetoric employed by the safety leader.

Rhetoric

Captivating language and the astute use of metaphors and stories are well-utilised skills by the master communicator. The importance of rhetoric was founded in the research around charismatic leadership where it has been shown that in the face of a crisis, the setting of a new vision or goal for the future is needed (Halverson, Murphy & Riggio 2004). Specific rhetoric captures the attention of employees (Davis & Gardner 2012). Once the attention has been captured by employees, then the safety leader can reinforce safety and use the moment as a platform to inspire others. A crisis from a safety leadership perspective can vary from an incident within the workplace or other upcoming challenges emerging on the horizon. If a call to arms is absent on a site where there has been a major injury, then unrest will sweep through the company and a level of uncertainty will be plaguing each person's mind. A strong safety leader who addresses the workforce and details upcoming actions can help minimise confusion and re-establish small goals and provide an immediate focus. On a site I visited in North Queensland, it was shared with me that a few major incidents had occurred but the leadership team had not addressed the workforce about the situation. As a result, the reporting of incidents had stopped because there is a general belief that nothing would be done by reporting the incident. When an organisation moves to this mindset, it is a powder keg of trouble as a major injury will be lurking around the corner.

The ability to connect with individuals with varied backgrounds and amplify your own personal flair through the use of expressiveness or the ability to share safety stories in public forums can captivate an audience to action. A stretched example of the power of rhetoric may be evident in the 2016 presidential campaign in the United States. At the time, Republican nominee Donald Trump was breaking all of the social taboos that politicians have been abiding by for years. The language utilised by Trump was able to cut through many levels of hyperbole and insincerity that are the common staples of politicians. In a political race that usually runs to a well-tested and well-prescribed format, the infamous Trump rallies were the playground of Trump's rhetoric, where he was able to drum up grass roots support, in the arguable absence of well-solidified policies. The crisis in motion in this example that often precedes charismatic leadership was the burdening influence and fear of a terrorist attack. When there is a collective goal, then the master communicator can shape language towards that goal.

There is a notable dark side of charismatic leadership which was detailed by Samnani and Singh (2013) which pertains to the use of influence to facilitate group pressure to conform. From a safety leadership paradigm, this dark side of charismatic leadership may be an advantage if the goal is to utilise group pressure for employees to conform to safe work practices. On the other spectrum is group pressure being applied to influence employees to take shortcuts. Leaders who establish such a deleterious environment can run the gauntlet of incidents, low morale and other consequences which may emerge.

Research from Ehrhart and Klein (2001) revealed that followers can differ in their attraction to charismatic leaders. The mediating factors that can gel alignment between the charismatic leader and their followers include the articulation of a values-based vision and the leader taking calculated risks. Davis and Gardner (2012) revealed that rhetoric that references leader similarity towards team members and information relating to children, family and friends can be the driving tools towards influence. Emotive language around the impact of safe behaviour on family members and friends can be the common language that allows team members to identify and empathise with the safety leader. Rhetoric can be astutely used as a tool for safety leadership by considering the following:

- What emotions and behaviours would you like to drive with your team by the kind of rhetoric that you use and when you use it? Aligning the masses post-incident can establish the boundaries, although such an approach may be deemed reactive as the centralising of the team is happening post event.
- Sincerity and simplicity of language are markers of effective communication. Over-stated metaphors or jargon may lose the broader appeal of any core safety leadership messages shared.
- Identify informal leaders within the group who may be utilised to apply benign group pressure towards others who allow them to conform to safe working practices and standards. Inter-group social pressure towards the desired behaviour can be an effective tool which relies on the strength of relationships within the team.

Influencing others through specific verbiage and the painting of a clear vision are integral tools for motivating and providing a sense of direction to team members. Unclear safety goals and misguided expectations can adversely impact employee behaviour. Exercising the full potential of safety leadership will need to be harnessed through effective engagement.

Engagement

One of the core components of the RAVE model has been based upon engagement. When applied to safety leadership, engagement is the overall outcome or behaviour comprising communication, openness and distribution of justice. Without meaningful engagement, it is expected that safety issues and concerns will decline, while organisational trust will be jeopardised (Cunliffe & Eriksen 2011). Picture a leader who barely interacts with their employees, regularly has their office door closed and has not established any group communication forums or regular team meetings. Through minimal engagement, minimal interaction will occur which can then result in minimal trust and minimal loyalty to the company resulting in minimal output.

Whilst consulting in the deep red hues of the West Australian Pilbra, I was analysing the processes and assessing the communication mediums on a piping job. There were about 100 employees, comprising a site manager, multiple supervisors and two superintendents. Upon speaking to the supervisors about the job, outcomes and set goals, it became clear that there was no alignment or thorough engagement from the superintendents and the site manager. In fact, one of the superintendents was witnessed to tell a visiting manager that she should fly back to the office in Perth because women should not be allowed on pipe-laying jobs. Through these sexist and outdated remarks, the visiting manager in question was never to be seen again on site. I was able to talk with the female manager and get some clarity around the situation. The female manager shared with me that such outdated views and philosophies have no place in the workplace and if that person remains on site and is not disciplined for their comments, then there is no point going back to site. Inadvertently, the superintendent's comments stopped the person from coming back to site which therefore limits engagement and reinforces their own behaviour. To thicken the plot, when I was consulting with the site manager about communication and whether everyone knows what their expectations are, it was clearly stated to me 'don't worry, they know ... trust me they know'. This sureness of communication was abundant even though there were no supervisor team meetings, regular debriefs or other forms of communication within the site. Alas, the only time there was any form of site-wide communication was after a major incident occurred on site. Limited communication and engagement are prime drivers for organisational rumours, which can further muddy organisational clarity and trust.

Benefits of safety engagement can be based upon the tenets of behavioural-based safety through safety interactions which can strengthen employer/employee relationships and improve communication (Geller, 2001). Engagement driven by open and honest communication may build capital trust between the safety leader and team member (Lapierre, Naidoo & Bonaccio 2012). In addition, engagement provides an avenue for open dialogue as opposed to monologue, which can then be exercised through team building, work training and leadership walk-throughs (Frankel, Leonard & Denham 2006). Safety leadership engagement can be epitomised through communication, openness and ensuring employee fairness through a distribution of justice.

Communication

A plethora of literature exists around the importance of communication, and many workshops are available that aim to enhance personal communication skills. When applied to safety leadership, the ability to communicate safety information and provide a personal connectedness to the end-user is a skill that is needed to negotiate organisational barriers. These organisational barriers can include distracting environments, poor group dynamics, nepotism and use of the wrong medium (Carmeli, Brueller & Dutton 2009). An example of poor group dynamics and the wrong medium being used to share information was based upon a leader I was working with who found out his position would be terminated by seeing it advertised on the internet. The leader asked me 'what do you think that means?' which I replied, 'probably means you need to look around for work'. Afterwards I was asking his colleagues about his job security and the advertised position and a few people said to me 'he is getting sacked, everyone knows it, except him', that was until he found his job re-advertised. An example of a distracting environment can include a supervisor I observed who was running a pre-start meeting on a resources project next to the ablution block where the sewage was being pumped. Even though effective communication and a clear safety vision were being shared by the supervisor, the smell of last night's dinner in faeces form was distracting from the core message.

Levels of employee satisfaction can also detract from broader organisational communication. If an employee has mentally left their job or are upset about an organisational issue, then there may be a possibility that core information will be kept to themselves and not shared with others. Safety shares are then jettisoned for resentment and reluctance. It would be similar to an employee having a brilliant idea about improving operational discipline, but keeping it to themselves so they can share it at the next company that they are looking to move to. Channels for capturing core information and lessons learned are needed to enhance organisational learning and to minimise the same mistakes or incidents from occurring again. Safety management systems can be the outlet for such processes.

During my research into safety leadership, many leaders outlined the importance of 'one on one conversations' and 'talking to the guys' in order to crystallise their safety message. Personal communication that is interjected with honest and truthful safety information can gather maximum impact and guide trust. Leaders who are not effective communicators may inadvertently send the wrong message to their team members. Countless times I have been to companies where senior leaders share with me that members of the leadership team may come across brash and uncouth which often results in people leaving the organisation. In some cases, such poor communication skills creates a trail of bruised people who are left behind who then become jaded and negative towards their company. The main reason why the person is kept on and not disciplined falls back to the common catch cry that 'they are very technically skilled'. If they are in a senior leadership position, importance should be equally placed on their communication skills as opposed to technical ability. If left unchecked, a message gets sent to the workforce that it is accepted to treat people poorly, providing you have technical competence. What is becoming a common occurrence in such situations is that leaders do not directly address such concerns with their employees. The tough conversations that may cause malaise are not being held and therefore unsavoury behaviour goes unchecked. If people are being belittled or not spoken to in savoury ways, then well-being and safety may be in jeopardy through an impact of someone's psychological health. Through the hallmark work of Scott (2004) it was well established that 'fierce conversations' need to occur. It was positioned that the relationships we have are the conversations that we have. Evolving from this could be the notion that the safety conversations that we have may become the safety that we live.

The inter-relating aspects of the RAVE model can be parried into the sub-element of communication. Individuals may be reluctant to hear the importance of safety due to an over-exposure of the topic. Other individuals may be reluctant to take information on board due to having established ways of approaching their work. When the signs of conflict arise, the deployment of personal discipline, empathy, established expectations and a clear vision can come to the rescue. Other interpersonal ways to improve personal communication which have been adapted from the work of Hogan (2003) include the following:

- Communicating through stories helps elevate a message and creates personal connectedness to the person speaking. In ancient civilisations, culture was passed on around the campfire through stories, which may reveal a natural evolutionary penchant to stories being shared.
- Learning preferences vary according to each person. By utilising language that appeals to the senses, a greater impact can be achieved to the receiver. Sensory language can include emotive words that tap into the visual, auditory, olfactory, and kinaesthetic or gustation senses.
- For an individual protesting or not wanting to heed the suggestions from a safety leader, the use of outcome-based thinking may be of benefit. Outcome-based thinking is the ability to provide the reason *why* someone should follow through with a behaviour. If a worker staunchly states 'I don't want to work with that person, as I think they are useless', the subtle reply could be 'that is why you should work with that person, as you can get to know that person in more detail'.
- The power of non-verbal communication can never be underestimated. Matching your non-verbal language through facial expressions, body movements, tone and inclination of voice can add credibility to the words being spoken. When there is a mismatch behind the words spoken and the body language displayed, it can create cognitive dissidence.

In the isolated security of an offshore resources project, I was able to see the dichotomy of the spoken importance of safety, although the communication mode suggested otherwise. Each meeting in the morning was started with the embedded 'incident and injury free moment' which was an opportunity to share some information around safety. This topic was shared with as much vigour as a mortician at a bachelor party. The tone was subdued, the leader was not making eye contact with anyone and subsequently not many 'incident and injury free moments' were shared. After about a week of observing these safety shares, it got to a stage where nobody raised anything and then the conversation was quickly moved onto the upcoming schedule and work duties for the day. Through the non-verbal communication being displayed, it was covertly suggested that the leader was not placing an importance towards safety and therefore their openness to suggestions may have been limited. Information being stifled can equate to the possibilities of innovation and shared learning falling to the wayside.

Openness

Leaders who I spoke to during my research emphasised the importance of safety leaders being 'open to feedback' and having an 'open door policy'. Outlining to employees that you are open to feedback differs from how feedback is received. I have met people who have told me that they have an open door policy, where they say that the door is open, but that doesn't mean they are open to suggestions or changing how they operate. Alternatively, I have worked with leaders who epitomise the open leader, where their open door policy equates to a slew of people lining up at the front of their door, waiting to see that person. The weight of seeing everyone often meant that the required work duties and priorities of that leader would be put on the backburner. Being open to feedback are the building blocks of building trust and increased organisational citizenship behaviour, which reflects participative leadership (Miao, Newman & Huang 2014). Being accessible provides an opportunity for impromptu conversations to occur.

There is always the chance that the information one has could be out of date or incorrect. Not being open to the possibility that you could be wrong can lead to failure and suppress personal growth. As a business coach, I would often share with junior consultants that people who are open and amendable are a dream to coach. Individuals who are unwilling to change or not willing to consider other possibilities may be an energy hog, as it takes a lot of energy and time to try and increase that person's level of insight. If an employee is not willing to adapt to the changing safety standards and processes that are implemented within an organisation, they may run the risk of being left behind and inhibit their own employment options. The level of openness someone has is one of the big five personality traits, with the other four personality traits being agreeableness, conscientiousness, extraversion and neuroticism (Mischel 1999). This psychological link can help explain why leaders who are open to new ideas may solidify work relationships and role model the desired behaviours of others.

Through an openness to new ideas, it is predicted that the integration of feedback can strengthen a working relationship and therefore improve a discourse into safety. Safety leaders would need to be present and accessible to their team for the relationship towards safety to be built. In the absence of face-to-face interaction, it is forecasted that relationships will not be as strong or solidified (Cunliffe & Eriksen 2011). For anyone that has facilitated or sat in a workshop on safety or leadership, you might have encountered the disgruntled individual who believes they have seen it all before and therefore are already numb to the ideas and suggestions being shared. Countless times I have heard from people that they may not need to sit through any safety training or workshops because they are already safe due to not having any injuries over the course of their career. When such information is shared, it provides a nice outlet to employ outcome-based thinking. I would often reply to the person that with such a perfect safety record, it demonstrates the value that they place on safety. Influencing individuals with such pre-conceived notions may be a call of action for the facilitator to pace out any objections and make that lasting impression which can open the doorway of possibilities. A point of personal resiliency for safety leaders is understanding that it may be egotistical to think you can change someone, instead what we say and do is the only way we can influence others. Safety has evolved over time from the implementation of guardrails in manufacturing companies in the early 1900s (Zinn 2003) to the presence of legislation. If an openness to change were not present, then the early recklessness and lawlessness of work would still be present today and therefore impacting the overall safety and morale of employees. The motivation for people to come to work when placed at immediate risk would be low and the resulting sick days would be high. Guiding points to aid one's level of openness include:

- Entering each meeting, forum or workshop with the mindset of learning. Asking yourself 'what can I learn from this?' or 'how can I apply this information to my job?' enables a level of openness and leaning to occur.
- Monitoring your own levels of defensiveness and identifying triggers which may cause slight frustration or stress. Self-awareness is the pathway to behaviour modification. Understanding that there is always more than one way to approach a situation can help someone accept the possibility that they may be wrong or incorrect.
- Change and innovation can be activated by asking employees questions about 'how can we do this differently?' or 'is there a better and safer way to approach this work?' Adopting an innovative mindset allows the benefits of creativity to come to the surface whilst acting as a catalyst for change.
- When suggestions and ideas are being shared by employees, it is important to validate any ideas being raised otherwise it may curtail the raising of future suggestions. Effective communication skills can help encourage further involvement.

Safety leaders who look to repeat the same habits and maintain the status quo will often reach a plateau in safety performance and overall performance. The fertile ground for change is even more apparent if an organisation has had a serious injury or incident. One worksite I went to had a fatality occur four months before my arrival. Upon talking with one of the contracting groups, I learned that the senior leadership team were not very open to change. I was flabbergasted by this; when such catastrophes occur, change is needed to prevent future fatalities. This is the ethos of any incident investigation, identifying root causes to prevent further incidents from occurring and ensuring that any proposed changes are equitable and fair across all key stakeholders. Fairness and distribution of justice are relevant to the safety leader if discipline needs to be applied.

Procedural justice

Imagine working in an organisation where there are different sets of rules for different people. Nepotism is running rife and consistency is applied on an as needs basis. If left unchecked, silos may occur, inter-team bickering emerges and organisational politics start to become common practice. The importance of fair and consistent treatment of others is paramount for credibility of safety leaders but also in guiding team expectations. Any hesitation to act may be perceived as favouritism. Procedural justice refers to how people are treated fairly across an organisation and whether there is consistency in organisational discipline (Krause, 2005). Organisational equity and a fair distribution of justice has been linked to increased likelihood of employees speaking out and the establishment of an environment that is conducive to increased engagement (Hsiung 2012; Zhu et al. 2011). When applied to safety leadership, fairness may increase the likelihood of workers speaking out against unsafe acts or behaviours.

First-hand experiences of when discipline was not applied and the organisational impact it had on employees was evident at a large coal mine I was working at. On this particular worksite, there was a zero tolerance policy for anyone who attended work with any alcohol in their system or other banned substances. Craft workers were quickly removed from site for violating this procedure. Through the fugue of alcohol, one senior leader might have forgotten this policy and attended work with alcohol in their system. It was quickly noted that this leader was not made redundant like many other craft worker would have been and instead only given a reprimand behind closed doors. The general workforce started to have a disregard for rules because of the inconsistency of discipline and the level of integrity for the leadership team was well below par. Incidents started to increase and levels of disengagement were running rife. Eventually the senior leader in question was moved to another mine site, although the damage was already done and the legacy of such actions was a point of discussion for many months afterwards. The importance of consistent discipline and employee fairness was attributed to ensuring procedural justice and setting up a culture of care (Read et al. 2010).

Inconsistent discipline for safety breaches may create confusion around established expectations. The articulation of strongly held beliefs and an overall commitment to the organisation are markers of the transformational leader (Bass & Bass 2009). Demonstrating such valued beliefs through tangible action is the ethos of the safety leader. Treating people fairly can allow mutual respect to be present which can further solidify the safety relationship. In office environments, the omission or exclusion of someone from core meetings can create a rift in the working relationship. Such social exclusion and unfair treatment can trigger the same neural activity that is equivalent to someone experiencing physical pain (Rock 2009). As indicated by Rock (2009) this may suppress someone's emotions and therefore place someone on guard where the free sharing of information is closed. Over the years, I have seen procedural justice and employee fairness facilitated by the following factors:

- Ensuring the pathway for promotion or access to any reward system is transparent and consistently applied. Perceptions of nepotism are increased if someone is promoted without due diligence being applied. This diligence can be based upon a merit-based or competency-based process.
- Open feedback channels minimise the hoarding of information and selective sharing of information which can inadvertently create 'in' and 'out' groups. Public recognition of new ideas or good performance minimises the possibility of someone taking credit for someone else's work.
- Safety incidents to be fairly investigated through one of the many investigation techniques with a just culture process being applied. Just culture was posed by Reason (1997) as a way to keep people accountable and to minimise unfair dismissal based upon actions and events leading up to an incident.

If conversations and actions are not carried out with a hint of fairness, safety leadership may be forsaken. Engagement through clear communication, openness to new ideas and exercising organisational fairness can allow safety influence to be galvanised. Other elements of the RAVE model flow together to create an overall framework for leaders to demonstrate and embolden safety leadership. The RAVE model was founded upon empirical research and validated through countless interviews across many leaders. Exercising safety leadership is pivotal to influencing others. Consideration of supporting safety management systems provides a complete picture of safety leadership.

Safety management systems

Leadership does not sit in a vacuum that is isolated from all other processes. Instead, leadership fluidly interacts with the external environment, culture, social system and internal processes in place. Safety leadership is heightened and strengthened through robust safety management systems. Capitalising on past learnings, capturing core information and managing safety processes would be difficult unless there is an effective management system in place. It has been shown that careful consideration into supporting safety systems will help foster a clear safety vision into a tangible reality which can help improve safety performance (Bottani, Monica & Vignali 2009). Any barriers to an effective safety management system may be due to external and internal factors such as market demands, competence and costs (Benjaoran & Bhokha 2010). A case in point of these barriers was evident with a large multinational company that I was working with. Outdated equipment and facilities were clearly visible across site and were often voiced as major concerns from the employee group. The potential costs of updating all of the machinery and equipment was quoted to be tens of millions of dollars. As a substitute to replacing all of the equipment in place, the organisation was engaging an outside party to focus on the attitudes and cognition of employees. On a balanced scale, the cost of training was a lot more favourable compared to dealing with the inflated costs of replacing plant machinery. Such an approach would be similar to making your beloved child more comfortable by merely talking to them instead of replacing the bed of nails they were sleeping on.

With the plethora of safety management systems available, the safety leader may need to navigate through the ocean of options to help utilise the best system for their company. To help clarify the importance of which safety management system to implement, Cheng, Ryan and Kelly (2011) stated that safety management practices that involve a dissemination of information are associated with positive performance. In practice, larger organisations that are not informed about safety risks happening within their own business may run the gauntlet of incidents and injuries reoccurring within the business. Not having a platform to capture and record such information limits the opportunity to learn.

Many smaller companies may not have the maturity or fiscal backing to implement effective safety management systems. Whilst working for a smaller consulting firm that specialised in safety, I was involved in an incident which was not managed well due to a lack of safety management systems. At the time I was working in Africa and heading the expansion of our business across the African continent. Working in such areas was new for the company and there were no set guidelines or protocols for travelling to such areas. Being foolhardy and addicted to travel, I relished the opportunity to work in Mozambique. In my haste, immunisations were not checked and there were no company requirements to be immunised. After spending two weeks scoping the client in mosquito-ridden areas, I soon returned to Australia. Upon my return I experienced fevers, headaches and nausea. As per the reactive nature of safety and well-being, I visited the doctor due to my failing health. Medical examination revealed that I had contracted malaria. Given the company I worked for was quite small, how to capture such an incident and track progress was void. Ongoing management and associated corrective actions was managed through ongoing conversations, without the aid of supporting safety management systems.

As with many organisations, after my incident, action was taken where a memorandum went across the country that informed all employees of the new safety expectations required by all. Actions are easier to implement after an incident has occurred. Being proactive in minimising such risk appears to be the core challenge. Safety leadership can provide the voice to promote inter-activity and educate others on the systems available to promote safety through increased knowledge, autonomy and motivation (Nahrgang, Morgeson & Hofmann 2011).

Whilst exploring and validating the applicability of the RAVE model, the majority of leaders I spoke to outlined aspects of safety management sys-tems which can influence overall safety leadership behaviour. Safety statistics were often mentioned as a core driver for many resource industries. Positive safety statistics and minimal injury rates were linked to an increased like-lihood of securing new work and retaining employees. Adhering to legal guidelines was also noted as a driving factor with legislative consequences being present if safe practices are not provided within the workplace. Branching from such legislative requirements is the importance of risk assessments and reporting processes. A study by Grote (2012) further backed up such findings that safety management systems need to be trans-ferable and take into account standards, procedures, training, incident reporting and incident investigations. Safety tools such as workplace inspections, personal risk assessments and audits can help drive compliance, whereas the application of the RAVE model can help drive embedded change and sustainable safe behaviours. An over-reliance on safety man-agement systems may start to generate the outcry from many workers that they 'don't get paid to think anymore'. Such comments reflect an over-pro-ceduralised workplace. If there is an over-emphasis on safety management systems then adverse consequences can start to occur where employees depend on such processes to keep them safe and therefore limit their safety focus whilst at work.

Swuste (2009) detailed that an over-reliance on administrative measures may serve as a platform for management avoiding responsibility for incidents which can in turn de-motivate workers and create added administrative strain. An organisation that prides themselves on the number of safe work method statements that they have alongside other risk protocols and compliance tools should be equally priding themselves on the balance of safety leadership behaviours that they promote. This in turn should encourage autonomy from their workers. If there is an over-emphasis on safety management systems, then the unpredictable aspects of the working environment may unglue the worker when faced with unplanned tasks. All aspects of risk cannot be man-aged out of a job as the socio-technical system of the workplace is more complex and nuanced than simply completing the task safely. The socio-complex systems of the workplace environment were further explained by Stoop and Dekker (2012), who posited that the non-linearity of work envir-onments needs to be considered when completing safety investigations. Such variables may fall beyond the scope of safety management systems and be better suited to the behaviours of an effective safety leader, prior to an inci-dent occurring.

Case study

A well renowned organisation was looking to implement a safety leadership programme across their multi-faceted oil and gas project. A slew of consulting companies were poaching for the work, each with their own detailed safety leadership programme. Some of the offerings included safety leadership that focused on risk management, other programmes focused on felt leadership or observing employees and providing effective feedback. After much deliberation a safety leadership process was chosen. Outcomes of effectiveness were measured upon the total number of people completing the workshop and attendance of follow-up coaching sessions. Millions of dollars were spent and after a number of years, the CEO wanted a stocktake of what information had been retained and what the tangible impact of their safety leadership process was. An outside consultant was contracted to assess the impact of the safety leadership process. Through countless interviews and a breakdown of safety statistics and metrics, some concrete conclusions were made. Participants saw the benefit in the safety leadership programme, although they were unable to specify what they learnt or decipher what being a safety leader was all about. The intent and outcomes of the safety leadership initiative was made clear to general managers although this information was lost as you went further down the organisational structure. Craft workers were able to 'feel' a change in their leader's behaviour, although they were unable to clarify exactly what it was. Due to the financial outlay and some of the conclusions reached, the executive team were freezing any further development into their leadership team. The thinking behind this was that money had already been spent and the leaders had already been upskilled based upon the completion of coaching and training sessions.

Questions

Q1. What could be the challenge or advantage with so many safety leadership programmes being on offer, all with their own take on safety leadership?

Q2. What could be some reasons why participants were unable to clarify the specifics of what they have learned?

Q3. The leadership team felt that their management group have been upskilled which precluded them from further training and development. What is the inherent assumption in this thinking and what could be the risk?

Q4. How could clearer safety leadership outcomes be made from the onset of the programme and what are some other ways to measure success, excluding the attendance of workshops or coaching sessions?

Epilogue

Inferring that development stops due to the completion of a coaching or training session inhibits further growth and implies that personal development has a definite start and finish point. After the 'cold eyes' review was completed, it was suggested that any future programme or process be linked to the larger organisational people development strategy with clear outcomes and goals developed prior to the commencement of the training sessions. The benefit of the safety leadership process was not able to be quantified beyond the attendance numbers of workshops. Presence at a workshop does not always correlate to a change in behaviour. The absence of a clear definition or empirical model to safety leadership impacted the knowledge transfer. Suggestions were made to improve the embedding and sustainability of the safety leadership process. Feedback from leaders when faced with these suggestions concluded that such activities would be an added cost for a potentially failed initiative. Instead it was better to 'cut our losses' instead of throwing good money after bad money. An executive decision was made to employ an outside specialist to develop any new programmes internally, where intellectual property would be owned by the company and costs would be minimised. Unless specific expertise is brought into the company based upon safety leadership, the risk might be that another initiative is rolled out which therefore minimises the previous work completed. A larger framework and strategy would help enhance the success of any future process as well as the integration with other existing internal or external courses. The employee who would be brought into the business would have to exercise their own level of safety leadership by building relationships, being honest, having a vision of the end goals and engaging with key stakeholders.

Organisational and personal application

The following suggestions can be integrated into your organisation or as part of your own personal safety leadership ethos. Comments are based upon the RAVE model and chapter content.

Organisational application

- Prior to embarking upon any safety leadership initiative, establish what the end outcomes are and how they align with the broader company vision. Does your organisation have a safety vision that inspires others and sets the foundations for desired behaviours? A vision that is co-created with a core team increases leadership buy-in and ownership.
- What organisational systems and structures are in place that enable effective working relationships to be formed? How can procedural justice be demonstrated and are the lines of communication clear between different job levels? The physical structure of an office can influence communication channels as well as any guidelines around virtual offices. If company expectations are not detailed at workplace inductions then the risk for

behavioural misalignment increases. Flat organisational structures may limit bureaucracy.

- Has a strong foundation or investment been set with supporting safety management systems? Are the safety management systems supporting safety or are they complicating the work being performed? If left unchecked, complicated safety management systems can take on a life of their own and become more complex than the work being carried out.

Individual application

- Consider the behaviours and actions that you will accept and not accept. Who can be some trusted colleagues or friends that can help act as your moral conscience in the face of ethical dilemmas? By understanding what you will not compromise on, you can influence others in terms of your safety expectations.
- What are some safety stories or metaphors that you can utilise to help influence others? Is the language you use captivating and tailored for the people who you want to influence? Rhetoric can be a tool of influence and help with the engagement of others.
- Reflect upon previous jobs or companies that you have worked for. Have you seen or experienced nepotism or being placed in the 'in-group' or alternatively the 'out-group'? Withholding information and being selective on who you share information with in your team may adversely impact the leader-member exchange relationship.
- How do you show genuine care and empathy to others? If there is an injury or incident at work, do you get involved in the investigation or assist the person in receiving medical attention? Attending a medical facility with an injured worker demonstrates the importance and value you place on the employee as opposed to delegating that task to someone else. Discussing the personal impact of an injury has more meaning than focusing on statistics or the mechanics of the injury.

Chapter summary

Safety leadership can encompass a broad spectrum of behaviours and if seen in isolation can be perceived to be quite broad and vague. Through the channelling of the RAVE model, safety leadership can be broken down to tangible steps that can help foster safe behaviours. The forming of relationships can be the precursor to self-awareness and authenticity. With rapport being established a broader vision can be communicated which can align a team towards a common goal. Through the facets of engagement, safety leadership can be translated to tangible safe behaviours. Effective safety management systems are needed to glue the transactional safety requirements with transformational safety leadership behaviours.

References

Appelbaum, SH, Habashy, S, Malo JL & Hisham, S 2012, 'Back to the future: Revisiting Kotter's 1996 Change Model', *The Journal of Management Development*, 31(8), 764–782.

Bass, BM & Bass, R 2009, *Bass Handbook of Leadership: Theory, Research and Managerial Applications* (4th edn), Free Press, New York.

Benjaoran, V & Bhokha, S 2010, 'An integrated safety management with construction management using 4D CAD model', *Safety Science*, 48(3), 395–403.

Bottani, E, Monica, L & Vignali G 2009, 'Safety management systems: Performance differences between adopters and non-adopters', *Safety Science*, 47(2), 155–162.

Carmeli, A, Brueller, D & Dutton, JE 2009, 'Learning behaviours in the workplace: The role of high-quality interpersonal relationships and psychological safety', *Systems Research and Behavioural Science*, 26(1), 81–98.

Carroll, AB & Shabana, KM 2010, 'The business case for corporate social responsibility: A review of concepts, research and practice', *International Journal of Management Reviews*, 12(1), 85–104.

Cheng, EWL, Ryan, N & Kelly, S 2012, 'Exploring the perceived influence of safety management practices on project performance in the construction industry', *Safety Science*, 50(2), 363–369.

Cianci, AM, Hannah, ST, Roberts, RP & Tsakumis, GT 2014, 'The effects of authentic leadership on followers' ethical decision-making in the face of temptation: An experimental study', *The Leadership Quarterly*, 25(4), 581–594.

Corey, G 2001, *Theory and Practice of Counselling and Psychotherapy*, Thomson Learning, Stamford.

Cunliffe, AL & Eriksen, M 2011, 'Relational leadership', *Human Relations*, 64(11), 1425–1449.

Davis, KM & Gardner, WL 2012, 'Charisma under crisis revisited: Presidential leadership, perceived leader effectiveness, and contextual influences', *The Leadership Quarterly*, 23(5), 918–933.

Dekker, SWA 2012, *Just Culture – Balancing Safety and Accountability*, Ashgate Publishing, Farnham.

Ehrhart, MG & Klein, KJ 2001, 'Predicting followers' preferences for charismatic leadership: The influence of follower values and personality', *The Leadership Quarterly*, 12(2), 153–179.

Epitropaki, O & Martin, R 2013, 'Transformational-transactional leadership and upward influence: The role of relative leader-member exchanges (RLMX) and perceived organisational support (POS)', *The Leadership Quarterly*, 24(2), 299–315.

Frankel, AS, Leonard, MW & Denham, CR 2006, 'Fair and just culture, team behaviour and leadership engagement: The tools to achieve high reliability', *HSR: Health Services Research*, 41(4), 1690–1709.

Gardner, WL, Cogliser, CC, Davis, KM & Dickens, MP 2011, 'Authentic leadership: A review of the literature and research agenda', *The Leadership Quarterly*, 22(6), 1120–1145.

Geller, SE 2001, *Keys to Behaviour-based Safety*, Government Institutes, New York.

Goleman, D 2002, *The New Leaders*, Time Warner, London.

Graen, GB & Schiemann, WA 2013, 'Leadership-motivated excellence theory: An extension of LMX', *Journal of Managerial Psychology*, 28(5), 452–469.

Grote, G 2012, 'Safety management in different high-risk domains: All the same?', *Safety Science*, 50(3), 1983–1992.

Halverson, SK, Murphy, SE & Riggio, RE 2004, 'Charismatic leadership in crisis situations: A laboratory investigation of stress and crisis', *Small Group Research*, 35(5), 495–514.

Hayes, J 2010, *The Theory and Practice of Change Management*, Palgrave Macmillan, New York.

Hofmann, DA & Morgeson, FP 1999, 'Safety-related behaviour as a social exchange: The role of perceived organisational support and leader–member exchange', *Journal of Applied Psychology*, 84(2), 286–296.

Hogan, K 2003, *The Psychology of Persuasion: How to Persuade Others to Your Way of Thinking*, Pelican Publishing Company, Gretna.

House, RJ & Shamir, B 1993, 'Toward the integration of charismatic, transformational, inspirational and visionary theories of leadership', in M Chemmers & R Ayman (eds), *Leadership Theory and Research Perspectives and Directions*, Academic Press, New York.

Hsiung, HH 2012, 'Authentic leadership and employee voice behavior: A multi-level psychological process', *Journal of Business Ethics*, 107(3), 349–361.

Jones, JW & Wuebker, LJ 1993, 'Safety locus of control and employees' accidents', *Journal of Business and Psychology*, 7(4), 449–457.

Jones, SM, Weissbourd, R, Bouffard, S, Kahn, J & Ross, T 2014, *How to Build Empathy and Strengthen Your School Community*, Harvard Graduate School of Education, Cambridge.

Joseph, C, Reddy, S & Sharma, K 2013, 'Locus of control, safety attitudes and involvement in hazardous events in Indian army aviators', *Aviation Psychology and Applied Human Factors*, 3(1), 9–18.

Kernis, MH & Goldman, BH 2006, 'A multicomponent conceptualization of authenticity: Theory and research', *Advances in Experimental Social Psychology*, 38(1), 283–357.

Koh, TY & Rowlinson, S 2012, 'Relational approach in managing construction project safety: A social capital perspective', *Accident Analysis Prevention*, 48(1), 134–144.

Kouzes, JM & Posner, BZ 2007, *The Leadership Challenge* (4th edn), John Wiley & Sons, San Francisco.

Krause, TT 2005, *Leading with Safety*, John Wiley & Sons, Hoboken.

Lapierre, LM, Naidoo, LJ & Bonaccio, S 2012, 'Leaders' relational self-concept and followers' task performance: Implications for mentoring provided to followers', *The Leadership Quarterly*, 23(5), 766–774.

Leary, MR & Tangley, JP 2003, *Handbook of Self and Identity*, The Guildford Press, New York.

Long, DG 2012, *Third Generation Leadership and the Locus of Control: Knowledge, Change and Neuroscience*, Gower Publishing Limited, Farnham.

Long, DG 2013, *Delivering High Performance: The Third Generation Organisation*, Gower Publishing Limited, Farnham.

Matsumoto, K & Tanaka, K 2004, 'The role of the medial prefrontal cortex in achieving goals', *Current Opinion in Neurobiology*, 14(2), 178–185.

Mayer, DM, Nurmohamed, S, Trevino, LK, Shapiro, DL & Schminke, M 2013, 'Encouraging employees to report unethical conduct internally: It takes a village', *Organisational Behaviour and Human Decision Processes*, 121(1), 89–103.

Menzel, DC 1996, 'Ethics stress in public organisations', *Public Productivity & Management Review*, 20(1), 70–83.

Miao, Q, Newman, A & Huang, X 2014, 'The impact of participative leadership on job performance and organisational citizenship behaviour: Distinguishing between the mediating effects of affective and cognitive trust', *The International Journal of Human Resource Management*, 25(20), 2796–2810.

Mischel, W 1999, *Introduction to Personality*, Harcourt Brace College Publishers, Orlando.

Mueller, BH & Lee, J 2002, 'Leader-member exchange and organisational communication satisfaction in multiple contexts', *The Journal of Business Communication*, 39(2), 220–244.

Nahrgang, JD, Morgeson, FP & Hofmann, DA 2011, 'Safety at work: A meta-analytic investigation of the link between job demands, job resources, burnout, engagement, and safety outcomes', *Journal of Applied Psychology*, 96(1), 71–94.

Nelson, SA, Azeveo, PR, Dias, RS, De-Sousa, SMA, De-Carvalho, LDP, Silva, ACO & Rabelo, PPC 2014, 'The influence of bullying on the well-being of Brazilian nursing professionals', *Public Money & Management*, 34(6), 397–404.

Rankin, B 2013, 'Emotional intelligence: Enhancing values-based practice and compassionate care in nursing', *Journal of Advanced Nursing*, 69(12), 2717–2725.

Read, BR, Zartl-Klik, A, Veir, C, Samhaber, R & Zepic, H 2010, 'Safety leadership that engages the workforce to create sustainable HSE performance', SPE International Conference on Health, Safety and Environment in Oil and Gas Exploration and Production, Rio de Janeiro, Brazil, pp. 1–18.

Reason, J 1997, *Managing the Risks of Organisational Accidents*, Ashgate Publishing, Aldershot.

Rock, D 2009, 'Managing with the brain in mind', *Strategy and Business*, 56, 2–10.

Samnani, AK & Singh, P 2013, 'When leaders victimize: The role of charismatic leaders in facilitating group pressures', *The Leadership Quarterly*, 24(1), 189–202.

Scott, S 2004, *Fierce Conversations*, Berkley Publishing Group, New York.

Shamir, B & Eilam, G 2005, 'What's your story? A life-stories approach to authentic leadership development', *The Leadership Quarterly*, 16(3), 395–417.

Steinbauer, R, Renn, RW, Taylor, RR & Njoroge, PK 2014, 'Ethical leadership and followers' moral judgement: The role of followers' perceived accountability and self-leadership', *Journal of Business Ethics*, 120(3), 381–392.

Stewart, I & Jones, V 1987, *TA Today: A New Introduction to Transactional Analysis,* Lifespace Publishing, Nottingham.

Stone, RJ 2007, *Managing Human Resources*, John Wiley & Sons Australia, Milton.

Stoop, J & Dekker, S 2012, 'Are safety investigations pro-active?', *Safety Science*, 50(6), 1422–1430.

Swuste, P 2009, 'You will only see it, if you understand it, or occupational risk prevention from a management perspective', *Human Factors and Ergonomics in Manufacturing*, 18(4), 438–452.

Toor, SR & Ofori, G 2008, 'Leadership for future construction industry: Agenda for authentic leadership', *International Journal of Project Management*, 26(6), 620–630.

Vlachoutsicos, CA 2011, 'How to cultivate engaged employees', *Harvard Business Review*, 89(9), 123–126.

Walker, A 2010, 'The development and validation of a psychological contract of safety scale', *Journal of Safety Research*, 41(4), 315–321.

Zhu, W, Avolio, BJ, Riggio, RE & Sosik, JJ 2011, 'The effect of authentic transformational leadership on follower and group ethics', *The Leadership Quarterly*, 22(5), 801–817.

Zinn, H 2003, *The Twentieth Century*, Harper Collins Publishing, New York.

4 Importance of culture

The DNA of an organisation

Understanding what constitutes a robust safety culture and how that can influence safety leadership is pivotal in establishing an interactive culture of care. Safety culture can vary over time, and safety leaders can directly influence culture. This chapter breaks down the influential elements that can constitute a strong safety culture and ideas and suggestions of shifting safety culture are shared. Throughout the chapter, the following questions will be answered:

- What are some of the differences between safety culture, safety climate and organisational culture?
- What are the elements that need to be considered when analysing safety culture?
- How can an organisation shift safety culture and develop a culture of trust?

Key objectives

Culture is complex and is unique to each organisation. Safety leaders who take into account the multitude of variances in one's safety culture will be better equipped in establishing the culture that they want to promote and work within. This chapter will help equip readers with multiple tools based upon the following objectives:

1 Working out the integral components that constitute a mature safety culture and how such elements can be measured, analysed and modified within one's own organisation.
2 Understanding different qualitative and quantitative tools that can be used to measure and analyse a safety culture and how such information can be used to shape, strengthen or modify culture.

Setting the scene

Safety leadership models and frameworks are plentiful and can be integrated well if contextualised wisely into an organisation's culture and safety processes. After being caught up in the tertiary system for a number of years, I vividly remember fellow professors touting research which in one way or another they were involved within. Whilst sharing an update on my research, fellow professors would say, 'have you read the work from Jones' or some other obtuse reference. When I replied 'no, can you tell me more about that author', the response would be along the lines of 'sure, it was an author I teamed up with and co-wrote a paper with'. Sometimes this myopic stance can be self-serving which can lead to confirmation bias, whilst stifling innovation. Not only does this self-serving bias exist within some university circles, it can exist within larger or smaller enterprises. A belief that your culture is the pinnacle of greatness may limit further growth and become a pathway for confirmation bias, where any problems or challenges are externally attributed to other factors as opposed to signs or symptoms pertaining to the workplace culture.

Comparisons between one organisation's safety leadership process over another safety leadership process can be like splitting hairs. Any safety leadership implementation should be rooted in research. Programmes that outline the differences between leadership versus management or the principles of behavioural psychology via ABC analysis are probably echoing relics of the past. Off the shelf programmes are most likely going to be broad attempts at addressing the nuances or each organisation's safety leadership challenge. Contextualising an organisation's culture to any chosen leadership process may have more sway then any 'off the shelf' offering.

A large top tier company I was working with shared with me some of their challenges with their attempts at implementing safety leadership within the company. After spending over a million dollars, the workshops and information that they were paying for was not resonating well with the top tier leaders. A mutual agreement was made that the outside company did not understand the company's unique and varied culture. Upon hearing this feedback, the consulting company then implemented changes to their leadership programme. The most notable change was a difference in PowerPoint slides. The parent slide deck was changed and that was their 'customisation' of the programme. Absent from this consulting company was an exposure to different parts of their client's business, focus groups, cultural observations or observation of different team meetings. Such initial scoping would provide more weight when considering the cultural variables that need to be considered when integrating a safety leadership programme. One of the biggest moot points was the perception that the company's culture is so unique that no outsider would understand the dynamics. Some may argue this viewpoint to be arrogant, whilst in contrast others may see the viewpoint as accurate. Outsiders will not always be privy to the internal politics, internal communications or cultural stories that make up the rich tapestry of an organisation's culture. Outside perspectives can, however, reveal blind spots of an organisation that others were not aware of.

Culture can directly influence behaviour and acts as the social glue for employees, whilst detailing the expected norms of workers (McShane,

Olekalns & Travaglione 2010). When comparing company policies and procedures to organisational culture, culture will devour process. Imagine an employee sitting through an induction that details all the required safety standards and expectations. Once that employee commences work and they observe all of their new team members doing the polar opposite of what should be done, confusion may set in. You can imagine the social pull for that individual to conform with their peers and jettison what was shared in the initial induction. Leaders set the culture of a company (Geller 2008) and therefore their actions will help set the tone and environment of the organisation. Managing directors that cross industries do not rely on their subject matter expertise of the industry, instead their leadership skills and mindset helps establish the desired culture. Toxic cultures of blind obedience and unethical practices have been well documented through the failed misgivings of Enron or more recently Lehman Brothers. Culture is such a complex and compelling aspect of business that, when applied to safety, nuances may start to emerge which are specific to safety. By understanding what makes up a robust safety culture, steps can be undertaken to unearth the hidden culture of an organisation as well as using culture analysis as a lead indicator when leading safety.

Safety culture

The notions of a safety culture have been well documented and have been used in the past to explain specific safety failures that may not be understood through conventional safety systems or controls (Mengolini & Debarberis 2012). The definitions of a safety culture are expansive, which range from the accepted way things are done to the attitudes, beliefs, perceptions and values that employees share in relation to safety (Guldenmund 2010). As Guldenmund commented, the depth and subtlety of what the term 'safety culture' means has been diluted over time without reference to the true behaviours of a safety culture. From this premise, Guldenmund outlined three different approaches to understanding a safety culture, which are founded upon the academic, analytical and pragmatic approach. An academic approach can become the compass from which pragmatic solutions can be unearthed. Through pragmatic application, results can be analysed which lends itself well to culture analysis. All three approaches to understanding safety culture will be looked at, through the sharing of relevant research, practical examples and how one can analyse the safety culture of an organisation.

When safety culture is spoken about, it can encompass the overall 'feel' or 'run-down' of an organisation. Changing culture can take considerable time and effort as the beliefs and behaviours of the organisation are going to be embedded through previous history. In contrast is the relevance of an organisation's *safety climate*. The differences between a safety culture and safety climate are based upon a safety climate having a temporary focus which is governed by the current actions of the leadership group (Fugas, Silva & Melia

2012). Safety climate is ephemeral whilst a safety culture is more long term. Over a period of time, the safety climate can influence and tie into an overall culture. In the fast paced global operating environment that businesses find themselves working within, the safety climate constantly changes, and how one navigates such changing conditions can influence the overall culture. An example of the differences between safety climate and safety culture can be evident through an organisation that I was consulting to.

Deep in the heart of Queensland, Australia, I was commissioned to analyse the safety culture of a coal mine. Before employing a scientific methodology, I picked up that the safety climate was heavily influencing the current zeitgeist which was attributed to a temporary focus on cost containment and minimisation of waste. The current focus on cost containment set up the climate of cutting resources which then minimised health and safety coverage on site. As a result, incidents started to increase and reporting levels of at-risk behaviours decreased. Prior to the focus on cost containment, the safety culture was stable with a healthy regard towards processes, the environment, team members and leadership. The climate of cost containment segued to a perception that leaders are not committed to safety and therefore the leadership team became the scapegoat for poor safety performance. This was attributed to the investment into safety being void or minimised, compared to previous actions. The culture was left unchecked, and the safety climate influenced the overall culture of the mine site where trust was diminished between the leadership team and employees. Safety climate therefore acted as the barometer of culture and changed accordingly based upon external or internal variables.

It would be similar to safety climate being the appetiser at a restaurant which can set the scene for the main meal. Depending on how the appetiser goes, it would influence the eagerness for the main meal to be brought out. If you were served a bucket of slop as an appetiser, reservations would occur about the main meal. As soon as you saw your waiter approaching you, a begrudging moan may be released in anticipation of the next meal. This is similar to a climate of cost containment being a precursor to increased trepidation by employees in regard to future events across the company. The overall feeling you get after you have finished eating the main meal could be considered the overall culture. Along the way, the overall feeling was influenced by the smaller meals in between, just like the overall culture of a company is influenced by the smaller focal points and events that have happened in the past. For the purpose of simplicity, when I discuss factors of safety culture, this will also encompass the notion of a safety climate.

A macro view of understanding safety culture can be easily traced back to the work of Geller (2008) where safety culture is broken down into four core elements. This includes the influence of leadership on an organisation, company processes and procedures, the environment of the company and lastly the individuals within the company, otherwise known as the person component of an overall culture. Geller's work creates a strong starting point to analyse culture. With the benefits of time and further research, the complexities of safety culture were further analysed. In an extensive study with over 25,574 participants, a confirmatory factor analysis found twelve hierarchal aspects of safety culture within the workplace (Frazier et al. 2013). The primary factors revolved around management concern, personal responsibility, peer support and safety management systems. Some of the second order factors included respectful feedback, cautioning others, supervisor concern, senior management concern, work pressure and communication. Safety leadership ties in well with these primary and secondary factors, specifically around management concern which has its safety leadership links towards empathy and personal responsibility and its ties with locus of control.

Diving in deeper to the nuances of safety culture is the work from Fugas, Silva and Melia (2012) who revealed that social mechanisms mediate the relationship between safety environment, safety compliance and proactive safety behaviours. In further detail, this can be focused towards perceived behavioural control and attitudes towards safety which tie into the RAVE model of safety leadership. Without engagement and effective communication, the specific behaviours of a safety leader are absent which therefore impacts the overall safety culture.

Within every organisation, the safety culture can be made up of a series of subcultures or micro cultures. This can be tailored to a specific department, function or work group. How an engineering team operate may be different to how a health and safety team go about their work. Similarly, how an accounts department operate may vary compared to a marketing department. When all of the subcultures are combined in a soup of activity, what emerges is the overall safety culture of the company which is harnessed by shared values or company objectives. It may be argued that the core moral/fiscal/humanitarian objective of a safety culture is to ensure the safety of employees. The interaction of so many subcultures can be vividly seen on construction and project environments. In such environments there could be multiple companies working towards an end goal. A graphical representation of such a relationship can be shown through the work of Fang and Wu (2013) in their Safety Interaction Culture model (Figure 4.1).

Behaviours in the below model are not explicitly detailed but can be deduced by the 'interaction' between the contractor, subcontractor and owner. What can sit above this model is the importance of safety leadership across all groups. The importance of safety leadership within an organisation's safety culture can set the mood as well as the long-term vision of a project or work environment (Beus et al. 2010). A further breakdown of the components that constitute a robust safety culture can help identify areas of strength and opportunities for improvement. It has been voiced that there is little consensus of the universal agreed components that constitute a safety culture (Frazier et al. 2013). A starting point of the key factors making up a safety culture will be looked at prior to establishing a framework of how safety culture can be analysed.

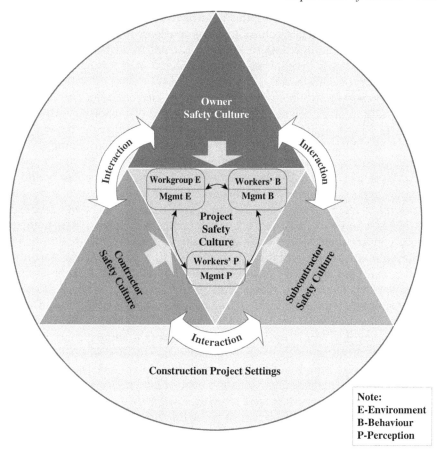

Figure 4.1 Safety Interaction Culture model
(Source: Fang and Wu 2013)

Components of a safety culture

A multitude of complexities exist within every organisation. Variances and nuances, when combined, can constitute the overall culture of an organisation. I have been in companies and on sites where all of the safety management systems are in place and are well implemented, although incidents still occur. A lot of the time, the breakdown could be based upon poor inter-team communication, low management credibility or impaired supervisor relationships. On one site I was at, the root cause of some of the incidents occurring was traced back to the core leader berating others for stopping the work due to safety concerns and the same leader publicly disparaging others in team meetings. Such actions outline that effective management systems are only one core pillar in an overall safety culture. If leadership is not providing a culture of trust and openness, the reporting of incidents starts to go underground. Further solidifying this point is the work from Toor and Ofori (2008) who revealed that a culture that has transparent and honest communication alongside an openness to share ideas tends to create a strong safety culture. This is based upon an increased likelihood of reporting injuries and sharing important information pertaining to safety.

Incident reporting within an organisation is one element of an overall safety culture. Work from Maslen and Hayes (2016) detailed that reporting an incident is a key to preventing injuries. It was further commented that the reporting of incidents should be framed up to employees as an essential component to sharing knowledge as opposed to previous descriptions as a learning opportunity. Incident reporting can be an individual behaviour which can be influenced by reporting systems and consequences of reporting such incidents (Mansouri et al. 2015). On one resources project I attended, it was revealed that incident reporting was well below the company average. After multiple candid conversations in the field, it was shared back to me that a lot of employees had stopped reporting incidents due to a lack of action once the incident had been reported. Such a breakdown in action birthed the overall perception that reporting is futile. With such a perception in place, it eventually lead to an increase in incidents, as the opportunities to learn from such scenarios was thwarted. Creating an environment that supports and encourages an employee to report an incident is pivotal in preventing further injuries.

Management systems are influential in supporting the overall safety culture. The motivation to report an incident is one factor, although ensuring there is an effective safety management system to capture core information is another story all together. Consistent and structured ways to manage occupational risks has been touted as a core way to prevent injuries (Vinodkumar & Bhasi 2011). Such importance can be evident in one large top tier resources company I worked with. One of their key mottos was to not be like other competitors and over-compensate on safety processes. The challenge though was when I spoke to the safety advisors within the company, they described to me the headache of working to a lack of established systems. As a result, confusion occurred and a clear message of how to approach safety was unclear. Audits and reviews can measure the effectiveness of established management systems, although the training, communication and dissemination of such information are just as important when utilising health and safety management systems (Mohammadfam et al. 2016). Employees who are uninformed about risk management processes can therefore not be held accountable for a lack of action or compliance.

Organisational support is an element that is needed to ensure that employees feel as though their company cares for them and they are valued. When employees feel supported via different training opportunities, recognition and empowered through working conditions, they are more committed to the company (Havaei, Dahinten & MacPhee 2015). Neglecting the well-being of employees can be a pathway to employee burn-out and increased exposure to risk. Such poor company support has been linked to adverse mental health of employees (Laschinger & Finegan 2005). With changing global economic conditions, companies may be faced with downsizing their workforce whilst expanding the span of work for remaining employees. Unless supporting structures are in place, a risk may exist where employees are over-burdened with work and start to look elsewhere for employment. Over the last few years, I have talked to many craft workers and employees who have mentioned to me that a decrease in wages or lack of a pay rise, combined with minimal money spent on equipment, is giving the impression that the company does not care about them. As a result loyalty is replaced with scepticism and employee turnover starts to increase. In contrast organisational citizenship behaviour can be increased through an expression of personal interest in one's work, generating employee morale and respect which can therefore lead to longer terms of tenure (Chen et al. 2013). Stability in the workforce can enhance the overall culture through established company norms and practices. Imagine working for a company where the longest tenure of employees is 12 months. In such cases, this can be an organisational clue that there are deep-seated issues or systematic problems that are impacting the happiness of staff. Levels of organisational support can be further complicated if there is an adverse relationship between the employee and line manager.

Leader-member exchange was previously shown to be an influential component of safety leadership. It is also a core ingredient in having a robust safety culture. Workers who have a strained relationship with their immediate boss are less inclined to converse with them and therefore safety conversations may be limited. Research from Wang, Gan and Wu (2016) showed that strong LMX increases employee voiced behaviour through the mediation of psychological trust and empowerment. Picture a worker who has a line manager who excludes them from the overall team or neglects to share pertinent information with them. Residual feelings of being on the 'out-group' start to occur where one may not have their boss's back when they are around. When I hear friends, colleagues or clients talk about the misgivings of their boss, it is a red flag to me that there is an issue of trust or line manager communication has floundered. From a cultural standpoint, the unenviable 'us versus them' culture emerges. What may influence the LMX relationship is employee performance and role equity through organisational fairness (Park et al. 2015). From the onset of the working relationship, if an employee is failing to meet work objectives or is perceived to be incompetent, then those perceptions can taint the future working relationship. Similarly if an employee is perceived to be a safety risk or a rule breaker, this may influence future safety interactions between the line manager and employee. In contrast if the line manager contradicts the touted safety message by displaying unsafe behaviours, this would not only impair the LMX relationship but impair the credibility of the overall leadership team.

Management credibility is aligned with a strong safety culture. If leaders are not seen as credible, then the information that they share with others will be taken with a grain of salt and a culture of mistrust may start to occur. During the downturn in the mining and resources sector, a lot of contracts were renegotiated which in some cases resulted in a drop in wages. One company I visited went through a similar ordeal. There was an overall vibe of mistrust between employees and the leadership team as the contract negotiations were perceived to be misleading and lacking transparency. Therefore, when the leaders addressed the workforce, their messages were filtered through a fugue of scepticism and a rise in union action occurred. Managing cynicism is important to restoring management credibility and, similar to a safety climate, management credibility can change over time due to it being attributed to an attitudinal state (Kim et al. 2009). Building management credibility goes beyond creating transparency. As mentioned by Dando and Swift (2003), responsiveness, learning, innovation and performance improvement are markers to improve levels of credibility. If leaders are not responsive to employee needs and if there is a lag period between any employee suggestions or concerns, then cynicism may exponentially increase. A safety culture that has poor management credibility is most likely a safety culture where the power balance lies with respected team members. When credibility is impaired, respected communication channels are left up to the organisational grapevine. If the grapevine is the source of core information, then messages may be diluted and miscommunication may start to occur. Just imagine a game of Chinese whispers being used as the core source of relaying integral information to the workforce

Communication can be the bloodline of an organisation's culture. When communication is open, widespread and encouraged, inter-team communication thrives. Therefore if someone is placed in an at-risk situation, it would be expected that an increase in voiced behaviour or safety conversations would be prevalent. This notion has been further confirmed through researchers who indicated that job satisfaction and workplace engagement are products of increased voiced behaviour (Koyuncua et al. 2013). To foster inter-team communication, it was shown that the education level of employees can influence team communication and should be placated through the driving of innovation (Valls, Gonzalea-Roma & Tomas 2016). A culture that is void of inter-group and vertical communication is most likely an organisation that is fragmented. A colleague once shared with me their experiences working within an organisation where information was the social currency. The more that one knew, the more power they had. This created a cesspool of nefarious behaviour where information was drip fed and only shared on an 'as needs basis'. The political game was apparently off the charts where everyone was cautious of who they spoke to and what they said. Given the fundamentals of safety leadership are based around strong relationships, such cautious behaviour created inauthentic transactional interactions. A culture that uses communication as a power tool runs the risk of alienating others and creating a subversive culture of ruthlessness and organisational games. An environment where employees feel psychologically safe to approach their colleagues about their safety and well-being is an organisation where safety conversations are occurring and knowledge is being shared. This can help solidify teamwork.

Teamwork can be the catalyst for workplace objectives to be achieved as well as a culture of support to be established. When teams are working well, employees are more satisfied and relish in the company of their peers, whom they can both learn and grow from. Collaborative teams are successful teams where diversity becomes a strength and networks are expanded on (Freeman & Huang 2014). When the true power of teams is unlocked, the sharing of ideas negates group think and innovation can thrive. Transformational leadership training and team building activities based upon goal-setting, interpersonal skills and problem-solving techniques have been shown to bolster teamwork and create a culture of learning (Aga, Noorderhaven & Vaellejo 2016).

Most people across the Western world spend a solid 40 hours a week at work. If you dislike the people whom you work with, those 40 hours can feel like 400 hours. Alternatively you might have worked in teams before where the hours fly by and frivolity, tenacity and fun allows objectives to be met. A safety culture that has solid teamwork is a safety culture where team altruism can be exercised due to shared similarities, friendships and goals. Whilst analysing the safety culture at an aluminium smelter, there was unresolved issues between two sets of craft workers. Such unresolved issues were not addressed and continued to fester to a point where healthy competition turned into ruthless competition. Incidents were not being reported and minor injuries were occurring due to the small innate safety conversations being jettisoned for people turning a blind eye. One of the guys I spoke to said to me 'fuck the other team, if they get injured, that is on them'. The conflict reached a point where the regard for someone else's safety vanished. To help turn this issue around, honest conversations and resetting the boundaries had to be done through the leadership team and core people involved. Re-establishing trust and acknowledging the past and envisioning the future was one of the keys to re-establishing the team. Outlining expectations and consequences were reiterated by the leadership team, which are core components of safety leadership.

Safety leadership can be the galvanising component that ties in all the core elements of a well-oiled safety culture. The influence that leadership has on safety culture can set the focus, legacy and outcomes of how safety is managed. Specific safety leadership behaviours have already been discussed in Chapter 3. A culture that lacks empathy from leadership or clear direction may result in employees who do not feel valued or cared for. The importance of safety leadership is integral in setting up a safety culture of inter-dependency and care. Safety leaders I have worked with in the past have gone through their list of injured workers and contacted each one to see how they are going and to see if anything else can be done to assist their recovery. Early in my career, I worked in occupational rehabilitation where I saw true genuine care emerge when an employee was injured. I also saw leaders who were focused more on their insurance premiums as opposed to getting someone back to work as safely as possible. During a plethora of counselling sessions I have run and working with injured workers for many years, it gave me incredible insight to the psychosocial issues that impact the daily lives of an injured worker. Employees who were supported by their leaders were motivated to get back to work. In contrast, leaders who minimised contact with the injured worker created a gap in the employment relationship, where the employee was less motivated to return to work. Safety leaders have a genuine care and when that is visible, a culture of trust exudes from the top levels of leadership and becomes the unwritten norm of what is expected around the workplace. If leaders do not value safety, then the perceptions of the company's overall value for safety starts to become diminished. Leaders' actions and attitudes can directly reflect the overall values of the organisation. Such is the responsibility of leadership to demonstrate the values of the organisation and to display authenticity and empathy.

Procedural justice is relevant to ensure fairness and equity across all employees and to make sure that the overall safety culture is just. A workplace that is characterised by nepotism and cronyism can create the inevitable 'in and out' group where feelings of unfairness emerge. Perceptions of unfairness could be based upon who gets promoted within the organisation or who gets rewarded. One allied healthcare organisation I consulted to had an issue with procedural justice. Clear pathways and distinctions for promotion were absent, where employees felt that promotion was based on who had the closest relationship with their manager. Without clear pathways of development in place, anyone who got promoted was often perceived to be a 'brown noser'. When this occurs, resentment may start to creep in with fellow colleagues, which can therefore influence the other components of a safety culture such as teamwork and leader-member exchange.

Respectful treatment between key stakeholders has been shown to increase perceptions around procedural justice due to feedback being received about one's standing within the group (Heuer & Stroessner 2011). The importance of fairness and procedural justice crosses multiple countries and different cultures and has been linked to overall well-being and life satisfaction (Lucas et al. 2016). You can just imagine the dinner table conversation one may have with their partner if they constantly get overlooked for promotion or are treated unfairly within the workplace. The lamenting of one's vocation may be an age-old venting mechanism that echoes the industrial revolution. In the modern era, technology and science has paved the way for the equitable treatment of employees which can generate a strong safety culture.

The complexities of an organisation's culture run deep. Other elements of a safety culture may emerge as newer research and zeitgeists emerge. Factors of innovation and knowledge management may become the new components of a robust safety culture. Harnessing this knowledge to allow a company to learn from previous mistakes to strengthen safety and employee performance may become the new norm. Certain parts of a safety culture are overt and can be easily traced back to tangible behaviours and practices. There are other components of a safety culture which are unspoken and can be equally as important in analysing the overall safety culture of an organisation.

Unearthing the true culture

Sometimes the things that you cannot measure count, as opposed to the things that you can measure. Culture can be talked about in company inductions and expressed through company values. What holds weight are the intangible actions of employees, which are not always documented or referenced. These finer points are alive and are evident in what is assumed in employees or reading the subtext in conversations. The work of Simpson (2007) labelled the nuanced subtext as 'unwritten ground rules', which can permeate all parts of an organisation. These unwritten ground rules are blueprints of behaviour or assumed knowledge. Examples can include such notions as people not talking at meetings because nothing ever gets done, and when the manager is around we say what they want to hear. Such summations may be based upon anchors in behaviour that have happened in the past where an employee was berated for speaking the truth to the manager or where information shared at meetings was never actioned. When applied to safety, the undesired message and unwritten ground rule may become apparent. This can help explain the notion that a company may preach the motto that 'safety comes first', but when you dig deeper, it may be production over safety. This may birth the unwritten ground rule that 'around here we talk about safety, but it's really about production'.

A term I use to reference the unwritten culture is 'cultural clues'. Indicators of normed behaviour could be overtly obvious or alternatively hidden through a range of innuendo and politics. Such cultural clues were noticed on a site I visited which was part of a large top tier mining company. Clues included posters dated back many years ago outlining how safety is everyone's responsibility to air conditioners being tagged out from three years prior and not being serviced. Such clues provided me a reference point, that the company on site did not see safety as a value or high on the agenda of desired outcomes. If one can master the art of picking up on cultural clues and unwritten ground rules of an organisation, they can start to address these clues before they turn into normed behaviour. It would be similar to using safety lead indicators as a marker for action before the lead indicator turns into a lag indicator through a safety incident.

Components of organisational culture are displayed through organisational stories, cultural legends and physical artefacts such as posters and awards (McShane, Olekalns & Travaglione 2010). From the safety paradigm, cultural indicators could be evidenced through previous stories of people who were injured or the display of safety statistics or HSE key performance indicators. At a manufacturing company I visited, there was an old plaque in the lunch room that was dedicated to a previous worker. It turned out that the plaque was a memorial plaque based upon a colleague who was killed on site more than 20 years prior. Such visible tokens served as a reminder to the workforce to commemorate the worker's memory and also a sombre reminder of the consequences of unmanaged risks. The workplace death that occurred 20 years prior became an organisational legend as the current workforce did not have any direct experience with the injured worker or were not even working in the industry at the time but knew of the worker.

As soon as you walk into an organisation, you will be surrounded by a number of different cultural clues. As is the penchant for human beings to focus on the negative side of things, it is important to keep in mind that not all cultural clues or unwritten ground rules are negative. Back in my early career, I used to work for an occupational rehabilitation company as a psychologist. Whenever a staff member's birthday came around, the leader of the company would make a cake for that person. Of course this was not a cake that was pre-purchased at the supermarket, rather a cake made from genuine care. In addition to the cultural clues at this company were the celebrations of success and lack of internal politics that plague many other larger companies. The culture was so strong that if someone started to complain about another behind that person's back, that person would be reminded to talk to that person directly as opposed to venting to others. This created a sense of group governance and developed the unwritten ground rule that 'around here we don't talk ill of others'. Sometimes an organisation may be unaware of their own cultural clues or unwritten ground rules. An outside perspective can allow a broader stocktake of cultural strengths and areas of opportunity. Very similar to an auditor coming through and assessing what is working or not, a cultural analysis can reveal the established norms which could be accounting for current behaviour. Prior to changing culture, first one has to measure culture to establish a baseline.

Cultural analysis

Undertaking a stocktake of an organisation's safety culture can be an exhaustive task. When culture is analysed, it will be time stamped by the dates of when the analysis has taken place. I have worked across the globe assessing workplace cultures and the safety culture of resource projects. In terms of a robust culture analysis, the more data that is collected from multiple sources, the richer the analysis will be. Mediums of information can include focus groups, observational data, past safety statistics, results from culture surveys and language used across the company. These data points can be in the form of qualitative or quantitative means. The power of a quantitative assessment of culture can be reflected in the tracing of data in an anonymous fashion whilst providing non-emotive factual data which can be normed and broken down to current organisational data (Kim, Lee & Seong 2017). Such information can take away the hearsay evidence and comments from employees.

Early in my time as a consultant, the company I was working with did not have any tangible culture surveys to administer to clients. A key focus was on identifying systematic issues and themes by talking to as many people as possible within a company. As part of my leadership debrief, I approached the manager of the company and provided some feedback based upon grouped themes. When sharing the hard truth, a wall of defensiveness was established quite quickly. Such questions as 'who have you been talking too?' and 'what areas have you visited?' were staunchly asked. As a reply, I mentioned that all information is confidential and that the core focus is on the shared theme that leadership are perceived to be aggressive and non-communicative. Ironically, the leader curtly told me 'that's bullshit and why would other companies want to analyse culture'. This experience can provide concrete validation that statistical data and quantitative methods are less emotive as the message can be on the constructs measured as opposed to the stories and feelings being shared. When both the qualitative and quantitative data points are combined, a richer more contextualised assessment of culture can occur.

The kind of safety culture survey tool being utilised, and the framing of such a tool to employees, will ultimately impact the information collected. If confidentiality is not assured, then the free flow of information and candid responses may be forsaken. As posited by Bjerkan (2010) surveys can have trouble affirming cause and effect relationships and self-reporting can be shaped by propensity to answer questions from a certain perspective. The strengths can lie in the sample size of numbers. The more people who complete a safety culture survey, the more valid and reliable the information will be due to the greater range of perspectives being accounted for. Any results from a safety culture survey can be utilised to tell a story of how things are going. How each of the constructs measured link up can reflect the organisational commentary that exists within a company. Figure 4.2 is an example of what some

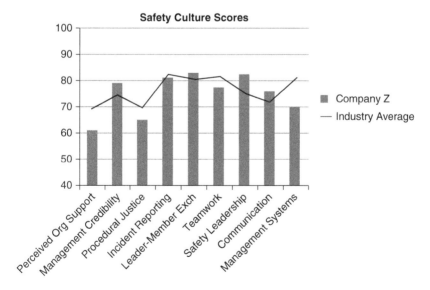

Figure 4.2 Snapshot of safety culture
(Source: Developed for this research)

of the outputs may look like if utilising safety culture surveys based upon some of the constructs discussed thus far.

The results in Figure 4.2 show a company's trending average against an industry average. Elements measured were, in this case, the ones discussed earlier. When interpreting results, it is important to understand the linkages between all the variables. As shown in Figure 4.2, when safety leadership scores are high, this may reflect well on management credibility. Scores that are a bit lower on the continuum were around organisational support and procedural justice. The narrative behind such scores could be based upon equity in reward processes or lack of company support around employee concerns. When used in isolation, the quantitative analysis provides a rough compass of what to focus on. Expanded narrative and reasons behind such cultural scores can be better garnered through qualitative means. If utilising a safety culture survey questionnaire, one way to capture some further insight is to include space on the questionnaire to write down any other commentary around the strengths and weaknesses of the company's safety culture. All comments can then be collated and coded to provide a thick description of data which can be further analysed to identify themes and provide a richness to the information procured (Shenton 2004).

Whilst analysing the culture of an Australian resources project, quantitative scores highlighted an issue with management credibility and upward com-munication. Prior to talking to any of the employees, there were written comments from two-thirds of the workforce outlining that the site manager 'is arrogant' and 'uses threats to get their message across'. When a general con-sensus exists, it holds weight to the information being shared. As safety leaders, if the use of threats and a hint of haughtiness exists, it can create a revolt where a subculture of mistrust occurs. Other qualitative means to capture information include focus groups and direct employee discussions.

The use of interviews and focus groups can help triangulate results for increased dependability and validity (Guba & Lincoln 1989). To gather the complete picture of an organisation's safety culture, many different data collection methods should be utilised to ensure any overall conclusions are sub-stantiated. Collating information from interviews is best achieved when employees are ensured that confidentiality will be maintained and only common trends or themes will be reported back on. If an issue occurs more than once and is voiced by multiple people, from different work areas, then some validity may start to exist around that commentary. The medium to collect such data could be through smaller sized groups or one-on-one inter-views. Over the years, I have found what works well is sharing some of the raw quantitative data from the safety culture survey and inviting input from employees in regard to why certain scores are high, low or otherwise. The sharing of such information can increase transparency and become an anchor point to start the discussion with employees. Depending on the organisation's culture, the level of candidness from employees can vary. I have had some experiences where the employees are thirsty to share information about what is working and not working, whilst other employees may be a bit more elusive or cynical of the process. If the words 'nothing will ever change' start to emerge, this can become a cultural clue that voiced issues have not been previously addressed or dealt with. Overall, any common themes emerging from the data can help provide commentary to the leadership team based upon the statistics obtained through the culture surveys carried out.

Other data collection methods can include direct observation of leadership meetings, weekly team meetings or other processes or forums which may exist. Direct observation may be classified as the research method of field work which can help explain behaviours and varying viewpoints (Richardson-Tench et al. 2011). Through the observation of group processes, a marker can be established for what is talked about, not talked about, who leads conversations, levels of engagement and what is set as a priority. The more meetings one can observe, the more data one can analyse. I have observed team meetings which are a monologue of information being dictated by the one individual, other meetings where the meeting is about what the meeting should be about, and well-run meetings where agendas are clear and there is equal input from all key stakeholders. With one company I worked with, I was able to analyse culture, and I quickly picked up on a core theme based upon employee comments. It seemed that communication was rather poor and on a 'need to know basis'. When I asked the leadership team if there were any meetings that I could attend, the leaders mentioned that most meetings were stopped due to them being non-productive. Upon hearing this, I was starting to empathise with employees of where the communication gap was starting to stem from. As safety leaders, communication is key as it drives a culture of learning. If a team is not learning, how can they improve upon a situation or prevent an incident occurring again? That company may be destined to repeat the same mistakes.

Safety culture can encompass the overall work environment as well as the attitudes and behaviours of all employees. Safety environment can be a distal antecedent for workplace injuries and it can be set by the actions and thoughts of management within the immediate environment (Kines et al. 2010). Fortunately the overall safety environment can be assessed prior to an injury occurring by looking at such variables as management commitment to safety, return-to-work policies and safety training (Huang et al. 2012). When analysing the safety culture of an organisation, a review of safety management systems, lead and lag indicators can provide further weight to the construct of management systems. Such observational data was discussed to be of integral importance by Kim, Lee and Seong (2017) when analysing safety culture across nuclear power plants. Other points of data can be gathered by cultural artefacts around a workplace; this can include posters, information displayed on screens, office layout, employee work hours and attendance rate of meetings or training sessions.

With a plethora of information being available across an organisation, there are multiple methods that can be infiltrated to capture a snapshot of the overall safety culture within an organisation. These methods and touch points have been graphically presented in Figure 4.3.

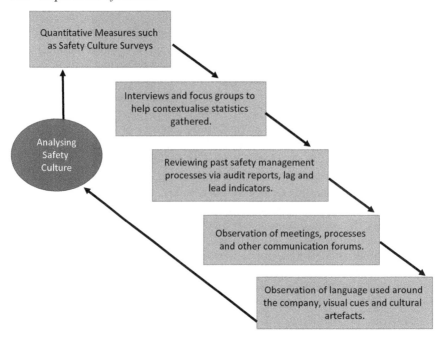

Figure 4.3 Component of safety culture analysis and process flow
(Source: Developed for this research)

Even in light of all the information collected and analysed, change will be absent unless some recommendations and interpretation points have been made. Whether or not a company chooses to take on board the overall safety culture recommendations is solely up the leadership team. Assessing what works and what does not work can be great for added insight, but better traction occurs when a tangible plan is implemented.

Changing culture

Now for the common conundrum that faces many leaders across many industries. If organisational culture needs to change, how do we do it? A myriad of strategies and approaches are available as the change management literature is plentiful. In essence, as mentioned by Dwan (2004), organisational change may start with a vision for the future, analysis of the current state, well-thought-out plan and involvement from key stakeholders. The importance of setting a vision has been well referenced in the change-management literature most often cited through the work of Kotter, which is still applicable today (Appelbaum et al. 2012). The principles that constitute Kotter's change management process include creating a sense of urgency, establishing a guiding coalition, creating a vision, communicating the vision and celebrating small wins. These components can be easily transposed into the safety realm. From a safety culture perspective, the change management process can be hastened as the sense of urgency can be stapled to an increase in workplace injuries or incidents. Being privy to many construction projects, I have seen a heightened version of change management. On one site I was at, there were multiple injuries on site, and the sense of urgency resulted in the site manager being removed from site and replaced with someone else.

Given that leadership sets a culture, the changing out of a leadership team is a quick way to change the safety climate and atmosphere on site. If a culture is toxic and at a point of no return, where management credibility is so low that nothing the leaders say can be taken on board, then such action may need to be taken. This action cannot only be in the form of changing out the leadership team, but in some instances changing out employees. The risk of removing certain employees is magnified due to company knowledge leaving the organisation and 'survivor guilt' emerging for remaining employees who were not made redundant. If the issue truly stems from leaders, then the same issues will keep emerging, even when new employees enter the organisation. If cultural issues run deep and the environment is unredeemable, the use of external change agents may be warranted and have been proven to be successful alongside self-advocacy (Miller 2015). Outside facilitation brings along neutrality and minimises bias or the individual being tainted by internal politics. Ensuring others are validated and heard through the change management process allows for self-advocacy to be nurtured.

Individuals who resist change may hold informal power within the company and therefore be influential in persuading others to be receptive or closed to impending changes. When painting the vision for the future, getting the individuals involved who have informal power can assist in influencing others. These individuals may then become toxic handlers, where they deal with others who are resistant (McShane, Olekalns & Travaglione 2010). A core example of this notion in place can be demonstrated by a heavily unionised site I was consulting at. As part of a behaviour-based safety process, a steering committee had to be established alongside a core internal facilitator. The culture on site was characterised by an 'us versus them' mentality where trust amongst the leadership group was minimal. The site was often disrupted through union strikes. Through outside consultation, it was decided that the best person to lead the steering committee would be the head union delegate on site. After some initial resistance and scepticism, the union delegate was able to wield their informal power and influence other core employees and educate them about the behaviour-based safety process that was being implemented across the company. Each organisation is unique with varying influences at play; sometimes broader culture change can be time consuming. To keep things in perspective, one may be best served to have an act local, think global mentality.

Etched into the bedrock of research is the technique of motivational interviewing that fosters a personal change in behaviour. First described by

Prochaska and DiClemente (1986), motivational interviewing is about increasing internal motivation by assessing where someone is at on the change cycle. Adapted from the drug and alcohol counselling methodology, this change model can also help explain motivation towards change from a cultural level. The change cycle could be based upon someone who is not ready for change (pre-contemplation), getting ready for change (contemplation), being ready to change (action), sticking with the change (maintenance) and possible learning through failure (relapse). The same steps can be traced when undertaking organisational change. By accounting for the individual differences, global change can occur.

Creating a tailored action plan to shift safety culture can be harnessed through the results of any safety culture assessment that might have been undertaken. In the absence of a safety culture assessment, diligent consultation with key parties may start to unearth some of the challenges and factors that may need tweaking. For instance, if management credibility is low, an action plan may be based upon building trust and following through with workplace requests. If procedural justice is low, actions may be undertaken to create transparency around reward and promotion opportunities. Actions that are contextualised for the issues at hand can ensure meaningful change lasts. The change that occurs now can be the future culture of tomorrow.

Case study

A safety culture analysis was undertaken with a company of 90 employees who were divided into three groups for analysis and comparison. The identified groups were craft workers (tradesman), white collar workers (engineers, health and safety advisors, etc.) and management. When answering the safety culture questionnaire, leaders answered based upon their perceptions of how they are operating as a leader. Key constructs of the safety culture were measured where results bucked the national norm, where white collar workers scored lower than craft workers. Overall company strengths were around incident reporting, safety management systems and teamwork. Figure 4.4 is a graphical representation of the quantitative data where a specific organisational narrative can be developed.

Prior to talking to the employees across the workplace, the leaders of the company were not aware of any core issues which might influence cultural scores. Further data obtained through direct observations and liaising with employees outlined that the teamwork and functioning of craft workers is well catered for, although the scope of work for the white collar workers was unclear and sometimes unorganised. Observations were made where white collar workers were civil to each other, although not as familiar or friendly compared to craft workers. In addition, white collar workers had to be prompted to discuss information about the leadership team and when doing so were diplomatic in their responses.

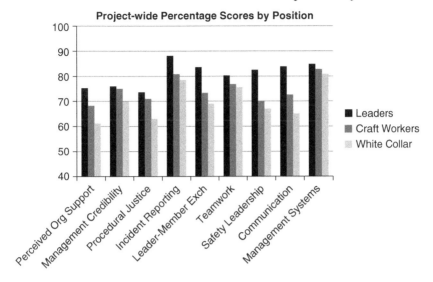

Figure 4.4 Company results across workplace positions
(Source: Developed for this research)

Questions

Q1. Looking at Figure 4.4, what could be the narrative behind the results obtained? Specifically around constructs that are strong and other areas which may need more work.

Q2. What could be some reasons why the leadership team are perceiving themselves to be operating well in comparison to other work groups?

Q3. How would lower scores across procedural justice and perceived organisational support be adversely impacting other cultural strengths?

Q4. What recommendations would you make in order to improve the overall culture on site, based upon the data presented?

Epilogue

Deeper analysis into the culture on site identified certain themes across the white collar workers. Across multiple individuals, an alleged issue had recently occurred where a colleague was acting in unethical ways which created general malaise for others. Concerns were raised with the core manager, although little action was taken. As a result, resentment started to build within the white collar team, and perceptions of favourites and nepotism started to occur. This issue was ongoing for over six months which started to influence the credibility of management. As a result, when leaders addressed the white collar workers, respect was already diminished. Craft workers were not privy to the associated issue as they were sheltered away from such concerns and operated in a different work environment. Upon broaching the issue with the leadership team, they were unaware of the angst amongst the white collar group and did not consider the concern a point of immediate action. What complicated matters was that the individual in question was still working within the company and recently received a promotion.

In terms of strengthening the safety culture scores, a focus was placed around safety leadership and communication. By focusing on these two constructs, clear communication can shift the current perceptions of nepotism and low organisational support. To address the grouped claims of unethical conduct, a separate investigation into the matter was raised. Safety leadership was exercised through increased management walk-throughs, additional engineering forums and weekly feedback sessions. Clarity around promotion opportunities was provided and further context was given around the recent promotion of the person accused of unethical conduct. Results of the HR investigation substantiated the concerns of the general white collar workforce and disciplinary action was undertaken with the person in question which resulted in termination. With these actions in place, a post-culture analysis was undertaken which showed a significant increase across the areas of procedural justice, safety leadership and communication. The follow up post-assessment was a powerful marker to demonstrate the effectiveness of the change management plan.

Organisational and personal application

The following suggestions can be integrated into your organisation or as part of your own personal safety leadership ethos. Comments are based upon the importance of safety culture and chapter content.

Organisational application

- How does your organisation currently measure and analyse culture? Prior to changing culture, what is the current measurement of cultural health? Undertaking a pre- and post-culture analysis can help ascertain if the changes undertaken have been successful or not.
- What are some of the unwritten ground rules that are present in your organisation? Do you have a culture that is mature enough to challenge some of these unwritten rules? If there is any mismatch in processes or procedures and actual work done, the unwritten culture could explain such discrepancies.
- Are there any toxic handlers that you can identify in your organisation? If implementing deep change within the company, what would be the benefits of an internal or external change manager? The nuances of your company culture will influence other strategic choices when looking to strengthening the overall safety culture.

Individual application

- As a safety leader, what are you currently focusing on which is influencing the current safety climate? The conversations you have and information you share will be creating a perception of how things are going across the company.
- When confronted with change, what is your immediate reaction? How quickly would you go through the personal change model? Individuals who are open to change are more likely to grow as individuals and adapt to new and varied challenges.
- How do you currently contribute to the organisation's culture? Do you feed an unhelpful unwritten culture or do you promote the behaviours of the desired culture? Undertaking a stocktake of individual leadership behaviours can help increase insight into your behaviours and how that influences the overall safety culture.
- How would you use the results of a safety culture analysis to inform, refine or create your company vision and purpose? Information that is not acted upon becomes an opportunity missed to capitalise on the current climate of the company. Without a clear vision for the company culture, a misalignment of cultural goals and behaviours may start to occur.

Chapter summary

The waters run deep when one attempts to analyse the safety culture of an organisation. There are a variety of different pathways that can help ascertain the cultural health of a company. Through combined qualitative and quantitative methods, a valid pulse check can be obtained. Unwritten processes and normed behaviours can provide a deeper perspective into workplace culture. Failure to recognise the unwritten ground rules of an organisation, may create a false reading of safety culture. Changing culture can be anchored through organisational change models or individual motivational change processes. Safety culture is driven through leadership, and safety leaders who link their behaviours to the organisation's overall vision are more cognisant of their breadth of influence.

References

Aga, DA, Noorderhaven, N & Vallejo, B 2016, 'Transformational leadership and project success: The mediating role of team-building', *International Journal of Project Management*, 34, 806–816.

Appelbaum, SH, Habashy, S, Malo JL & Hisham, S 2012, 'Back to the future: Revisiting Kotter's 1996 Change Model', *The Journal of Management Development*, 31(8), 764–782.

Beus, JM, Payne, SC, Bergman, ME & Arthur, W 2010, 'Safety climate and injuries: An examination of theoretical and empirical relationships', *Journal of Applied Psychology*, 95(4), 713–727.

Bjerkan, AM 2010, 'Health, environment, safety culture and climate – analysing the relationships to occupational accidents', *Journal of Risk Research*, 13(4), 445–477.

Chen, S, Yu, H, Hsu, H, Lin, F & Lou, J 2013, 'Organisational support, organisational identification and organisational citizenship behaviour among male nurses', *Journal of Nursing Management*, 21, 1072–1082.

Dando, N & Swift T 2003, 'Transparency and assurance: Minding the credibility gap', *Journal of Business Ethics*, 44(2/3), 195–200.

Dwan, S 2004, 'Changing organisational culture', *NZ Business*, 18(5), 36.

Fang, D & Wu, H 2013, 'Development of a safety culture interaction (SCI) model for construction projects', *Safety Science*, 57(1), 138–149.

Frazier, CB, Ludwig, TD, Whitaker, B & Roberts, DS 2013, 'A hierarchical factor analysis of a safety culture survey', *Journal of Safety Research*, 45(1), 15–28.

Freeman, RB & Huang, W 2014, 'Strength in diversity', *Nature and Scientific American*, 513, 305–306.

Fugas, CS, Silva, SA & Melia, JL 2012, 'Another look at safety climate and safety behavior: Deepening the cognitive and social mediator mechanisms', *Accident Analysis Prevention*, 45(1), 468–477.

Geller, SE 2008, *Leading People-based Safety: Enriching Your Culture*, Coastal Training Technologies Corp., Virginia Beach.

Guba, EG & Lincoln, YS 1989, *Fourth Generation Evaluation*, Sage Publishing, Newbury Park.

Guldenmund, FW 2010, '(Mis)understanding safety culture and its relationship to safety management', *Risk Analysis*, 30(10), 1466–1480.

Havaei, F, Dahinten, VS & MacPhee, M 2015, 'The effects of perceived organisational support and span of control on the organisational commitment of novice leaders', *Journal of Nursing Management*, 23, 307–314.

Heuer, L & Stroessner, SJ, 2011, 'The multi–value basis of procedural justice', *Journal of Experimental Social Psychology*, 47, 541–553.

Huang, YH, Verma, SK, Chang, WR, Courtney, TK, Lombardi, DA, Brennan, MJ & Perry, MJ 2012, 'Management commitment to safety v. employee perceived safety training and association with future injury', *Accident Analysis Prevention*, 47(1), 94–101.

Kim, T, Bateman, TS, Gilbreath, B & Andersson, LM 2009, 'Top management credibility and employee cynicism: A comprehensive model', *Human Relations*, 62(10), 1435–1458.

Kim, YG, Lee, SM & Seong, PH 2017, 'A methodology for a quantitative assessment of safety culture in NPP's based on Bayesian networks', *Annals of Nuclear Energy*, 102, 23–36.

Kines, P, Andersen, LP, Spangenberg, S, Mikkelsen, KL, Dyreborg, J & Zohar, D 2010, 'Improving construction site safety through leader-based verbal safety communication', *Journal of Safety Research*, 41(5), 399–406.

Koyuncua, M, Burkeb, R, Fixenbaumb, L & Tekinc, Y 2013, 'Antecedents and consequences of employee voice behaviour among front-line employees in Turkish hotels', *Anatolia – An International Journal of Tourism and Hospitality Research*, 24(3), 427–437.

Laschinger, HKS & Finegan, J 2005, 'Empowering nurses for work engagement and health in hospital settings', *Journal of Nursing Administration*, 35, 439–449.

Lucas, T, Kamble, SV, Wu, MS, Zhdanova, L & Wendorf, CA 2016, 'Distributive and procedural justice for self and others: Measurement invariance and links to life satisfaction in four cultures', *Journal of Cross-Cultural Psychology*, 47(2), 234–248.

Mansouri, M, Shaqdan, KW, Aran, S, Raja, AS, Lev, MH & Abujude, HH 2015, 'Safety incident reporting in emergency radiology: Analysis of 1717 safety incident reports', *Emergency Radiology*, 22(6), 623–630.

Maslen, S & Hayes, J 2016, 'Preventing black swans: Incident reporting systems as collective knowledge management', *Journal of Risk Research*, 19(10), 1246–1260.

McShane, S, Olekalns, M & Travaglione, T 2010, *Organisational Behaviour*, The McGraw-Hill Companies, Sydney.

Mengolini, A & Debarberis, L 2012, 'Lessons learnt from a crisis event: How to foster a sound safety culture', *Safety Science*, 50(6), 1415–1421.

Miller, R 2015, 'Changing organisational culture: Another role for self-advocacy', *Tizard Learning Disability Review*, 20(2), 69–76.

Mohammadfam, I, Kamalinia, M, Momeni, M, Golmohammadi, R, Hamidi, Y & Soltanian, A 2016, 'Developing an integrated decision making approach to assess and promote the effectiveness of occupational health and safety management systems', *Journal of Cleaner Production*, 127, 119–133.

Park, S, Sturman, MC, Vanderpool, C & Chan, E 2015, 'Only time will tell: The changing relationships between LMX, job performance and justice', *Journal of Applied Psychology*, 100(3), 660–680.

Prochaska, J & DiClemente, C 1986, 'Towards a comprehensive model of change', *Treating Addictive Behaviours: Process of Change*, Pergamon, New York.

Richardson-Tench, M, Taylor, B, Kermode, S & Roberts, K 2011, *Research in Nursing: Evidence for Best Practice*, Cengage Learning Australia, South Melbourne.

Shenton, AK 2004, 'Strategies for ensuring trustworthiness in qualitative research projects', *Education for Information*, 22(2), 63–75.

Simpson, S 2007, *Cracking the Corporate Culture Code*, Narnia House Publishing, Sanctuary Cove.

Toor, SR & Ofori, G 2008, 'Leadership for future construction industry: Agenda for authentic leadership', *International Journal of Project Management*, 26(6), 620–630.

Valls, V, Gonzalez-Roma, V & Tomas, I 2016, 'Linking educational diversity and team performance: Team communication quality and innovation team climate matter', *Journal of Occupational and Organisational Psychology*, 89, 751–771.

Vinodkumar, MN & Bhasi, M 2011, 'A study on the impact of management system certification on safety management', *Safety Science*, 49, 498–507.

Wang, D, Gan, C & Wu, C, 2016, 'LMX and employee voice: A moderated mediation model of psychological empowerment and role clarity', *Personnel Review*, 45(3), 605–615.

5   Innovation and emerging paradigms

Shifting the needle on safety: progressing from dogma to science

This chapter was written in collaboration with:

Michelle Oberg, Sarah Colley, Jonathan Lincolne, Laura Graham and Sidney Dekker

Overall assumptions: what context is relevant before you proceed?

This chapter provides a framework for leaders to progress safety by taking a fundamentally different approach to the role people have in creating safety at the front end of their businesses. This approach centres on autonomy, decluttering bureaucracy and compliance, and searching for the sources of success rather than just counting the occasional failures. The intended audience consists of both safety and operational leaders in organisations of all kinds. A case study of a real-world safety intervention is described throughout to show how the framework can be applied.

For brevity, this is a high level account of the ideas that inspired the new approach, as well as of the framework, methods and applications. The framework has been developed over 15 years from researching and implementing innovative human-focused processes that change culture and enhance the health, safety, well-being and engagement of people across industries. This chapter contains a high level overview of the approach in an innovative and thought-provoking application to safety which shifts the needle from safety dogma to safety science.

Key objectives

The following chapter is designed to help paint a picture of what is possible in terms of shifting the safety needle to progress safety from dogma to science by addressing four overarching questions:

- What organisational values help and hinder safety across industries?
- Can shifting towards values that focus on people and innovation advance safety?
- Does effective change management have a role in progressing safety?
- What can we learn from real-world research to advance safety?

After you read this chapter, it is our intent that you can take what is effective and working in your current safety approaches, and build on them through raising awareness of:

1   A framework to integrate people-focused change management with rigorous scientific methods to:

a   Identify and retain only that which is effective and supports safety, and
b   Remove any redundant approaches that are based solely on safety dogma.

2   Practical tools and skills to adopt and facilitate real change in safety for the people in your organisation.

What is the dilemma part #1? Valuing bureaucracy versus valuing people

After nearly two decades of observing and participating in both the research and implementation of safety efforts around the world we have observed two very concerning phenomena. As the discipline of safety continues its maturation, this seems like a good time to voice these topics. Past experience tells us that some people will be angry or indignant by the end of the chapter. Others will be curious, and some of you will agree that the time is right to make these topics available for the global safety discussion.

> Businesses are in the stranglehold of health and safety red tape ... We are waging war against this excessive health and safety culture that has become an albatross around the neck of businesses.
> David Cameron, UK Prime Minister (Cameron 2012)

There is a saying that 'a fish doesn't know it lives in water until you take it out'. The Germans have a word for this. They call it the Umwelt. Umwelt is a psychological construct that describes how human beings have a need to believe that which we see, and the way that we see it, is reality. As a result, we have significant difficulty seeing outside of our own belief systems and the environment that we consequently construct from these beliefs. The Umwelt serves an important psychological purpose. By giving us the impression that our perceptions about the world are right, it makes our world. In essence, our Umwelt lets us see what we need to see to be effective while at the same time keeping us blind to reality. Within the discipline of safety, we have our own Safety Umwelt. That is, there exists a collective belief system regarding safety that gives us the feeling that we are doing it right, which simultaneously limits our reality to see the situation at hand. We are referring here to the bureaucratisation of safety.

A bureaucracy is a system of administration distinguished by 1) a clear hierarchy of authority, 2) the rigid division of labour and 3) written and inflexible rules, regulations and procedures. Once instituted, it is difficult to dislodge or change. The eminent German sociologist Max Weber argued that bureaucracy constitutes the most efficient and rational way in which one can organise human activity, and that systematic processes and organised hierarchies were necessary to maintain order, maximise efficiency and eliminate favouritism. By this definition we can easily see why, with few exceptions such as Sweden, the regulation of health and safety has become so pervasive.

Consistent with Weber's observations, the bureaucratisation of safety has brought many benefits, including an immediate reduction of harm and greater motivation for business owners and their management teams to create safer working environments through legislated consequences, standardisation, transparency and control. All of this has been of immense importance and great benefit to those exposed to risk in the workplace.

However, like most things, you can have too much of a good thing. Weber, while able to clearly articulate the benefits of imposed regulations, also saw unfettered bureaucracy as a threat to individual freedom. He wrote that 'bureaucratisation of human life can trap individuals in an impersonal iron cage of rule-based, rational control'. He said bureaucracy led to the great depersonalisation of work and the worker (Swedberg & Agevall 2016). If Max Weber was to take a look at the state of our safety systems currently, he may define them as 'unfettered bureaucracies' and may express his concerns that they have gone from being a source of safety improvement to a safety hindrance. Seeing its impacts for the last 20 years, we suggest that in the current state, safety bureaucracy is one of the single biggest hindrances to safety performance we face today.

Bureaucratisation of safety has been driven by a number of factors, including legislation and regulation, changes in liability and insurance arrangements, a wholesale move to outsourcing and contracting, and increased technological capabilities for surveillance, monitoring, storage and data analysis. Bureaucratisation tends to see people as a problem to control (e.g., by standardising and fixing rules, expecting compliance) and generates secondary effects that run counter to its original goals. These effects include an inability to predict unexpected events, a focus on bureaucratic accountability, quantification and numbers games, the occasional creation of new safety problems and constraints on organisation members' personal freedom, diversity and innovation.

One of the defining qualities of the Umwelt is the continuation of behaviour in the face of evidence that suggests it is ineffective. Many organisations in industry and government perpetuate safety bureaucracy as 'the way safety is done'. It is easy to make things more difficult; it is easy to add more rules, and it might help assuage people's fears of liability. There is, however, a better way. Just as Max Weber predicted it would, safety bureaucracy has dehumanised safety. It has taken the power, the accountability and control away from the people doing the job. We have instead empowered policy, procedure, paperwork and checklist to (ostensibly) keep us safe. The situation is at best nonsensical, at worst it is bordering a form of social insanity.

Clearly of course, *some* overarching regulation is required. There is a growing body of evidence to suggest there is genuine value in the calm reassessment of what regulations are actually required, paired with the re-humanising of our workforce. The people doing the job are the experts on the job. Our experience, and a growing body of research, shows that it takes surprisingly little to engage people in the process of both engineering and implementing safe work practices that are more practical, more efficient and more effective than those imposed by a safety bureaucracy. What it takes is autonomy, giving the workforce a pride of ownership and craftsmanship, a sense of mastery and a purpose they themselves want to rally behind. This is exemplified in the story of WorkSafe Victoria.

Bureaucracy in action – WorkSafe Victoria example

In 2014, WorkSafe Victoria, Australia published a report detailing its mistakes and learnings from the time of its inception in 1980 through to present day 2014 (WorkSafe Victoria 2014). In this report WorkSafe Victoria cites the findings from an inquiry into the health, safety and welfare of Victorian workers way back in 1981. This inquiry was chaired by Alfred Robens and was commissioned due to massive problems with existing legislation, which were considered 'outdated, reactive, lacking in uniformity and non-inclusive of employers and workers in the setting of standards'.

Robens' inquiry directly recommended that 'a system be adopted that was self-regulating, whereby each party (employer and employee) would take responsibility for workplace health and safety, and whereby a consultative and inclusive approach be adopted between each party in setting standards and approaches to safety'.

These consultative and inclusive approaches – humanising approaches that focus on engaging people – were ignored in totality. Instead, a more 'comprehensive' OHS programme was established – bureaucracy. This more 'comprehensive' approach established a commission, increased the powers of inspectors to issue harsher penalties and became inextricably intertwined with compliance. Heavier fines for safety breaches and the introduction of a licensing system for workplaces reinforced more command and control approaches that increased policing, auditing and punishment to combat safety – more bureaucracy. As a senior safety manager summed it up well by saying 'compliance protects the office holders of the business, safety protects the guys on the ground.'

The WorkSafe Victoria system continued to be in peril and was on the verge of ongoing financial collapse for the next 20 years. It wasn't until 2000 that things began to change when new management adopted a much-needed new approach. Ironically, it was one of collaboration and consultation – a human focus – which had been recommended some 20 years earlier by the initial inquiry. Keri Whitehead, who began working for the scheme at its inception, claims that in terms of the scheme's efficiency 'the difference was phenomenal', citing WorkSafe's consultative and collaborative approach as a major factor in its success and improvement.

Bureaucracy is dependent on the adherence of those it governs to be effective. However, as far back as 1917 the Australian philosopher and pioneer in industrial psychology, Bernard Muscio, argued that health and productivity would be managed much more effectively by a combination of enhancing worker discretion and effective work practices rather than working people harder and longer under a stop-watch. He argued that people could not be treated like machines because the antecedents to the productivity and safety of people were clearly different from the antecedents to the productivity and safety of machines. Muscio's words are offered modern support from the Competing Values Framework.

Safety research: organisational values and safety

The Competing Values Framework has been studied and used within organisations for over 25 years and has been often posited as one of the 40 most important frameworks in the history of business. The Competing Values Framework provides a way of examining the competing demands placed on an organisation. These values have long been recognised as determinants of organisational success. Recent research (Colley, Lincolne & Neal 2012) looked at cultural values using the Competing Values Framework which proposes that four sets of cultural values exist in unison in any one organisation. The four cultural types, or quadrants, are collaborate, create, control and compete. Each cultural quadrant achieves certain ends (i.e., outcomes) via specific means (i.e., activities and actions), and has distinct characteristics. Depending on the demands placed on the organisation, each cultural quadrant will be more or less dominant. Further, the strength of each cultural type within an organisation can vary in response to both internal (e.g., leadership) and external (e.g., industry, financing, etc.) factors. An organisation's emphasis across the four types creates a specific 'cultural values profile' (represented like a web spanning across the four quadrants).

Research from Colley, Lincolne and Neal (2012) conducted across construction, mining and rail organisations found three distinct cultural patterns, each with its own impact on safety performance. Organisations that possessed the first pattern, comprised of strong control and compete types (quadrants), displayed lower organisational safety climate and supervisor support, as well as more incidents and unsafe behaviours (see left, Figure 5.1). More broadly, a controlling or bureaucratic and proceduralised type hinders safety performance. Organisations that possessed the second pattern, comprised of a very high collaborate type, displayed higher organisational safety climate and supervisor support, as well as fewer incidents and unsafe behaviours (see center, Figure 5.1). Interestingly, however, organisations that possessed the third pattern, comprised of a combination of high collaborate, high create, high compete and low control, displayed the same positive outcomes as the collaborate type (see right, Figure 5.1). This highlights that a focus on both people (collaborate) and the market (compete) can foster innovation (create) that benefits the organisation.

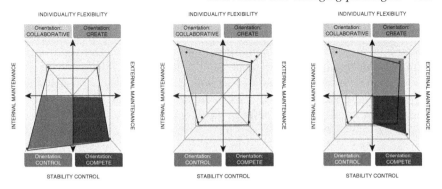

Figure 5.1 Competing values framework
(Source: Adapted from Colley, Lincolne & Neal 2012)

As part of our work with safety leaders, we recently assessed the perceived organisational values of several hundred leaders we were working with, all from mega-projects/construction, across four regions: Asia (sampled 100 leaders), USA (sampled 45 leaders), India (sampled 75 leaders) and Australia (sampled 43 leaders). When we analysed the data, it highlighted that across locations, perceived organisational values were mostly similar, with the exception of India. India possessed a much higher collaborative type, which is conducive to higher safety performance, however, anecdotally, Indians are pressured to conform to 'west is best'. Conforming to these Western values patterns would reduce their collaboration, therefore, and may adversely and unnecessarily impact safety. A second consistent finding from this data was that all companies had low levels of values emphasising the create quadrant, highlighting the lack of focus on innovation within companies across the globe. This data has been graphically represented in Figure 5.2.

What is the dilemma part #2? Safety dogma

The belief systems or dogma that have accrued and ossified around safety are persistent and highly resistant to change even in the face of empirical

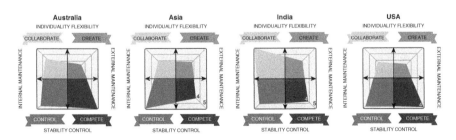

Figure 5.2 Cultural patterns
(Source: Adapted from Colley, Lincolne & Neal 2012)

evidence. Dogma is defined as a principle or set of principles laid down by an authority that are incontrovertibly true; a belief or set of beliefs that are accepted by a group without being questioned or doubted. Derived from the Latin word *dokeîn* meaning 'to seem good', the word was the name given to various collections of canon law. Throughout time, examples of dogma stifling innovation and necessary change are evident. As an example, Nicolaus Copernicus initially presented the thesis of heliocentrism – that the planets orbit around the sun at the centre of the solar system. He kept his ideas between his friends and colleagues for around 28 years before they were published. Why did he wait so long to publish material so revolutionary? His peers urged him to not publish the material out of fear of scorn due to his ideas being too novel and incomprehensible as they challenged the dogmatic public beliefs prevailing at the time.

Parallels can be drawn between the origins of dogma, the Christian church, Copernicus and the state of safety today. Safety is currently heavily dogmatic and proceduralised with leaders often passing down doctrine to frontline workers without any science justifying its use. Doctrine without science becomes dogma both in Safety 1 and Safety 2. Safety 1 is the term used to describe traditional safety, where safety is interpreted as when the fewest things go wrong. Contrarily, a newer approach, Safety 2 (or Safety Differently), describes safety as when the most amount of things go right. Without a scientific basis and justification for the safety approach, it does not matter about the safety definition or type; dogma will prevail and drive negative outcomes. We need a doctrine of a safe and better outcome for workers.

To summarise: Safety 1 believes that people are the problem to control, that we need to tell them what to do (through procedures, rules, compliance demands), and that the best way to learn about safety is to check how many things are going wrong (incidents, injuries). Safety 2, or Safety Differently, in contrast, suggests that people are the solution to harness; the experts to rely on. We shouldn't be telling them what to do, we should instead ask them what they need. And we shouldn't be counting negatives as a marker of our progress on safety: instead, we should be identifying and harnessing the positive capacities and capability in our people that make things go right, despite the resource constraints and goal conflicts that operate in everybody's work. Safety 2, if based on dogma at all, is more philanthropic and open-minded than Safety 1. It acknowledges that there are multiple pathways to successful outcomes, that this doesn't always involve exact compliance with pre-specified routines, and that it takes expertise at front-line work and explorations to develop ways of working that are both safer and more efficient.

To shift the safety needle from a reliance on dogma, we propose that more rigorous scientific methods are needed to advance and innovate how we address safety. Research suggests, however, that high-risk organisations tend to under-value innovation and experimentation (Colley, Lincolne & Neal 2012). The need for control and predictability – which supports bureaucracy – stifles innovation. However, to address this, this chapter reports on a real-world evidence-based quasi-experiment, that attempts to progress safety through a focus on experimental methods, controls and measurement.

How can we facilitate change? Applying the 5i approach

> Seventy per cent of all organisational change efforts fail.
>
> Kotter (1995)

This is a widely quoted statistic which is horrifying. While the actual failure from Kotter has been heavily debated in recent years, a modern study by Towers Watson found that only 25% of change management initiatives were successful in the long term. For those of you who are bad at maths, this means that the true number is closer to 75% and that involved over 276 organisations from North America, Europe and Asia (Towers Watson & Willis 2013). The cost of failed change efforts is estimated that for every dollar spent, the company loses 65 cents – this equates to a 35% return on investment (ROI) (McKinsey Quarterly 2002). Over the past 15 years our team have worked in organisations to improve the outcomes of change projects using our 5i approach.

The 5i is an integrated people-focused change management and scientific method of safety change. This approach has been developed over many years through real-world research driving change in complex organisations. Table 5.1 provides an overview of the 5i approach. In short, the 5i approach was designed to consistently address the needs of businesses and, as such, possesses a framework of operation at each stage of the change model. These needs range from setting an initial focus before any change occurs, gathering the correct data from the correct source to inform change, performing short-term engagements with a long-term focus, pilot testing and reiterating the change process, and embedding the necessary knowledge and skills within the organisation.

While many change management frameworks and models exist, they often remain just that – a framework or model. Unlike most change frameworks, the 5i approach:

- is a practical methodology that has definable skills and tools for applying it in practice.
- allows organisations to fluctuate between its principles according to the iterative demands of safety change within their organisation.
- is nonlinear. It is challenging, iterative, adaptive and focuses on continual improvement. Complex change is not solved by following a neat linear recipe.
- defines the actions and skills needed to enact change, and which support the embedding of long-term safety change. This allows the 5i approach to succeed where other models may not.

Table 5.1 An overview of the 5i approach, key skills and evidenced benefits

5i approach	Key skills	Evidenced benefits
Intent 1. Set a human-focused intent 2. Build capability to understand the psychology and the complexity of human behaviour to effectively orientate the purpose of the change effort; and effectively collaborate in enacting the change process	• Applied knowledge about the psychology of human behaviour • A range of soft skills • Strategic visioning • Stakeholder analysis • Leading a team • Perspective taking • Research skills	• Increased long-term buy-in for designed initiatives • Reduced cynicism and change resistance
Intelligence 1. Gather intelligence from data and people 2. Build internal research capability	• Communication and engagement • Relationship building • Empathy • Listening • Critical thinking • Strategic thinking • Data analysis	• Accurate identification of employee/end user problems • Increased satisfaction, productivity and engagement • Evidence-based actions and outcomes
Instigate 1. Collaborate with experts in the short term to insource the expertise to deliver change in the long term 2. Develop skills to implement and sustain change 3. Acknowledge the 5i approach is nonlinear and requires some stages to be conducted concurrently and others to undergo iterations	• Listening • Small-group process facilitation • Large-group facilitation • Decision making • Applied skills in mitigating cognitive biases • Collaboration	• Improved internal capability in the listed key skills • Improved adaptability to changing business environment • Internal support for change agenda • Less future dependence on external consultants

5i approach	Key skills	Evidenced benefits
Implement 1. Start small, pilot, iterate, replicate 2. Focus on top-down and bottom-up approaches in tandem	• Research methodology and analysis • Stakeholder engagement • Planning and organising • Political nous • Communication • Problem solving • Reflection	• Maximise organisational learning, collaboration and growth • Increase in long-term change support
Internalise 1. Start with the end in mind – internalising change – and develop practices to support the embedding of behaviour change 2. Support and reinforce behaviour change through a focus on team practices	• Regular feedback loops • Regular interactions • Team-based accountability • Team-based coaching • Communication • Empathy	• Enhanced organisational learning through a learning culture which was evident by individual champions taking up the cause • Reduced blame culture

(Source: Developed for this research)

To paint a clearer picture, the following sections describe the fundamental philosophies and science behind each of the 5i elements and how they have been brought to life through real-world research within the context of the Woolworths Project. A brief overview of the Woolworths Project is described below. Following this project overview, the 5i approach will be explored, and the research will be used through the rest of the chapter to illustrate how the 5i methodology can be applied.

The case for conducting real-world safety differently: the Woolworths Project

The Woolworths Project (detailed throughout) describes the approach of one of the first ever real-world 'quasi-experimental' research projects undertaken to move from safety dogma to rigorous safety scientific with one of the biggest food retailers in Australia. It was designed to provide evidence that safety could be done differently when the right conditions and approaches were adopted.

Below is a brief overview of the research design and conditions within the experiment.

Research design

The experiment is described in more detail under each of the 5i stages. The company volunteered sites across south-east Queensland, Australia. The 30 sites, varying from low, medium and high performance, were assigned to one of the three conditions:

1   *Control condition:* In the control condition, sites remained the same – no activities changed – to allow us to compare the impact of the quasi-experimental design across the other two conditions.
2   *Leadership condition:* In the leadership condition, all safety rules were removed. Processes and procedures were not required by law, and site managers had the control, responsibility and power to manage safety on the front lines. While this is an interesting topic and necessary for debate, we are not delving deep into the theory or the philosophical reasoning behind the approach in this chapter.
3   *Ownership-support condition:* In the last condition, ownership-support, each site participated in two half-day workshops focusing on thinking about safety differently and forming a strong team supporting network for the site itself.

While each condition varied in its manipulation, we ensured that the activities done by the researchers regarding data collection and observations were consistent across all three conditions. This ensured that the Hawthorne effect was managed and the same baseline measures across the conditions controlled for other placebo effects. The following sections describe the

Woolworths Project, examining it through the lens of the 5i approach, highlighting valuable and practical benefits and key lessons learned.

Intent

The two key learnings from this section on intent are:

1   Set a human-focused intent.
2   Build capability to understand the psychology and the complexity of human behaviour to effectively orientate the purpose of the change effort; and effectively collaborate in enacting the change process.

The following section outlines why intent is important, what the research says, the key actions and skills required for setting intent, and a set of reflective questions to get you started.

Intent: what intent is and why is it important?

Understanding people and accepting them as they are is the first principle that underpins the effectiveness of the 5i process. We will reiterate this point as it is essential: setting a human-focused intent is the key ingredient, the secret sauce and the essential component needed to drive effective changes in safety. Intent is defined as the state of mind with which an action is performed. The intent stage is just that, deliberately setting the mindset required to effectively understand, accept and manage human complexity. This begins with the first principle which for any effective change or innovation – inside a complex system that involves people – is very specific: 'accept and understand people as they are, while believing in their inherent capability to be a part of the solution, and not the problem to be solved'.

Why is this principle so important? Well, being a very intelligent, capable and complex human being yourself does not exempt you from the inherent challenges of leading or working with other complex human beings. People are impossibly complex – they have different perceptions, preferences, values, skills and challenges. So dealing with people means dealing with this complexity. This complexity is a contributing factor in why we have a preference to 'proceduralise' safety as opposed to 'humanise' safety. Despite this, the essential 'human skills' continue to be widely referred to as 'soft skills' in the business vernacular. This is not the 'soft stuff'; people are the hard reality of our daily work life! People are the source of your businesses productivity and deliver the return on investment to stakeholders through investing their precious time and energy to your organisation over their work life.

So to ignore this and not see them as people who have hopes, dreams, fears and needs is not only dehumanising but also lacks business savvy. Whether you like it or not, people, and all their complexity, are the hard reality of business. If we fail to understand and accept this reality, we will continue to be frustrated and unsuccessful in influencing any real change. This is part of the reason why we so frequently hear leaders blaming others for the predictable failure of their well-planned process improvements, or lack of adherence to regimes and procedures that they themselves rarely have to adopt or enact because they don't perform the work at the coal face. This leads them to look elsewhere hoping that a consultant-informed or *New York Times* bestseller-based programme will be the panacea cure for their woes.

Too often organisations set out with the intent of introducing a new system or process divorced of people, to overcome safety issues. This results in ineffective change because more processes does not necessarily address the issues that people face. When we consider the psychology of people, we understand that most people want to experience autonomy, freedom within limits, support and be competent and capable in their work. When we see people in this manner, we are able to entrust and support people to own their work and contribute ideas about ways they can address the issue of keeping themselves safe at work. It is unlikely that many people come to work wanting to be harmed. When we focus on trusting in our people's capability, we start to focus on the more effective activities that foster safer outcomes. So in this regard, simplifying safety process does not mean simplifying safety thinking. In fact, we would suggest that when we focus on people, we are engaging in more complex and sophisticated safety thinking. When we refocus our approach and adopt a human-focused intent, we see them as a resource to be harnessed, rather than as a problem to fix.

This is not just opinion or magical thinking. Recent research in the tenth anniversary edition of Towers Watson and Willis (2013) found that organisations were three times more likely to have effective change outcomes when they focused on engaging employees. We would recommend approaching every change initiative with an acceptance and understanding of human complexity, that they are a resource to be utilised and the philosophy of 'love the crap out of your people first and foremost'. With this intent you are able to design and deliver initiatives people understand, relate to and will apply in their lives.

Intent: what does the research say?

For brevity and simplicity, below are four key areas of research that help us understand why making a shift toward a human-focused intent works and is foundational to shifting current safety paradigms.

1   Focusing on people enhances organisational commitment. Research shows that the levels of support people believe they receive from their organisation both indirectly and directly impact the effectiveness of change processes (Iverson 1996).
2   Focusing on people drives proactive actions. Research shows that when people feel supported by their organisation, they also feel more committed. Moreover, when people feel they have positive exchanges with

their leader (leader–member exchange), they are more likely to choose to engage in more constructive and proactive actions in their role and on behalf of the organisation (i.e., positive citizenship behaviours; Kraatz & Rousseau 1994).

3   Focusing on people enables change. Research shows that change readiness is linked to an employee's beliefs, attitudes and intentions (e.g., Armenakis et al. 1993).

4   Focusing on people has a positive impact on safety. Research shows that when an organisation values people through investment in training, leadership, collaboration and relationships, people report stronger and more positive safety climates and report fewer incidents (Colley, Lincolne and Neal 2012).

Intent in action: what happened at Woolworths?

Intent as applied to the Woolworths Project is described below.

Researchers' assumption

When setting your intent, it is not one conversation. It is an evolving and ever-growing process with the people you engage with in your project. In this case, we were involved in running a Learning Lab for company executives and safety people, and we showed a picture of a so-called 'shared space' traffic square in Drachten, the Netherlands. It is a square where there is no top-down traffic management, no obvious rules, no lines, no lights, no barriers, no sidewalks. There is just an expanse of uniform bricks. The square used to be gridlocked frequently and produced eight pretty bad accidents per year. More top-down imposition of safety rules was not going to help either. In fact, the opposite was done. Everything was taken out, creating just a square for people to figure out by themselves how to cross it, whether by foot, bike, car or scooter. The results were spectacular, and we talked through them in the Learning Lab. Accidents went down to about one per year. People now looked each other in the eye to decide who went first: it became a space where the creation of safety became a collaborative, jointly negotiated activity, full of interaction and humanity. Interestingly, and consistent with psychological literature on risk compensation, the riskier things looked, the safer the behaviour became. It was obvious that you couldn't enter this square and not be engaged in your own safety. Then one of the Woolworths executives asked: 'What if we were to do that, take everything out? What would happen to safety then?' It was the question that kicked off the Woolworths' Experiment.

About three months later, we met with the Woolworths Queensland Head Office safety team and the National Manager for safety. In this meeting, we discussed why the organisation wanted this project to happen. The QLD head office safety team spoke about how they believed that the effectiveness of their current safety approach was plateauing, that they were interested in seeing if there was a different way to address safety in their sites and to have a greater people-focus. This was their intent. The research itself was occurring with frontline site managers, team leaders and employees in several sites.

It was important that our intent and the organisation's intent were communicated to the participants to ensure that they were bought-in, engaged and committed to the research. This process involved an initial email and a phone call from the QLD head office safety team to ensure the sites were prepared to talk to us and had an opportunity to opt out of the research at an early phase. Next, a member of the QLD head office safety team accompanied us in visiting each of the sites to discuss the project. While there, we answered questions and addressed any concerns or comments. We also provided the site with collateral outlining the vision for the project and the project's purpose as well as their rights and responsibilities as a research participant. Once the site manager had signed on to the project, we also visited each site's morning huddle where many employees gathered to check in and to share information. In these huddles, we communicated the intent and expectations behind the research.

Later in the project, the intent was addressed again for the individual site in the experimental condition. While we had an overarching intent for the project, for the success of the project it was important that each site set their intent for how they wanted safety to be in their site. Teams undergoing the workshops were shocked and delighted at this approach. Within the organisation's context new initiatives, especially around safety, were referred to as 'Launch and Leave', meaning that the new ideas were thrust upon them with little consultation and little support. The workshops provided the space, time and support needed for each site to set their intent and their purpose.

Benefits

- Being clear and committed to the intent of the project and inviting people to create their intent reduced cynicism and change resistance.
- Initiatives work over the long term because they were designed with the people they affect. One solution for one site did not suit another.

Lessons learned

- If we had emphasised the person-led design process, it would have increased buy-in from the beginning.
- The researchers managed the majority of the project. The organisation would have gained greater benefit and insight if their members were involved in these conversations rather than rely on second-hand reported information.
- In the future, we would have each of the site managers' report to each other what inspired their intent to gain a greater understanding and sense of community.

Intent: where to start?

So you have read about the philosophy, research, applications and benefits of setting a human-focused intent. The next thing to consider is how you start to shift the safety needle in the right direction inside your organisation if this element is missing.

The intent stage could be described as 'the invisible made visible'. By that we mean you cannot see someone's intent, it is invisible. Intent is made visible through the actions it drives. In order to initiate a shift in intent, a series of key actions and processes can be adopted. The key actions are listed below:

- Establish a team of willing volunteers comprised of internal and external people with the motivation to make a genuine change and the willingness to learn on the job.
- Establish the ground rules for the way the team will work together.
- Identify and align on the human-focused values driving the project.
- Identify the envisioned end state the organisation is needing to achieve.
- Identify a critical safety issue, that cannot be solved by a single person.
- Identify all relevant stakeholders.

In addition to simple actions and processes, there are also an essential set of skills and attributes that are required, and may need to be developed, to support your organisation to adopt a human-focused intent. That being said, people have enormous untapped potential to be brilliant, and these skills are able to be developed and learned when people are simply provided the necessary information paired with encouragement to be – well – human in the workplace. The key skills relevant to bringing the intent to life include:

- an understanding of people, and a genuine care and concern for others
- a range of soft skills – such as communication, critical thinking, team-work, listening skills
- strategy visioning
- stakeholder analysis
- perspective taking.

To help you and your organisation assess where its safety intent is focused, and to prime them for change, we have provided a set of reflection questions for organisations and individual leaders. You can use these as either personal reflection questions or to facilitate a discussion within your organisation to establish where you are at and what safe next steps your organisation can take to move toward a human-focused intent.

Organisational reflection questions (intent)

If you recognise the need to make changes to safety in your organisation, the following questions will get you started on setting a human-focused intent:

- To what degree is the intent of our change consciously chosen for the change?
- To what degree do we communicate this intent before and during the change process?
- What is our safety vision for the future?
- What are the drivers beyond safety performance?
- What is the real, critical, important and complex issue that we will impact on through the project?
- How will we ensure lasting and sustained commitment to the project and what will hinder this sustained commitment?

Personal self-reflection questions (intent)

To what degree do you adopt a human-focused intent? If you're curious to know if you are personally adopting a human-focused intent, take a few moments to sit quietly with yourself and answer these questions honestly:

- If you were really honest, to what degree do you see your people as a resource that can be harnessed or as a problem that needs to be solved?
- How many front-line workers, who carry the greatest risk of being harmed, do you know the names of?
- Do you know them well? What do you know about them? Do you know their kids, family situation, hobbies, interests, hopes, dreams?
- How often do you engage them? Weekly, monthly?
- Are you curious to learn about them and what their unique skills are that enable them to do the work they do – which delivers the product/output for your business?
- Do you value what they do above what you do for the business?
- Do you feel your role is to serve them and create a workplace that is challenging, rewarding and supportive for them – because you as a leader have the ability to create that?

Intelligence: inquire | learn

The two key learnings from this section on intelligence are:

1 Gather intelligence from data and people.
2 Build internal research capability.

The following section outlines why the intelligence phase of the 5i process is important, what the research says, the key actions and skills required for effective intelligence, and a set of reflective questions and some of the foundational skills required to get you started.

Intelligence: what is it and why is it important?

After setting your intent, before you embark on any change initiative, gather intelligence. Intelligence is the process of gathering the right data from the right sources so you get the right outcome. There are two key types of intelligence that are important. The first type of intelligence comes from facts, figures and numbers gathered from sources including internal reports, research reports and industry trends. The second, and possibly most powerful, type of intelligence comes from your people. This intelligence is gathered by authentically and curiously engaging your people by asking great questions. Asking great questions is a marker of curiosity. Curiosity is a marker of intelligence. Curious leaders want to know 'What is happening, how it is happening and what needs to happen?' This second type of intelligence is frequently the most underutilised source of intelligence. However, it is an essential type of intelligence that enables you to understand the real issues to be solved to effect real change.

Many change initiatives however are doomed from the beginning because leaders spend all their time listening to each other and third parties with impressive resumes when they should be listening to their people. If they did, they'd hear exactly what needs to be done. While leaders of an organisation may believe they have an accurate picture of its challenges or believe they must provide the solution, the experts of the organisation are actually on our frontline. Organisations often fail to gather the right intelligence to understand the problem before implementing change. Challenges are approached with the thinking 'we need to have the right answers, we need to solve the issue on our own'. This results in top-down strategies being implemented across the organisation, which gain little buy-in at the bottom and increase cynicism. Organisations fail to harness the wealth of knowledge within their business that can be leveraged for superior outcomes.

Leaders often think that they have the big picture. More accurately, they have a picture, certainly not the complete picture. The world is far too complex for one person to have the entire picture of the situation. The picture that frontline workers see is different. It is drawn from their first-hand knowledge of the company's operations, strengths and weaknesses. What is important about the frontline workers' view is that these people capture a fuller picture of what the organisation faces and what it can actually do. In most cases, they see more chances for bold action than the executives at the top

In a *Harvard Business Review* article, Gallo (2010) quotes CEOs referencing the benefits of employee-lead solutions. One CEO was quoted as saying: 'Let people figure out how to best accomplish the goal', says Merchant. Ask your frontline employees, How can we achieve our objectives? This question will likely uncover new approaches to execution that senior management hadn't thought of. 'Often the best strategies don't come from the top of the organization,' Simons points out. The frontline can be a well of ideas. 'New ideas pop up from the pressure of trying to solve a problem for the customer,' says Simons (cited in Gallo 2010).

Moving the safety needle in complex organisations requires leaders to gather intelligence from the front line because no one person alone has all the answers, experience, or solutions to ensure consistency in safety performance. While this sounds simple and straightforward, why is it that leaders prefer to base decisions on the 'hard numbers?' Is it because for most leaders the safety numbers are easily accessible? Or that in most organisations leaders' key performance indicators (KPIs) are set by these numbers? Or is it even that the numbers are believed to be a more reliable indication of the state of safety? Or are our leaders just more comfortable with numbers than they are dealing with people? What this means is that in the end, safety is often directed by numbers, as opposed to lead by people.

To foster effective intelligence capabilities, mature organisations build internal research and implementation skills in their people. Gathering effective intelligence requires an essential set of skills that enable the creation of a learning organisation. Developing these skills enables your people to effectively identify, diagnose and develop solutions that work.

Intelligence: what does the research say?

For brevity and simplicity, below are four key areas of research that help organisations understand why utilising the insight and wisdom from both sources of intelligence enhances the identification of the right issues and possible solutions:

- The integration of multiple standpoints including both management and frontline level perceptions are necessary to understand health and safety within organisations (Eakin, Champoux & MacEachen 2010).
- People who work on the frontlines are the closest to the constrained end of the system so should be involved in designing any systems, processes or interventions that affect that work (Eurocontrol 2014).
- Organisations perform better when management involve employees in decision making (Spreitzer & Mishra 1999).
- Procedures or processes written without frontline employee involvement produces a gap between the procedures written to standardise work and the actual tasks completed at the sharp end (Blandford, Furniss & Vincent 2014).

Intelligence in action: what happened at Woolworths?

To bring the philosophy and research behind intelligence to life, the ways in which different intelligence methods were utilised to facilitate change in the Woolworths Project are described below.

Researchers' assumption

Gaining a preliminary understanding of the organisational context is essential for designing and implementing real-world research. Just as we define and understand the theory and concepts that influence intervention and measurement, we need to explore the organisational contexts and to be aware of the complex components which we are trying to change. There was no one best intervention or solution for the project. Sites differed in size, configuration, the location of teams and offices, and, of course, the work they did.

In the project, the research was occurring in the complex, confusing and ever-changing real world. To hone in on the outcomes of the experiment, multiple sources of data needed to be monitored and evaluated over the life of the project, what was typically considered intelligence. In fact, our sources of intelligence occur a lot earlier in the process with our people. The intelligence gathering of the project started at the initial meeting that occurred three months after the Learning Lab.

Intelligence methods

This experience and insight were collated and used to formulate the research project using rigorous research mixed-methods. Mixed-methods research:

- is a combination of both qualitative and quantitative research approaches. The selected measures were included to capture the different elements of safety and to allow us to parse out the differences in safety perspectives between conditions.
- has been shown to succeed in the organisational context where other traditional approaches have failed. The organisational environment is rich and complex in nature, so it requires converging methods to investigate it adequately (Plano Clark 2005).
- allows for strategic research processes to understand and achieve evolving understanding (Plano Clark, 2005).
- is said to provide significant enhancement and a deeper understanding of complex phenomena as well as ensuring instrument fidelity and participant enrichment (Collins, Onwuegbuzie & Sutton 2006; Plano Clark 2005; Creswell et al. 2009).

The *quantitative method* utilised one form of data – surveys – at the beginning and end of the project. The project incorporated a battery of measures including demographic items, employee engagement, safety climate, safety leadership, safety behaviours and transformational leadership. Cronbach's alpha for the ten subscales ranged from medium internal consistency to high internal consistency (α = 0.66 to 0.86). Survey validity has been demonstrated through the comparative fit index (CFI).

The *qualitative method* was the dominant form of data collection and analysis within the project. The reasoning behind this was that qualitative research is flexible and can be readily changed to match the fluid and dynamic demands of the situation (Lee 1999). Passive techniques are collection strategies that occur in a nonintrusive manner (Martin 1995). This project utilised observations, archival data, and safety incident and accident reports as its passive data collection techniques. Active techniques are collection strategies which involve the interference of staff from normal every-day work (Martin 1995). This project utilised interviews, workshops and weekly manager emails (with feedback loops) as the active data collection (this component is later mentioned in the internalise phase).

Intelligence at the organisational level

During the meeting with the head office, we asked the question about what were the safety procedures and the effectiveness of them. Through this process, we gained an insight into their perceptions and beliefs about safety in their sites. As one of the ideas of the project was to remove a lot of the safety procedures currently in place, we asked how staff members would react and if they thought they would feel an increase in their personal risk. The response was: 'They won't notice; I doubt there are very many people in the site who even know what our safety documents look like as it is normally done in the management office.'

Following this conversation, we hit the books and trawled through the current research, best practice and legislation available that could have an impact on our experiment. The pilot study was devised using the literature, the new ideas of the team and the perceptions and beliefs of the head office QLD team. A preliminary understanding of the organisational context was essential for designing and implementing real-world research. The intent of the pilot study was to gain a deeper insight into the ways of working of a site, test some of our assumptions and have the opportunity to include the frontline guys in the design of the research project.

Intelligence at the local level

The intervention itself varied from site to site. In the ownership-support condition, site team leaders and site managers participated in a workshop. One of the core intelligence activities used within this phase – which was used to set the intent – was a visioning activity. Vision creation ensured that the team had a shared purpose where actionable targets could be established and achieved. A funnelling effect was used to ensure that the planned actions were feeding into an overarching goal leading to the site vision. Within the programme, this involved the team brainstorming questions such as: 'what would the site look like if safety was being managed effectively in two years' time?' resulting in five high-level targets that did not have an immediate solution. The five key areas were then broken down into a maximum of four key actions or tasks. The process was an established practice to develop goals and objectives ensuring actions and targets were realistic (Doran 1981). It is interesting to note that such activities correlate well with the RAVE model.

Benefits

- We accurately identified the main problems and issues for the individual sites which maximised return on investment.
- Employees in the experimental conditions reported having increased satisfaction, productivity and enjoyment. They felt they had an input into how safety was managed at their site so felt greater responsibility to safety at that site.

Lessons learned

- While the researcher provided answers to some interesting questions, the individual sites should have had a say in the design of the research questions themselves.
- A greater focus on how and why the workshops were conducted in that way so that leaders could feel confident conducting their intelligence gathering missions.

Intelligence: where to start?

So you have read about the philosophy, research, applications and benefits of gathering intelligence. The next thing to do is consider how you start to shift the safety needle in the right direction inside your organisation if this element is missing.

In order to initiate a shift, a series of key actions and processes can be adopted. The key actions are listed below:

- As a team, set your intent to learn about your employees and their needs.
- Identify key sources of collateral internal to the organisation which could add information to the problem (e.g., reports, systems, processes).
- Create an interview guide to engage and learn from the workforce. What do you want to learn and how will you use the data?
- Whom do you want to learn this from – will you go broad and interview from the CEO to the front line or is there a specific division or department?
- Capture the data from the interviews. Note what people say, what they are feeling, what you observed, and capture insights you deducted from the interviews.
- Cluster the information and identify themes from across the interviews.
- Critically think about the linkages and meaning behind the themes to identify key issues.
- Formulate initial ideas for possible ways to address these issues (then move to the instigate phase).

In addition to simple actions and processes, there are also an essential set of skills and attributes that are required, and may need to be developed, to support your organisation to adopt human-focused intelligence. The key skills are listed below.

- Communication and engagement skills
- Relationship building
- Interviewing skills
- Listening skills
- Critical thinking
- Research skills
- Data analysis skills.

To help you and your organisation assess where its safety intelligence is coming from, and to prime them for change, we have provided a set of reflection questions for organisations and individual leaders. You can use these as either personal reflection questions or to facilitate a discussion within your organisation to establish where you are at and what safe next steps your organisation can take to move toward holistic and people-focused intelligence.

Intelligence: organisational reflection questions

If you recognise the need to make changes to safety in your organisation, the following questions will get you started in gathering the right intelligence:

- What types of data are we currently using to make our decisions – do we use both facts and people data?
- How effective are we at including everyone in the organisation in change design?
- Do you know if there is a disconnect between the 'safety polices' and the 'way work is done' – if so, have you considered changing to adapt to your employees' needs?
- How do we evaluate the effectiveness of our safety approach?
- Do we know what works and what doesn't work for safety for our people?
- What data motivates us to make significant changes – a death, a near miss or people's feedback?
- What data do we use to inform our safety strategy?

Intelligence: personal self-reflection questions

If you're curious to know how strong your intelligence gathering skills are, take a few moments to sit quietly with yourself and answer these questions honestly:

- I frequently (weekly) engage my people to ask what can I do to improve your safety?
- I feel comfortable and confident approaching my people to seek feedback?

- Do your people frequently approach you with suggestions for improvements?
- When you receive safety report data, do you then follow up with conversations to understand what can be improved?
- In the last month, have you changed a safety process based on feedback from your people?

Instigate: teach a man to fish

The two key learnings from this section of instigate are:

1　Collaborate with experts in the short term to insourcing the expertise to deliver change in the long term.
2　Develop skills to implement and sustain change.

The following section outlines why instigate is important, what the research says, the key actions and skill required to effectively instigate, and a set of reflective questions to get you started.

Instigate: what is it and why is it important?

Instigate is a distinctive element of the 5i approach. It is listed as the third phase; however, it runs through the entire process. It explicitly focuses on developing the internal skills and capabilities required to implement sustained change. When instigating change, a range of skills are required, including internal consulting, collaborative decision making, action learning/research and small-group coaching. While some change models make mention of the need for certain skills to support change, they do not explicitly build capability development into the change process itself.

The instigate stage, however, has an explicit focus on developing internal skills and capability as part of the 5i process to ensure leaders and organisations are able to sustainably deliver change into the future. Within the 5i approach, we refer to this development of skills as 'The Brody Method' which refers to teaching a man to fish. It is important to remember that this development, and the 5i process as a whole, is nonlinear. The instigate element is often performed concurrently with other elements of the 5i approach and by engaging in one element, gaps in a previous element may appear. This highlights the importance of acknowledging that 5i is an iterative process.

This is a significant shift in mindset for most businesses. While investment in upfront skills development is uncommon in Australian business, it pays big dividends. A recent review by Deloitte (2017) showed that employees who utilise soft skills are worth $2,000 more per year to the business and a published study from Harvard University stated that human-skills training boosts productivity and retention by 12% and immediately delivers a 250% ROI on total investment. Great, that's the business case, but what about safety? Well research has shown that soft skills are directly related to improved safety performance.

Too often organisations outsource significant change initiatives to external consultants who are asked to deliver a result often in isolation. This means that much of the tacit knowledge gained from being actively involved in the change process, as well as the expertise to instigate the change, leaves with them so they need to keep coming back. The main reason for this is that executives and leaders overlook the critical soft skills needed to gain buy in for any change initiative. This leads to a failing to instigate change across the business and failing to see the change results delivered. There is nothing soft or easy about these sorts of skills. Remember: the soft skills are the hard reality of business.

Soft skills (also referred to as transferrable skills) refer to the qualities and capabilities of an individual separate from the technical-task-based skills. Soft skills are skills that are not job specific, but rather are adaptable skills able to be readily applied across contexts. Soft skills that support change management include critical thinking, problem solving, communication skills, teamwork, emotional judgement and innovation.

For organisations, influencing change is hard and influencing sustained change in people is sometimes harder! One of the challenges in this area is the skills and backgrounds of safety leaders. Safety leaders come from varied backgrounds – there is no single discipline or pathway that leads to the role. Some come from more technical and tertiary educated backgrounds with degrees in safety, human resources and management. Some come from more practical backgrounds, working on the frontline. One of the challenges associated with the diverse backgrounds of safety professionals results in soft-skill development that is vastly varied. However, this is not just a challenge facing the safety profession. Deloitte (2017) reported that three out of four businesses report a workforce skills gap in soft skills. This is a critical capability gap affecting all industries and reinforcing factors associated with ineffective change. Mature organisations collaborate with external experts to create a diverse team, who work alongside your people to build your internal capability during change – meaning your organisation develops and retains the expertise in the business.

Instigate: what does the research say?

For brevity and simplicity, below are five key areas of research that help organisations understand why building internal capabilities and skills enhance safety performance, employee engagement and improved adaptability to the changing safety environment.

1   Technical skills may get you the job but soft skills can make or break you as a leader. Soft skills were once thought to be 'nice to have' for business leaders, we now know, for the sake of performance, leaders 'need to have' soft skills (Goleman 2000).
2   Innovation and adaption is related to an organisation's ability to learn (Jimenez-Jimenez & Sanz-Valle 2011).

3   Soft-skills are directly related to individual, team and organisation performance (Deloitte 2017).

4   Soft-skills enhance employee performance and reduce error rates which have a significant impact on safety (Rhona, O'Connor & Crichton 2008).

5   To maintain a focus on the long term, our capacity to engage others and enable their mutual needs to be met, while maintaining the viability of the systems in which we operate, is indispensable. Stress management, resilience, self-awareness and engagement are all important competencies for surviving challenging times, and these skills are grouped under the general category called 'soft skills' (Milanovich-Eagleson, Howes & Fattahi 2015).

Instigate in action: what happened at Woolworths?

To bring the philosophy and research behind instigate, the way in which instigate was utilised to facilitate change in the Woolworths Project is described below.

Researchers' assumption

Most research strategies and change management approaches focus on the design and implementation of the research, strategy or intervention. The key assumption that has a long-term impact on the efficacy of these projects is the assumption of skill.

An explicit focus on instigation was not a specific focus of this project. However, in some regards, the researchers themselves had the skills in consulting, engagement, collaboration, facilitation and programme design to act as effective change agents. A focus on developing instigate skills in the workplace would be a recommended next step to further this research in the future.

Instigated at the organisational level

One component of instigating – collaborating with internal and external experts – was semi-achieved in the project. We did engage and communicate with the sites and the safety team regularly; however, we did miss including other key functions within the business such as HR, legal and maintenance. At different points within the project insight, guidance and supports from these functions would have made the project stronger in the long term.

Instigate at the local level

Retrospectively, we did observe the need for a focus on developing these skills, however. For example, we observed that even if a site manager or leader had a strong passion towards safety, if they could not communicate that passion, then they were the lone pioneer. Moreover, the research design built into the workshops an instigate 'soft-skill' component' via a team-based approach. This was observed to enhance results in the 'ownership-support condition' and lead improved project results. In one group, within this condition, a member of the team said 'No one here cares about others, they only care about their work and getting their job done. They don't care if anyone else is struggling and no one offers to lend a hand'. This sentiment was discussed and debated in the group at length and given the time to resolve. Moving forward six months, the staff member later said, 'It's completely different, I don't know the safety stats, but the way we work together and support each other has definitely improved.'

We understood that teamwork and the effects of teaming with a group of people made an impact. By building teaming skills – which could be considered as soft-skills – before the implementation process, we ensured support for the teams in the third condition, and they were no longer lone pioneers.

Benefits

- Sites that were upskilled through a teaming focus experienced greater performance in safety and could maintain the project more easily.
- The teaming approach also ensured that the team leaders participated for the entirety of the project.
- Teams who used evaluation techniques were also able to adapt to their changing environment.

Lessons learned

- In Kotter's 8, the change process assumed knowledge. It would have been beneficial to understand the leadership skill (e.g., communicating, influencing and supporting team members) before the project implementation to ensure appropriate support and guidance were offered.
- Departments outside of safety should have been included in the project such as HR, as other avenues of support and resources.

Instigate: where to start?

So you have read about the philosophy, research, applications and benefits of having the internal skills to instigate. The next thing to do is consider how to start to shift the safety needle in the right direction inside your organisation if this element is missing. In order to instigate a safety change, a series of key actions and processes can be adopted. These are listed below:

- Following on from intelligence, present your themes and initial ideas to a fresh audience for consultation and engagement in designing a pilot change process/approach.

- Plan a pilot intervention and establish measures of success to assess impact and effectiveness.
- Conduct a skill and competency gap analysis to identify necessary skills needed to support the successful design and implementation.
- Develop the necessary soft skills through investing in long-term skills development, that is carried out while working on the implementation of the change.

In addition to project specific skills, there is also an essential set of skills and attributes that are required, and may need to be developed outside of the project team, to support your organisation to instigate change. The key skills are listed below:

- Listening skills
- Small-group process facilitation
- Large-group facilitation
- Decision making
- Applied skills in mitigating cognitive bias
- Collaboration.

To help you and your organisation assess its readiness to instigate a process to innovate safety, we have provided a set of reflection questions for organisations and individual leaders. You can use these as either personal reflection questions or facilitate a discussion within your organisation to establish where you are at and what safe next steps can be taken to build the key instigate skills.

Instigate organisational reflection questions

If you recognise the need to make changes to safety in your organisations, the following questions will get you started in identifying how to support and instigate a change.

1 Do we have the skills to re-design our safety approach inside the business?
2 Do we promote based on technical or soft skills?
3 How successful have we been at internally implementing significant safety change initiatives?
4 How do we capture and share organisational wisdom – so we cross-skill knowledge before we lose it?

Instigate personal self-reflection questions

If you're curious to know what instigate skills you can leverage or develop, take a few moments to sit quietly with yourself and answer these questions honestly. Table 5.2 has a list of key soft-skills involved in instigating change.

Table 5.2 Soft skills for change management assessment

Soft skills for change management	1	2	3	4	5
Listening skills: Capacity to pay attention to and effectively interpret what other people are saying.					
Small-group process facilitation: Capacity to create an experiential and relational environment in which diverse individuals develop as a group (under 30).					
Large-group facilitation: Capacity to create an experiential and relational environment in which diverse individuals develop as a group (over 30).					
Decision making: Capacity to make effective and important decisions.					
Applied skills in mitigating cognitive bias: Capacity to prevent or reduce the negative effects of cognitive bias.					
Critical thinking: Capacity to analyse and evaluate an issue in order to judge its quality.					
Problem solving: Capacity to analyse and develop solutions to problems.					
Communication skills: Capacity to convey or share ideas and feelings effectively.					
Teamwork: Collaborating effectively with colleagues to complete tasks.					
Emotional empathy: Ability to understand your effect on others and manage yourself accordingly.					
Innovation: Ability to develop new ideas and opportunities.					

(Source: Developed for this research)

Rate yourself on a scale of 1 (I don't know where to start) – 5 (It's my clear strength). If you're brave, ask a peer, spouse or member of your team to also rate you.

Considering both your self-rated scores and your peer scores:

- Do you believe soft skills benefit your role in the organisation?
- What training or education do you need to enhance your soft-skills?
- How will you practise your soft skills, gain helpful feedback and reflect on your skill?
- How will you know when you have achieved the soft-skill?

Implement: top-down | bottom-up

The two key learnings from this section on implement are:

1 Start small, pilot, iterate, replicate.
2 Focus on top-down and bottom-up approaches in tandem.

The following section outlines why implementation is important, what the research says, the key actions and skills required for effective implementation, and a set of reflective questions to get you started.

Implement: what is it and why is it important?

Effective implementation starts small with a pilot; adopt an iterative process to ensure improvement and focus on concurrent 'bottom-up and top-down' strategies. The first key to effective implementation is starting small with pilot implementations. This process is adopted to engage employees in continuing to collaborate in the design and implementation to enhance their experience and meet their needs. Adopting a one size fits all approach which fails to iterate and continually learn about the employee experience is an erroneous approach. One size does not fit all. Far too often, team leaders and managers jump into solution mode before truly understanding the problem. Truly understanding a problem involves continuing to re-clarify and make adjustments throughout the implementation process just like you would to construction plans and blueprints when building a skyscraper. The true extent of this issue became publicly known when a report by *Harvard Business Review* revealed that 85% of people strongly agreed or agreed that their organisation was bad at problem diagnosis and 87% strongly agreed or agreed that these mistakes carried significant costs (Guest 2017). These costs may be amplified exponentially in the case of safety implementations. The response is clear: to accurately begin to implement solutions, a detailed understanding of the problem is required.

For effective implementation, both bottom-up and top-down strategies are needed. This important component of implementation requires us to break a commonly held misconception that implementations and safety initiatives should be simply handed down from management to frontline employees. This process is defined as a 'top-down' strategy, as safety information is conceived by people in higher positions within an organisation and then passed down to subordinate teams of employees to facilitate compliance. But compliance only gets you so far. Indeed, research has highlighted that pure top-down strategies fail to development enough implementation commitment from employees (Stewart, Manges & Ward 2015). An example of the unsuccessful nature of a pure top-down strategy is described in the story of Captain Marquet of the US Navy.

Captain Marquet was a highly intelligent man, and was originally assigned to take charge of the highest performing ship and team within the Navy fleet; however, close to his starting date, he was re-assigned to a ship with technology that he did not understand and which also possessed the lowest performing team. Captain Marquet began to give orders as he thought a leader should according to his knowledge of another ship's technology. However, upon completing a training exercise with his new crew, he quickly learned that his crew would follow any order he gave, even if they knew it was impossible or incorrect, simply because their leader gave it. Captain Marquet realised the issue with this blind obedience and instead shifted responsibility to crew members and not just himself. Through this, his crew acquired ownership of their actions and, under Captain Marquet's guidance, began to think for themselves and not simply comply. Over time, his crew became the highest performing US Navy team ever, and fostered a culture of leaders, with several of his crew going on to take charge of their own ships. In Captain Marquet's own words, 'Those at the top have all the authority and none of the information. Those at the bottom have all the information and none of the authority' (Sinek 2014, p. 144).

High safety-performing organisations adopt this advice and incorporate an iterative implementation process that includes a concurrent 'bottom-up' strategy to the top-down strategy. The key here is concurrent. Bottom-up strategies involve the engagement of the employee teams who are undergoing the change. Bottom-up strategies, much like top-down strategies, are largely unsuccessful, but for different reasons. Change programmes require a mandate from the top to implement. Pure bottom-up strategies are unable to gather the resources necessary to distribute widespread change (Stewart, Manges & Ward 2015). Instead, an implementation that concurrently harnesses the respective benefits of both top-down and bottom-up strategies allows organisations to adopt a 'we' mindset, where a bureaucratic leader structure gives way to a culture of shared learning and engagement from both leaders and employees, and everyone in-between. By harnessing the information and needs of employee teams, those in leadership positions can use their skills in direction to help facilitate a successful implementation. This collaborative process is one that follows the method of *pilot, iterate, replicate*, where ideas developed by all levels of the organisation are tested, revised and performed again to enable constant learning, adaptation and wide-scale uptake. The use of iterative approaches, such as pilot programmes, with intact teams from both the top and bottom, means you implement more engaging programmes that are supported at all levels of the organisation.

Implement: what does the research say?

For brevity and simplicity, below are four key areas of research that help organisations design effective implementation techniques through top-down and bottom-up approaches:

1   Iteration and piloting is essential to adapt an implementation across an organisation's context. The one-size fits all approach commonly used by managers does not work. Even within one organisation, different teams often possess different conceptualisations of the issue, different pockets of information, and different resistances to change. These differences grow enormously when comparing across industries (Kotter & Schlesinger 2008).
2   Top-down and bottom-up approaches are needed in tandem. While top level leaders are essential to organisational change, including a bottom-up process encourages employees to innovate, be empowered, problem solve and learn (Daniels 2010; Lupton 1991; Stewart, Manges & Ward 2015).
3   Changing safety – innovating it fosters a learning organisation. Innovation and adaption is related to an organisation's ability to learn. Organisational learning and innovation contribute to business performance, and organisational learning influences innovation. For teams to innovate, they must be included in the iterative implementation process (Jimenez-Jimenez & Sanz-Valle 2011).
4   Developing internal capability to implement safety initiatives is critical. Organisations, people and safety are all complex dynamic social elements, and research supports that developing the skills and knowledge in implementing interventions are often missing and needing to be developed (Olsen et al. 2008; Pawson 2002).

Implement in action: what happened in the project?

To bring the philosophy and research behind implement to life, the way in which implement was utilised to facilitate change in the Woolworths Project is described below.

Implement at the local level

Implementation of the project involved both the pilot study previously mentioned and the project itself.

Implement at the organisational level

Top-down implementation was not a specific focus, however, we did have visual and consistent support from the safety teams at the Queensland level and national level. This occurred predominantly during the start of the project, and site managers consistently sought advice and guidance from their safety representative throughout the project lifespan.

Implement at the local level

A small-steps approach was adopted starting with a pilot study across seven sites of varying size, location and performance which were approached to participate in the study. It was important that all sites participated voluntarily in helping ensure commitment across the project. The sites varied in characteristics to make sure that we understood the ways-of-working in the different contexts of a project's site. During the pilot phase, we interviewed all levels of the site, conducted site observations and completed surveys. This approach fed into the intelligence for the overarching project confirmed the intent of the research and engaged the frontline people early. We used the pilot results, process learnings, the safety findings and the feedback from the employees to iterate and devise the experiment itself – a wider scale roll-out. The experiment, as mentioned, was designed to be customisable at every stage, yet the approach had a common framework. The steps involved in the experiment were:

1   Conversations with staff and site managers to ensure they were true volunteers.
2   Removal of rules and procedures from the workplace for the two experimental groups with clear communication and warning.
3   A check-in with the site immediately after the change.
4   Two half-day workshops (for the third group only).
5   Weekly emails to the site managers to act as a check-in.
6   Fortnightly/monthly site observations and interviews.
7   Three monthly and six monthly evaluation focus groups (for the third group only).
8   Start and end of the project survey.
9   Communications with head office, site managers and employees as needed.

The framework was stable, but the information at different stages changed. For example, the weekly manager questions were adapted based on observations and interviews from the month before. Interview questions changed based on contexts, such as time of year or survey information. The process was the same, but the content modified to ensure it was relevant.

Benefits

- Managers believed the new approach was more effective and that site-specific initiatives were more beneficial to the usual launch and leave approach.
- Sites increased collaboration behaviour significantly and focused on problem-solving through communication.

Lessons learned

- Consideration was given to the method of measure delivery and collection to ensure there was sufficient time built into the timeline (e.g., paper survey).
- It would have been beneficial to teach all managers a simple iteration and replication process, which would have helped those not in the experimental group improve safety.
- It would be useful to have a site debrief of the project – everyone was involved with the process yet not everyone received readily accessible feedback and results, and this hinders the iteration and replication process.

Implement: where to start?

So you have read about the philosophy, research, applications and benefits of having the internal skills to implement. The next thing to do is consider how to start to shift the safety needle in the right direction inside your organisation if this element is missing. In order to implement a safety change, a series of key actions and processes can be adopted. These are listed below:

- Conduct a small, safe next-step pilot to test the intervention and measurement strategies.
- Review and evaluate the intervention from all available sources – feedback reports, participant experiences, impact on the ground, etc.
- At the end of the pilot, reflect on the lessons learned and adapt the next phase to include these processes in another adaption of the pilot in another area of the business.
- Continue to pilot, iterate and replicate each implementation across the business – after several iterations you will likely find that there is an 80:20 rule; whereby 80% of the approach is effective and can be implemented across the business. However, 20% generally needs to be adapted to the specific context of different pockets within the organisation.
- To scale the implementation across the business, you will revisit the previous 5i stages to enable you to identify the 20% changes required to effectively adapt the implementation and enhance the organisational uptake and effectiveness of the change.

In addition to project specific skills, there are also an essential set of skills and attributes that are required, and may need to be developed outside of the project team, to support your organisation to implement change. The key skills are listed below:

- Stakeholder engagement skills
- Planning and organising
- Political nous
- Communication skills. This is not limited to just written communication, but also interviewing skills as interviews enable you to gather feedback from participants in the pilot and improve your change strategy through subsequent iterations
- Problem solving skills
- Reflection skills. These allow you to critically analyse your pilot study and make the correct changes to ensure the success of future iterations.

To help you and your organisation assess its readiness to implement a process to innovate safety, we have provided a set of reflection questions for organisations and individual leaders. You can use these as either personal reflection questions or to facilitate a discussion within your organisation to establish where you are at and what safe next steps can be taken to build the key implementation skills.

Implement organisational reflection questions

If you recognise the need to make changes to safety in your organisation the following questions will get you started in identifying how to support and implement a change.

1   Who is our change leader on the executive team?
2   How will we engage willing volunteers in the pilot?
3   Are we sure we can implement a top-down, bottom-up roll-out?
4   What is the process to iterate, reflect and adapt our process?
5   Do we have the internal skills (soft skills) to sustainably deliver this change?

Implement personal self-reflection questions

If you're curious to know what implement skills you can leverage or develop, take a few moments to sit quietly with yourself and answer these questions honestly:

1   Do I ensure that employees are included in planning processes?
2   Am I able to get the appropriate change leaders on-board?
3   Am I strong at correctly diagnosing problems in my organisation?
4   Do I possess the skills and knowledge to be able to pilot and test a change process?

Internalise | personalise | embed

The two key learnings from this section on internalising change are:

1   Start with the end in mind – and develop practices to support the embedding of behaviour change.
2   Support and reinforce behaviour change through a focus on consistent team practices.

The following section outlines why internalising is important, what the research says, the key actions and skills required for effective internalising, and a set of reflective questions to get you started.

Internalise: what is it and why is it important?

While internalise is the last phase in the 5i approach, we would suggest at the outset you start with this end in mind. Internalisation of change is the resulting shift in behaviours that the change was intended to effect. To facilitate effective internalisation, planning for it from the outset of the change process, the planning and subsequent 5i stages are essential. This will ensure that learning from the process continues to support teams and people to adapt, change and learn on the job.

The 5i internalise phase is where we demonstrate the success of the implementation through long-term embedding and maintenance processes that support sustained change. In most change models, internalisation of change is assumed, however, in the 5i model, processes to support internalisation are explicitly adopted. *Harvard Business Review* found that globally, companies invested $356 billion on training and education with little return on investment because people reverted to their old ways of working (Beer, Finnstrom & Schrader 2016). Internalising change through maintenance and embedding is the final stage of the 5i process.

Any change that fails to consider a maintenance and embedding process will not deliver the desired ROI. The internalise stage enables your people to embody, personalise and apply their new learning to demonstrate a shift in capability, behaviour or attitude on the job engaging people to integrate their learning and experiences from the process into their safety leadership profile. This will enable change to stick. This links back to the First Principle of the 5i's, intent.

The real benefits of your investment in any change initiative are realised by the internalisation of that change into day-to-day habits. Organisations often fall into the trap of rolling out quick fix initiatives. They implement strategies that don't support the transfer of learning into changes of people's habits. As a result, most learning is lost and an ROI is not realised. It is essential to implement strategies for change where employees take ownership by providing supporting tools and frameworks. Changing habits is hard. However, when you understand the brain and the psychology that underpins successful habits, strategies can be adopted which facilitate this change.

The *American Journal of Psychology* (Andrews 1903) defined habit as a 'fixed way of thinking, willing, or feeling acquired through previous repetition of a mental experience'. All habits have three things in common: a cue (trigger), a routine or reaction (the behaviour) and the reward (the payoff the behaviour brings). During this process (performing a behaviour), the brain releases a chemical called dopamine, which is one of the feel-good hormones. The repetition of this habit process also causes the brain to develop specific neural pathways. The brain likes repeating patterns and enjoys the stimulation of the dopamine release, so we unconsciously repeat the habitual pattern without thought, and gain the benefit. Habits are like superhighways in the brain which allow for an easy and mindless approach to life. Unfortunately, an unconscious, automatic behaviour makes it challenging to choose an alternative behaviour. Choosing a new behaviour would be like taking a difficult dirt road. Therefore, changing habits is hard, but worth it.

The 5i approach supports the long-term embedding of habit change through a focus on team accountability – not individual accountability. Why? It is easier to change behaviour through a focus on shifting social norms, rules and behaviours of a group, than through individual will-power or accountability. This is because we are social creatures and are more likely to adopt the habits and behaviours of those around us.

The 5i approach supports habit change and embedding at the team level though a range of approaches, including regular feedback loops, regular team interactions, team-based accountability and team-based coaching. Over time the sustained change creates brilliant workplaces where people are more connected with their teams, more resilient, more purposeful and more likely to go home to their loved ones as better parents, friends and partners. This is the ripple effect of brilliant workplaces creating brilliant teams.

Internalise: what does the research say?

For brevity and simplicity, below are four key areas of research that help organisations see the value in internalising the 5i process.

1   One key to effective and lasting change is embedding the necessary knowledge, procedures and behaviours within members of the organisation. Not all organisational changes stick, no matter the purported benefits. If the organisation does not learn during the change process, they will not retain the changes (Roberto & Levesque 2005).

2   The focus of change initiatives must be on people, not process. Teams within organisations must have the space to provide input on the change and possess a long-term future benefit focus (Eaton 2010).

3   Effective changes utilise constant two-way communication, feedback loops, training and development. Throughout this process of continual

information, the focus should always be on building confidence within the teams that are undergoing change, and making use of their feedback (Longenecker & Rieman 2007).

4   Effective change is supported through setting achievable goals, recognising that no two brains are alike, therefore individuals require support and understanding from leaders to embrace and internalise change (Berkman & Lieberman 2009).

Internalise in action: what happened at Woolworths?

To bring the philosophy and research behind internalise to life, the way in which internalise was fostered to facilitate change in the Woolworths Project is described below:

Internalise at the organisational level

Within the Woolworths Project, there were no pre-specified plans for the future to internalise the process of the experiment or the conditions themselves into the larger organisational structure for to two main reasons:

1   It was unknown at the point of planning if the project would be effective or indeed harmful to the staff's health and safety.
2   The organisation itself went through massive internal disruption and change that disconnected the advocates of the project from the project itself.

There was a deficit in our intent setting at the beginning as there were pockets within the organisation who had no idea that the project existed. Participants were then left unsupported at the end of the project.

However, this story does have a happy ending. The QLD head office safety team were open and receptive to the findings and recommendations of the project. They were devising their own strategy to continue the learnings within sites. From the employee perspective, a site manager in the third condition stated, 'I understand we have to go back to the old way for now, but we now know that to get safety right, it takes a lot more than what we were doing before, and we are committed to that conversation.' The internalisation process in many change management approaches might only be addressed with a throwaway sentence or ignored completely in the scientific approach.

Internalise at the local level

One of the core factors contributing to this can be linked to the research design, whereby we had a visual presence in the sites at least once a month where we spoke to team members about safety and we communicated weekly with site managers weekly via emails. Site managers themselves made a concerted effort to engage more actively with QLD head office. So it was no longer a 'launch and leave' safety initiative. There was regular feedback loops and follow-up, which echo the pillars of the RAVE model.

Benefits

- Enhanced organisational learning through a learning culture which was evident by individual champions taking up the cause.
- Initiatives that work over the long term because they were designed to change habits: Projects constructed in isolation to the company would remain isolated from the company.

Lessons learned

- Initiatives that work over the long term because they were designed to change habits.
- Projects constructed in isolation to the company would remain isolated from the company.
- For future safety research, a plan should be developed at the time of intent formation to support internalisation.

Internalise: where to start?

So you have read about the philosophy, research, applications and benefits of having the internal skills to internalise. The next consideration is how to start to shift the safety needle in the right direction inside your organisation if this element is missing.

In order to internalise a safety change, a series of key actions and processes are listed below:

- Develop a support programme that encourages outcomes to be sustained.
- Feed the results back to all key stakeholders in the organisation.
- Review and celebrate with the project team.
- Debrief the process and capture lessons learned, to feed into future projects.
- Evaluate the original intent/question with the end outcome. Decide on the next phase of research and where you would like to learn more.

In addition to project specific actions, there are essential practices that support your organisation to internalise change. These key practices that support internalisation are listed below:

- Regular feedback loops: Annual surveys (top-down) don't work. Implement regular lead safety indicators via visual management approaches to monitor performance and behaviour change at the team-level.

- Regular interactions: Use regular team-based processes to self-monitor agreed team accountabilities via 'facilitated' team meetings; not chalk and talk.
- Team-based accountability: Action is taken locally by the team to identify what's going right and what wins they have had.
- Team-based coaching: undertaken by leader to support changes when indicators of performance fluctuate.
- Communication skills.

To help you and your organisation assess its readiness to internalise long-term safety innovation, we have provided a set of reflection questions for organisations and individual leaders. Use these as either personal reflection questions, or facilitate a discussion in your organisation around these questions to establish where you are at and what safe next steps can be taken to internalise safety change.

Internalise organisational reflection questions

If you recognise the need to make changes to safety in your organisation, the following questions will get you started in identifying how to support and internalise a change:

1   What is our sustainability plan and how will our teams be supported to adopt the changes in their day-to-day work context?
2   What is fixed and what is flexible – what are the fixed outcomes the business needs to achieve, and what are the flexible approaches that can be adapted to differing contexts to make the change relevant to different teams to enhance internalisation?
3   What is the feedback loop from suggestion to management, back to the suggestion maker?
4   How are we moving from top-down measures of performance to localised team-based measures which foster engagement and localised accountability?
5   How are we leveraging technology to provide teams with the leading indicator data required for them to internalise change?
6   How are we feeding our new insights, learnings and skills back into the organisation?

Internalise personal self-reflection questions

If you're curious to know what 'internalise' skills you can leverage or develop, take a few moments to sit quietly with yourself to answer these questions honestly.

1   How do I support the desired change in my organisation?
2   How am I communicating feedback and learnings back to my team?

3   Do I facilitate regular (weekly) collaborative, data-based conversations focusing on leading indicators to support my team's change journey?
4   Do we focus on what goes right on a weekly basis?
5   Do I celebrate small wins and success to facilitate motivations to sustain the change?

Where to from here? Summary and future directions

We began the chapter with the intent to paint a picture of what is possible in terms of shifting the safety needle from dogma to science. To do this, our intent was to 1) raise awareness of a framework to integrate people-focused change management with rigorous scientific methods and 2) provide practical tools and skills to facilitate real changes in safety for the people working in your organisation.

A short summary of where we have come from and where to next is provided below:

1   We first examined the common organisational values that help and hinder safety across industries. We reviewed the literature and identified a preference for 'control' type values exemplified through procedures, bureaucracy and standardisation. Through the lens of the Competing Values Framework, we highlighted that organisational values underpinning the Control Quadrant resulted in poorer safety performance. Conversely, we highlighted research which suggests that organisational values that underpin the Collaborate quadrant – exemplified via a focus on people, teams, training and development – resulted in safer outcomes. This provided grounds for suggesting that a shift from a focus on procedures and bureaucracy to a focus on valuing the human-aspects of an organisation were needed first and foremost to shift the safety needle.
2   Next, we examined how we shift from dogma to science. We suggested that the dogma that has accrued and ossified around safety are persistent and highly resistant to change even in the face of empirical evidence. We proposed the idea that the dogma that surrounds safety may be analogous to, and as dangerous as, some types of early religious dogma, that refused to see the realities brought to the world through a scientific methodology. We suggested that to progress safety, the adoption of values that focus on innovation through the adoption of scientific methods would be a valuable step forward.
3   To this end we explored a human-focused change management approach, through a retrospective analysis of a case study of real-world safety research – to see if a shift could be made in how we address safety into the future.
4   The 5i approach was examined, along with the supporting research and analysis of the Woolworths Project to highlight benefits and lessons learned.

The merits of the 5i approach, paired with a scientific method, are summarised by the following key points:

1 *Adaptable approach to support change.* Change is constant, and only by changing constantly can organisations hope to survive (McKinsey Quarterly 2008). To remain competitive organisations need effective change approaches to continually evolve their safety approaches.
2 *Mitigates risks associated with change.* The 5i approach helps organisations mitigate three common mistakes that increase the risk of failure: 1) failure to understand the people, 2) failure to build trust and confidence, 3) failure to gain support and commitment (Maurer 2011).
3 *Supports sustained change.* The 5i approach helps organisations deliver sustainable change starting with the right intent. Long-term sustained change needs the right intent (O'Neil 2000). Furthermore, this approach focuses on critical aspects for sustainable organisational change that most change approaches gloss over. Specifically it focuses on providing support and care, building internal capacity, facilitating learning and reducing silos (Moffett 2000). The deliberate internal development of the knowledge, skills and processes required to implement successful safety strategies is a key difference that is often overlooked.

Future directions

The research team who authored this chapter collaborate with industry to co-create future directions and next steps. Immediate future directions we are exploring with industry are summarised below. These future directions aim to address current limitations and provide pathways to build on the method and research presented in the chapter:

1 Applications of 5i approach and scientific method to a wider array of industries, across higher risk environments.
2 Integration of learnings into educational programmes for safety leaders.
3 Integration of effective lead-indicators to cycle back into the intelligence phase to monitor embedding and change following an implementation.
4 Exploration of technology to support the embedding phase through a focus on lead indicators, and constrictive 'Safety 2' type feedback-loops (i.e., focus on learning not just incidents).

In closing, and in keeping with the intent and style of this chapter, we thought it fitting to pose two final questions to orientate you toward the future directions you can take within your organisation:

1 What is the smallest and most successful step you can imagine taking to help shift the safety needle tomorrow? (e.g., Start an elevator conversation

to share what you have learned? Host an internal meeting and use the reflection questions to stimulate conversation?).

2   Do you feel comfortable to champion a small-scale safety research project in your organisation? If not, what is one small thing you could do tomorrow to enable you to feel comfortable taking the next step?

References

Andrews, BR 1903, 'Habit', *The American Journal of Psychology*, 14, 121–149.

Armenakis, AA, Harris, SG & Mossholder, KW 1993, 'Creating readiness for organizational change', *Human Relations*, 46(6), 681–703.

Beer, M, Finnstrom, M & Schrader, D 2016, 'Why leadership training fails and what to do about it', *Harvard Business Review*, https://hbr.org/2016/10/why-leadership-training-fails-and-what-to-do-about-it

Berkman, ET & Lieberman, MD 2009, 'Using neuroscience to broaden emotion regulation: Theoretical and methodological considerations', *Social and Personality Psychology Compass*, 3, 475–493.

Blandford, A, Furniss, D & Vincent, C 2014, 'Patient safety and interactive medical devices: Realigning work as imagined and work as done', *Clinical Risk*, 20, 107–110.

Cameron, D 2012, 'Business boosting measures announced', www.gov.uk/government/news/business-boosting-measures-announced

Colley, SK, Lincolne, J & Neal, A 2012, 'An examination of the relationship amongst profiles of perceived organizational values, safety climate and safety outcomes', *Safety Science*, 51, 69–76.

Collins, KM, Onwuegbuzie, AJ & Sutton, IL 2006, 'A model incorporating the rationale and purpose for conducting mixed methods research in special education and beyond', *Learning Disabilities: A Contemporary Journal*, 4(1), 67–100.

Creswell, JW, Fetters, MD, Plano Clark, VL & Morales, A 2009, 'Mixed methods intervention trials', *Mixed Methods Research for Nursing and the Health Sciences*, 161–180.

Daniels, F 2010, *Top-down vs. Bottom-up Management Approach: The Effect on Employee Motivation and Retention*, Capella University, Minneapolis.

Deloitte Access Economics 2017, *Soft Skills for Business Success*.

Doran, GT 1981, 'There's a S.M.A.R.T. way to write management's goals and objectives', *Management Review*, 70(11), 35–36.

Eakin, JM, Champoux, D & MacEachen, E 2010, 'Health and safety in small workplaces: Refocusing upstream', *Canadian Journal of Public Health*, 101(1), 29–33.

Eaton, M 2010, 'Why change programs fail', *Human Resource Management International Digest*, 18(2), 37–42.

Eurocontrol 2014, *Systems Thinking for Safety: Ten Principles. A White Paper. Moving towards Safety-II*, Eurocontrol, Brussels.

Gallo, A 2010, 'Making your strategy work on the frontline', *Harvard Business Review*, https://hbr.org/2010/06/making-your-strategy-work-on-t

Goleman, D 2000, 'Leadership that gets results', *Harvard Business Review*, https://hbr.org/2000/03/leadership-that-gets-results

Guest, G 2017, *Soft Skills Training Boosts Productivity*, University of Michigan, http://ns.umich.edu/new/releases/24468-soft-skills-training-boosts-productivity

Iverson, RD 1996, 'Employee acceptance of organizational change: The role of organizational commitment', *The International Journal of Human Resource Management*, 7, 122–149.

Jiménez-Jiménez, D & Sanz-Valle R 2011, 'Innovation, organizational learning, and performance', *Journal of Business Research*, 64, 408–417.

Kotter, JP 1995, 'Leading change: Why transformation efforts fail', *Harvard Business Review*, https://hbr.org/2007/01/leading-change-why-transformation-efforts-fail

Kotter, JP & Schlesinger, LA 2008, 'Choosing strategies for change', *Harvard Business Review*, https://hbr.org/2008/07/choosing-strategies-for-change

Lee, TW 1999, *Using Qualitative Methods in Organizational Research*, Sage, Thousand Oaks.

Longenecker, CO & Rieman, ML, 2007, 'Making organizational change stick: Leadership reality checks', *Development and Learning in Organizations: An International Journal*, 21, 7–10.

Lupton, T 1991, 'Organisational change: "Top-down" or "bottom-up" management?', *Personnel Review*, 20, 4–10.

Martin, RR 1995, *Oral History in Social Work: Research, Assessment, and Intervention*, Sage, Thousand Oaks.

Maurer, R 2011, 'How to avoid the pitfalls of change', *The Journal for Quality and Participation*, 34(1), 12.

McKinsey Quarterly 2002, *Change Management That Pays*, McKinsey & Company, Seattle.

McKinsey Quarterly 2008, *Creating Organizational Transformations*, McKinsey & Company, Seattle.

Milanovich-Eagleson, N, Howes, S & Fattahi, B 2015, 'Soft skills committee: The role of soft skills in a challenging environment', *Journal of Petroleum Technology*, 67, 102–108.

Moffett, CA 2000, 'Sustaining change: The answers are blowing in the wind', *Educational Leadership*, 57, 35–38.

O'Neil, J 2000, 'Fads and fireflies: The difficulties of sustaining change', *Educational Leadership*, 57(7), 6–9.

Olsen, O, Albertsen, K, Nielsen, ML, Poulsen, KB, Gron, SMF & Brunnberg, HL 2008, 'Workplace restructurings in intervention studies – a challenge for design, analysis and interpretation', *BMC Medical Research Methodology*, 8, 1–11.

Pawson, R 2002, 'Evidence-based policy: The promise of realist synthesis', *Evaluation*, 8(3), 340–358.

Plano Clark, VL 2005, '*Cross-disciplinary analysis of the use of mixed methods in physics education research, counseling psychology, and primary care*', doctoral dissertation, University of Nebraska.

Roberto, MA & Levesque, LC 2005, 'The art of making change initiatives stick', *MIT Sloan Management Review*, http://sloanreview.mit.edu/article/the-art-of-making-change-initiatives-stick/

Sinek, S 2014, *Leaders Eat Last: Why Some Teams Pull Together and Others Don't*, Penguin Group, New York.

Spreitzer, GM & Mishra, AK 1999, 'Giving up control without losing control: Trust and its substitutes' effects on managers' involving employees in decision making', *Group and Organization Management*, 24, 155–187.

Stewart, GL, Manges, KA & Ward, MM 2015, 'Empowering sustained patient safety: The benefits of combining', *Journal of Nursing Care Quality*, 30, 240–246.

Swedberg, R & Agevall, O 2016, *The Max Weber Dictionary: Key Words and Central Concepts*, Stanford University Press, Chicago.

Towers Watson and Willis 2013, *2013–2014 Change and Communication ROI Study*, 10th Anniversary Report.

WorkSafe Victoria, Australia 2014, *VWA Annual Report*, WorkSafe Victoria, Australia.

6 Embedding learnings and ensuring longevity

Making the information stick

Understanding the roadblocks and barriers that can impede the learning process can help leaders negotiate such barriers and provide a clear pathway for others to succeed. By the end of this chapter, individuals will understand the pitfalls that can impede someone's learning and development, and understand how one can support and maximise such learning activities as applied to safety leadership. The content of this chapter will aim to answer the following questions:

- What role does leadership have in ensuring a successful transfer of learning and what processes can be set up to maximise learning activities?
- What are some facilitator hints and tips that can help ensure core messages are being crystallised with potential learners?
- How can the lack of a learning organisation influence the notion of 'zero harm'?
- What needs to be done to ensure knowledge shared is knowledge applied?

Key objectives

Capitalising on any learning and development process will be influenced by a range of factors. Safety leaders that are conscious of their role in the learning process are better equipped to enable the development of others. After reading through this chapter, individuals will have a greater awareness and understanding of the transfer of learning process that is facilitated by the following key objectives:

1   Understand the importance of the learning organisation and how establishing a learning organisation can enhance learning for employees whilst increasing organisational capability.
2   Establish practical steps and tools to help increase inter-team learning and to ensure a successful roll-out of any proposed safety leadership initiatives.

Setting the scene

An investment into developmental programmes can serve the dual purpose of developing employee capability whilst at the same time increasing organisational responsiveness and corporate knowledge. Participating in the most ground-breaking and engaging workshop in the world may have an immediate impact; however, transferring that impact into a lasting change in behaviour is where the challenge starts. After running a plethora of workshops across the globe, I have personally seen the positive reaction to training. Most of my workshop engagements were carried out over a few days. Post-workshop, I was not privy to the embedding of information or change in conduct once that person left the training room. Deep down, I had a sense that unless there were supporting mechanisms in place, the vigour and energy leaving the training room may dissipate over time.

The return on investment into any training initiative has often been measured by the Kilpatricks' model of learning. This constitutes a measurement of the initial reaction to training, retention of learning, change in behaviour and impact upon final results (Kirkpatrick & Kirkpatrick 2006). Without a well-thought-out embedding strategy, the transfer of learning into meaningful behaviours may never eventuate. I always smirk when HR or learning and development professionals base the success of a workshop on the feedback forms that are received. Especially when the feedback forms are handed out immediately after a workshop where the energy of the workshop is still present and the feedback forms are completed under the watchful eye of the facilitator who may be patiently peering over the participants whilst they are filling in their forms. Despite the validity of this process, it is still one of the most fluid and convenient ways to get feedback from a group. The catch is that the success of the training may be based upon the likability of the facilitator as opposed to the content shared. Such likability is one of the most common laws of persuasion (Hogan 2003). When implementing any proposed leadership initiative, a well-thought-out strategy that aids the transfer of learning needs to be implemented.

Companies that invest into safety leadership workshops, coaching or any other processes aimed at building internal capability within an organisation need to consider the potential pitfalls and risks which can limit the overall investment. Through an understanding of such pitfalls, actions can be taken to side-step such challenges. Once these pitfalls have been explained, some empirical data will be shared that helps maximise the impact of any developmental programmes. How one measures success or the fiscal return on investment will be explored, with a blueprint being laid out for organisations to play with. Safety leadership can maximise and reinforce the safety of an organisation, but other metrics can also be measured which may have benefits outside the realm of safety.

Potential learning and development risks and failures

Likeability of the facilitator or coach

An executive that I was once talking to explained to me the failure of a previous external leadership engagement that his company invested in. An exhaustive list of workshop showstoppers was quickly fired off to me. This included poor logistics, messages not being contextualised for the audience or poor presentation of material. The biggest flaw shared with me was the personalities involved in facilitating the leadership programme. In the past you might have had your own experiences with an arrogant presenter or under-prepared facilitator who lectures as opposed to leading discussions. If participants cannot connect with their coach or the facilitator of a workshop, it may inhibit the transfer of learning as automatic filters may start to cloud the judgement of the participant. In vivid detail, the executive I was talking to mentioned to me that they attended a workshop and then participated in a few coaching sessions. Apparently the person running the workshop was self-indulgent and lectured to the group as opposed to involving the group and leading a robust discussion. Out of mild respect, the leadership group sat through the workshop and patiently endured the training. Complications started to occur when the same presenter was also the personal coach for the executive where old reservations and negative thoughts came swarming back into the mind of the executive. From a cultural perspective, such poor experiences that participants have with training can adversely impact future training opportunities within the company.

Whether an organisation embraces growth and places knowledge and learning as a value can influence how training opportunities are received. If employees have been tainted by poorly run workshops, then the collective groan can be heard across oceans when employees are first informed that they will be participating in further training courses. The skills of the facilitator need to rise to the occasion when presenting to groups who may be jaded or in some cases over-trained. Turning resistance around and creating an open learning environment can be achieved by activating the amygdala, establishing trust and creating an environment of openness and fun (Hrybouski et al. 2016). Suggestions to enhance the learning experience and to ensure the facilitator starts off on the right foot include the following:

- Ensure the facilitator has ownership of the room prior to participants arriving and ensure the room is set up to allow free discussion. Seats that are set up in linear fashion can generate old frames of school-based learning. Similarly tardy attendance by the presenters is a poor reflection of organisation skills.
- Impressions and judgements are going to be made within moments of the presenter meeting and interacting with the audience (Uleman, Saribay & Gonzalez 2008). The use of stories is captivating and allows a personal

reference to the facilitator whilst setting the scene for the workshop session. Linking up stories with the workshop content and work performed allows greater applicability and engagement.

- Without collaboration and input, information shared may fall on deaf ears. Discussions can be facilitated through the effective use of questions that can kick-start an open discourse into the topic at hand.
- Catering for all different learning types can ensure that the information shared is more readily absorbed by participants. Experiential learning activities and tasks can cater for kinaesthetic learners whilst at the same time injecting energy into the group. The core content shared can be amplified by the learning activities. A powerful debrief that links the activity to the content is imperative.
- Exercising the laws of persuasion by building upon likeability, similarity, expert power and attractiveness allows a greater span of influence by the facilitator (Hogan 2003). If a connection is not made between the presenter and the participant, then the information shared will be less likely to be translated to observable behaviours.

The above vignette points are based upon my many years of facilitating. Further guidance notes and elusive tricks of the trade were not included. The main point is that if the facilitator of a workshop is not connecting with the audience, then any learning activities may become futile.

Organisational support post learning activities

Colleagues and associates of mine have often shared the blind approach to learning activities from their parent companies. Examples of such follies include leaders contacting the learning and development department and asking what training courses are available for their staff members. When quizzed further about their request, the collective response is often 'I just want to put them on a course and for them to become better leaders'. Specific behaviours outcomes or learning objectives are often unspoken and assumed. A common recipe for development is the workshop approach of developing leaders through classroom-based learning and expecting an automatic change in behaviour. This is done without consideration of how to apply the content or learnings of the workshop into the workplace. Empirically it has been shown that even unmotivated participants that have been through a training module will be more likely to apply the training materials in the workplace if given greater organisational support (Futris et al. 2015). The same study also referenced that individuals who reported a high learning impact from training modules do not need additional support from the company to solidify the information into the workplace.

One of the large blue chip companies I worked with invested heavily into a safety leadership process that was specifically targeting safety leadership behaviours. Initial scoping was able to allow contextualisation of the course content and apply that content to the corporate culture. Matched with this was the support from leadership who voiced their full support behind the programme. Post workshop, the organisational support stopped. Ongoing support or opportunities to share what the participant's learned was absent. In the eyes of the leaders, paying for the course and saying that they support it was in their way sufficient enough to ensure organisational support. Simple things like supportive communication, information emails, posters, discussion groups and even peer coaching were absent. Initially there was a strong decline in safety incidents over the 12 months, although after the 12 months when the training workshops were all completed, the information learned started to dissipate as there was no mechanism to ensure the retention of information within the business. When such scenarios occur, it breeds scepticism as the next leadership initiative may be seen as a fad and the latest ephemeral attempt at improving safety. Enhancing the transfer of learning can be applied from Geller's (2008) safety culture model with a specific focus on the environment, practices, the person component and leadership. After years of consulting with multiple organisations and liaising with thought leaders across the globe, the following supporting mechanisms have aided the retention of knowledge from any organised training programme:

- Post-training, provide an outlet via a team meeting or other established medium for participants to share what they have learnt from the session and how they will modify their behaviour. Sharing such information provides an antecedent for the individual to follow through with their commitment.
- Ongoing coaching based upon the core content from the workshop can uncoil the information and make it personalised and relevant for the individual. Coaching that provides positive psycho-social support enhances development for the coachee (Stewart & Palmer 2009).
- Depending on the information being shared in the workshop, core concepts and catch phrases can be embedded into safety documentation and other written material. This provides a visible memory mnemonic to workshop content.
- Utilise technology and internet-based systems to create supportive post-training learning environments to help share knowledge and insight. Blogs, web forums and email groups can be the pathways for creating a supportive post-course learning environment.
- For information to be embedded into the culture, leaders following through with their stated behaviours and constantly referencing the information allows the core content to be rooted into the organisation. An example of this that I have seen has been with leaders who share a safety leadership moment at the commencement of any meeting as discussed in the workshop they attended.

Endless possibilities abound in terms of integrating workshop content into the organisation. It is pivotal that any organisational support process will be contextualised and suited for the culture at hand. The absence of such an integration can result in embarrassment and loss of faith from the workforce.

On a large site I was visiting, an example of the cultural nuances not being taken into account when sharing key concepts resulted in a fair chunk of the workforce cringing. This cringe factor was evident by a large American company that was trying to implement their commitment to safety with a large Australian-based resources project. For the parent American company, it was expected that energy and vigour be amplified at the commencement of the workday by sharing what is held most important to them and why they will work safely. Of course the intent was to show that their investment into safety allows them to spend time with their most valued friends and family members. When implementing this process with a sceptical cross-cultural Australian workforce, the initial implementation was met with a rolling of the eyes as many individuals thought the concept was 'cheesy' and not suited to the Australian culture. Without full buy-in from the Australian leaders, the proposed implementation vanished as soon as the American counterparts left the workplace. This example indicates the importance of ensuring any organisational support processes are suited for the organisational culture. A pivotal element to ensure a successful post-course implementation of core information is the role of leadership.

Support from leadership

A common occurrence across many industries is the reality that many leaders yearn for training for their team but then they fail to release individuals from their normal work duties to attend such training. A previous safety leadership implementation across the coal seam gas sector saw a company I was working with implement safety leadership training for front-line supervisors. The training was mandated by the general manager as compulsory. Despite this, the challenge occurred when my colleague and I went to site, and only three out of the nominated 15 people attended. The reasoning behind the low numbers was attributed to operational requirements. Ironically, the production over safety argument starts to carry weight when such events occur.

Safety leadership training that is put on the back burner for operational requirements can be a facsimile for ensuring the job gets done before we develop our staff. In the above example, a breakdown of expectations was apparent as the core message from the general manager was not resonating with operational leaders. If such poor attendance rates continue, the costs of any planned implementation start to sky-rocket, due to the training being cancelled at the last minute because a quorum is not being met. I have seen first-hand the mad scramble to get numbers into the training course to bypass cancellation. This often results in individuals that are ill prepared being shoved into a training room, when their role or position may not be suited for the training at hand. If not planned well, the implementation budget may run into the red by millions of dollars due to poor leadership support and subsequently poor planning.

A gauge of leadership support can be shown through the number of senior leaders attending any proposed leadership programme. Given that leadership helps shape a culture (Krause 2005), it is often astute to start any planned leadership roll-out from a top-down perspective to help embed core information. The common catch cry from participants starts to arise when they complete a successful workshop and they ask the facilitator 'how come our leaders haven't gone through this workshop yet?' Any pertinent information shared in the workshop may be stifled in the workplace, if there is a clear distinction between the trained and consciously untrained leaders, who have skipped training on purpose. A potential double culture may start to emerge, where the old versus new start to intersect, where the dividing piece is dictated by who have been trained and those who have not been trained. If core leaders do not attend the learning sessions that they have introduced into the workplace, the embedding of core concepts, referencing key learnings and internal coaching opportunities are missed out on. As safety leaders, credibility will be shaved in half if safety leaders promote the importance of safety leadership in the workforce, although they plead immunity when it is time for themselves to be trained. Imagine a leader attending the newest leadership development workshop being implemented in the company, where all leaders will be going through the training, including their subordinates. Let's say this leader did not pick up any useful information in the workshop, and in fact deeply disagreed with the content and philosophies in place. If this leader then shared with all other leaders and their subordinates that the training is a waste of time and not worth the effort, how many other leaders will be motivated and energised to attend the training session? What a leader says has a weight of influence on others due to their positional power (Atwater & Yammarino 1996). In saying that, there could be some cases where a specific leader is on the social/work out-group where their voiced misgivings of any training course secretly validates its relevance to others. A point to consider is that transparency of information is a core attribute of being an effective safety leader. Choosing the audience and thinking about the core impact of messages being shared needs to be considered to minimise the harpooning of a companywide leadership implementation. Effective coaching can sometimes address such misgivings or lack of continuity between what was delivered in a workshop and what was retained.

Leaders that openly promote development and support further education can be seen as the activators for developing a learning organisation. There is a business case for leaders to support the learning transfer based upon their support being strategically linked to the business outcomes of the organisation (Marsick & Watkins 2003). This is further backed up by Kim and Callahan (2013) who summarised that leaders who support learning tend to foster an increase in overall organisational knowledge. Practically this can equate to an organisational culture that is flexible and adaptable which is powered by the knowledge of the employees of the company.

In one organisation that I consulted with, the leaders openly encouraged people to continue their professional development and factored into their budget a professional development allowance for each employee. The health care professionals that worked within this company relished their training and development days for two core reasons. Cheekily, it was an escape from their normal routine of work. Secondly, the employees were able to choose their own course which was aimed at building their own skill set which can have immediate benefits for the company. In adjunct to this is their increased employability outside of their current company. When I spoke with the general manager, they insightfully shared with me that a workforce that is developing and thriving will be more engaged and committed compared to a workforce that practises the same set of skills. In addition, an untrained workforce would not have any opportunity to try different or innovative ways to solve their organisational challenges. In this company, a strong culture of learning was further facilitated by the general manager sharing their own learnings from workshops or courses that they have attended and therefore encouraging their team members to do the same. In contrast, a sure way to set a handbrake on the transfer of learning is by leaders voicing their opposition to any learning activities, not providing any assistance to aid the transfer of learning and vocalising negative feedback based upon established training courses (Holton et al. 2007). Apply such a philosophy towards managing incidents within an organisation. An employee outcry may ensue if leaders fail to act and learn from incidents that occur in their organisation. It is even more paramount that leaders are involved in aiding knowledge and supporting a learning organisation. The failure to do so can lead to the macabre and sombre aftermath of human pain and suffering caused by a workplace incident. In general, it may be expected that leaders would want to quickly learn any root causes for workplace injuries and get that information out to the workforce as quickly as possible. If this same alacrity was applied to learning in other areas, then such knowledge can be the new leading indicator that can potentially prevent further injuries. Some practical leadership tasks and activities that can aide the knowledge transfer can include the following:

- Leaders to speak benignly about future training activities and to outline the importance of acquiring knowledge for the benefit of the individual and how it links to the company's business objectives. If learning and development is seen as a value, then such training courses will be seen as an opportunity to learn as opposed to training that 'has to be done'.
- Professional development days or allowance to be provided to employees or alternatively provisions made to workers who wish to further their skill base or knowledge. Denying employees to acquire new skills may run the risk of employee stagnation and disengagement.
- Leaders to drive and embed into their business processes miniature in-services or group sessions for individuals who have recently attended a workshop or some form of training session. If individuals are forewarned

that they will be sharing their key learnings back with the workforce, this may become a trigger to listen more intently under the guise that information will have to be shared back with others. Being able to learn from colleagues is also a great avenue to enhance informal learning.

- Establishing growth, learning and development as a value or pinnacle part of the business that is supported by leadership and referenced often. Any mistakes can therefore be seen as an opportunity for growth. When applied to safety, the unwanted workplace incident can then become the opportunity for learning.

Leadership support is only one piece of the puzzle in terms of embedding the knowledge and ensuring a healthy transfer of learning. Organisational structure and establishing a learning organisation can have an influence on how one retains knowledge and applies that knowledge as part of their leadership ethos.

Organisational structure applied to the 'zero incident' dilemma

Companies and workplace cultures may be constituted by a mechanistic structure dictated by routine structures, practices and in some cases politics. Alternatively organic structures are characterised by flexible sharing of knowledge, flat reporting structure and responsiveness to workplace challenges (Alavi et al. 2014). Organisational structures that have a flat structure often promote clear communication as employees can be empowered to liaise and talk with all members of the company without positional power or pretence being a barrier and increased organisational agility being present (Alavi et al. 2014). An informed and communicative workforce is most likely a workforce that is sharing information where learning opportunities abound. Developing a learning organisation in terms of health and safety may go against the grain with such safety slogans as 'zero-harm' or 'zero-incidents' due to the implied absoluteness of such slogans.

The overall intention of safety metrics that revolve around 'zero-harm' are rooted within the moral philosophy that each organisation will not accept a workplace injury. Whilst I was exploring the ethos of what constitutes a safety leader, the hot topic of 'zero harm' was raised multiple times, where 90% of leaders interviewed outlined their dismay with such a safety vision or slogan. Prior to this disillusionment, there was a solid grounding to the notion of 'zero incidents'. The goal of zero incidents within the workplace started to emerge in the 1990s and may be an offshoot of socio-cultural policies of zero tolerance. The vision of zero incidents is closely aligned with high-reliability theory that states all injuries are preventable if suitable organisational practices are implemented (Weick & Sutcliffe 2001). Zero incidents started to become the ultimate safety goal, which contradicted normal accident theory that explains injuries are an unwanted natural process of hazardous work due to a complex socio-technical system (Cooke & Rohleder 2006). When used as a metric as opposed to a vision, the goal of zero incidents may denigrate safety efforts and cause disillusionment and minimise a learning organisation.

Behaviours that constitute a zero incident culture have been linked to people feeling empowered to take action, being knowledgeable and having the right attitude (Vecchio-Sadus 2012). The challenge is that these behaviours may not be directly observable or tangible, especially when looking at the covert factors of attitude. The importance of a strong safety culture in achieving zero incidents is evident though espoused slogans and associated organisational artefacts and posters, although the direct impact on employee safety behaviour may remain questionable. Relating to the goal of zero incidents or zero harm are the overarching elements of zero tolerance.

Outside the realms of safety, zero tolerance can be applied to criminal misdemeanours, gun control or drug policies. Research from Evans and Lester (2012) concluded that the results of such strategies vary upon the context and application of the policy. Further to this, Evans and Lester found zero tolerance policies do not cater for the social, emotional and behavioural support that provides long-term change. Similar notions can be applied within the safety culture realm where multiple events may be contributing to an overall safety incident. In contrast, the benefits of zero tolerance include outlining clear consequences for deviating from a clear mandate as well as enhanced collaboration across all departments (Blair 1999). Although the intentions may be clear for the desired behaviour, it creates a clear dichotomy for all behaviour that falls outside this scope. Other socio-technical influencers can affect individual behaviour. From a safety paradigm, zero tolerance can be inclusive of zero tolerance of injuries. In an absolute framework, the factors of safety culture and safety leadership are not considered; just the outcome is measured. Human behaviour is complex, and satellite factors of social influence, personality, client demands and production pressures provide the grey area that does not fit into the goal of zero incidents (Long 2012). Organisations that continue to espouse zero harm philosophies may be inadvertently shirking away the learning possibilities that abound within any organisation.

Many years ago I was sitting in a safety induction on a large scale oil and gas project where the company slogan was based around the goal of zero incidents. The safety advisor quipped that the project had already failed because there have already been incidents on the site. It was definitely an interesting start to an induction. Such comments outlined the literal and absolute stance that can be taken when such verbiage around zero is spoken. Another project manager shared with me his firm belief that achieving zero incidents can never occur as the site that he works at is an A Grade nature reserve where any oil spill is categorised as an incident. This included such miniscule oil spills of 20mls. This viewpoint is normal accident theory in action.

After talking to many workers across the globe, it has been shared with me multiple times that any pre-start meeting or daily meeting that commences with the number of days that have occurred on site incident and injury free is futile. This is based upon increased anxiety as the number of injury-free days start to edge closer to such milestones as 100 days or 500 days. It is always wise to celebrate safety wins and successes. Such celebrations may be better served by not celebrating a set number of incident and injury free days and instead focusing on safe behaviours that demonstrate the company's values. I always remember one site that I was working at where the safety record was abysmal, and the workers were constantly reminded of this record by a massive billboard that overlooked the company bus bay where the workers stepped off the bus and commenced their 12-hour shift. The framing of their day commenced with a visual reminder of how the site has not been able to achieve at least three weeks without an incident occurring, a sure way to inject confidence into the workforce. Such billboards and large signs reflect the vintage mindset of focusing on the undesirable to help motivate workers. Such a behavioural approach to motivation is the antithesis to innovation and therefore limits the learning organisation. Any learning from such an approach will be based upon how the workers are not performing as opposed to what they are doing well.

One colleague of mine shared a story with me that he was consulting to a large company that were quick to tout how they have had no incidents of any kind for 1500 days in an environment where hazards are abound and work is conducted in isolated areas. The authenticity of such a milestone was one thing, what was more telling was that the company was focusing on numbers as opposed to innovations, learning opportunities or other helpful lead indicators that can ensure the safety of the workforce. To help promote a culture of learning and openness, the following behaviours and actions can be incorporated into a company's practices:

- Minimise any verbiage associated with 'zero harm' or 'zero incidents' and instead focus on the desired behaviours that you would like to see within your company. The focus on 'zero' may minimise opportunities for learning and therefore have the undesired result of incidents being pushed underground or not reported at all.
- Embracing learning opportunities for any incident that occurs as opposed to focusing on punitive measures for incidents in the workplace. Any associated fear of reporting or being involved in an incident may decrease the opportunity for other people to learn from the same incident.
- Track any safety goals or measurements in the background and celebrate success as it occurs. The daily charting of incident free days that are visible to the workforce becomes arbitrary and places the focus on numbers as opposed to safe behaviours.
- Creating a safety vision that is contextualised for the workplace culture and site that is palatable enough for all sections of the workforce group to identify with. A mismatched safety vision or slogan can cause malaise and create a counter-culture of identity.

The importance of enabling workers to feel supported in reporting safety incidents and providing opportunities to report back any findings is paramount in preventing further injuries from occurring. On a smaller scale, I have seen first-hand the misgivings of failing to report incidents.

Whilst managing a rehabilitation company, I was flown to the head office to provide some mentoring for one of our junior psychologists. Hard polished floorboards, stainless steel appliances and copious amounts of glass doors and walls characterised the city-based office. The glass walls and doors were kept crystal clean, which did cause some slight confusion as there was no frosting on the glass and it gave the illusion that you can walk straight into another room without fuss. Whilst down in this office, I was wrapping up a conversation with a colleague based upon our psychological reporting format, as I got up and turned to walk away, I walked straight into the glass wall. After the typical profanity was uttered, I apologised and made my way to the bathroom to inspect the damage. What was staring back at me was an open gash on my forehead that needed 14 stitches to close up. As characterised by many companies, safety actions were taken post-incident and company-wide communication went across the nation suggesting that each office should get frosting on any glass wall or door.

Upon return to my regional office, one of my colleagues approached me and shared that the same incident nearly happened to her a few months earlier. Of course, when I asked if she told anyone about it, in a surprised tone she said 'no'. This lack of communication and reporting resulted in an incident that could have been prevented. This scenario only had dire cosmetic consequences to my medium-sized forehead. Amplify the factor of the non-reporting of incidents on a larger scale and the consequences could range from major injury or death. Openly encouraging reporting and sharing the learnings from such near-miss incidents or injuries on site can help enhance the transfer of learning but also embed the acquired behaviours into the organisation.

Role of self-leadership

Historical research from Argryis and Schon (1978) detailed three forms of learning which pertain to single loop learning, double loop learning and deutero learning. The differences between these learning styles are based upon identifying and solving problems, changing the way we think and learning to learn. Deutero learning can be the pinnacle of the leader who is thirsty for knowledge and has an unyielding quench for knowledge. To facilitate this quest for knowledge, the role of self-leadership comes to the foreground. Self-leadership may be defined as an individual's capacity to improve their own performance through self-regulation strategies which can be based upon motivational, behavioural or cognitive strategies (Napiersky & Woods 2016).

A failure of self-leadership may lead to a potential wastage in learning and development activities. Previous colleagues who facilitate a lot of workshops have shared with me their dubious feelings towards previous individuals who openly opt out or mentally resign during any potential training course or workshop. As a result, my colleagues started to feel a sense of resentment towards such individuals which therefore feeds into the reluctance of the potential participant to participate. This can then confirm the participant's reservations and reinforce the person's negative self-fulfilling prophecy towards training workshops. An exercise of self-leadership from both my colleagues and also the potential learning participant could mitigate such spiralling dire reservations.

To allow self-leadership to strengthen the transfer of learning, Napiersky and Woods (2016) found that setting self-guided goals, working towards such goals, being cognisant of your own motivation and a healthy level of optimism are strong predictors of learning success. One of the realities that may face many leaders is that certain individuals may attend a workshop or seminar reluctantly and therefore any learning opportunities may be cloaked in pessimism. To help foster self-leadership in these situations, the line manager or even facilitator of the session may ask the individual what their goals are and what they will do to help achieve such learning goals. Without desire or openness from an individual, the best pearls of wisdom may vanish into the ether and therefore limit potential growth and learning.

Behavioural strategies that can assist in self-leadership as applied to a learning context can be the self-observation of performance towards set goals, provision of self-rewards and regulating one's own behaviour (Neck & Houghton 2006). In addition, if the training is relevant and effective, it becomes a powerful factor towards motivating others to learn (Renta-Davids et al. 2014). One of the documented cognitive strategies to promote self-leadership as it applies to learning is the concept of reflexivity. This cognitive strategy may be dictated by the individual reflecting back on their own thinking and learning which can therefore allow greater integration of any new awareness into their current pattern of thinking (Meixner 2010). Other cognitive strategies may range from developing memory mnemonics, repetition of learning and ensuring there are no distractions when initially learning core information.

When individuals have challenges recalling information, it has been shown that it may be an issue with the initial encoding of the information as opposed to direct recall of information (Shelton et al. 2016). Pairing information with a visual cue may improve the learning outcome. Needless to say, any training or workshops conducted in chaotic environments may therefore impact the overall transfer of learning for participants. Some of my first-hand experiences that showcase poor encoding environments include workshops that were held in lunch rooms where there was a constant stream of individuals coming through to have their lunch or alternatively workshops held outdoors due to the electricity going out in the main training room.

A memory that sticks with me is a workshop I ran that was booked by a client at a local lawn bowls club. Upon reflection, the location was chosen due to the fiscal savings that were readily at hand. The problem was that there was no closed off training room, instead the training room was the open dining room turned into a training room, complete with a makeshift screen and sheets of A3 paper doubling up as a whiteboard. Given the training conducted was over an eight-hour period, it collided with the lunch time beers and afternoon drinks of the local patrons who would often stumble into the training room and ask for change for the nearby poker machines. The encoding process of the participants may therefore be impaired due to background noise of intoxicated patrons, the dazzling sound of poker machines and the open environment of the workshop which limited candid conversations about workplace strategy and culture.

If individuals are coachable then growth can occur, alternatively if they are closed and resistant to growth then opportunities will pass them by. One of the pathways to open up the doors to self-leadership for resistant individuals could be based upon the latest research into neuro-psychology. Neural activity in the insula and putamen areas of the brain has been associated with enhanced memory performance enhanced by emotionally charged events (Dirnberger et al. 2012). In addition, research by Gerraty and colleagues (2014) outlined that intrinsic brain dynamics can be precipitated by flexible learning behaviour, based upon fronto-parietal networks. The neuroscience therefore suggests that enhancing participant involvement can be guided through emotionally charged information and autonomous learning. From a safety leadership perspective, the route of emotions may be played upon the grim realities of poor safety leadership leading to potential incidents, whilst fun and interactive training sessions can kick start the amygdala and enhance memory retention. Oscillating between these emotions is the moderating factor of self-leadership.

Setting up for success

All efforts aimed at building the capability of safety leaders may become futile unless a range of precursory steps have been established. To counter the above risks and failures of learning and development programmes, additional hallmarks can be implemented that can foster a successful embedding of core information for both the individual and the company. Pre-cursory steps that have already been outlined include the gregariousness of the facilitator, leadership support towards learning initiatives, flexible organisational structure and the enabling of self-leadership. On a macro level, one of the ways that an organisation can establish a smooth transfer of learning is by seeding a learning organisation. The work from Tait and Blinco (2014) outlined the importance of all staff being involved in informal learning and having supportive leadership that provides a shared purpose and clear direction. Further pathways to create a learning organisation include allowing opportunities for individuals to share their learnings with others.

From a safety leadership paradigm, the seeding of the learning organisation may be evident through leaders openly supporting the reporting of incidents and sharing any corrective actions that result from an incident. Ensuring that employees are informed about the success of any implemented actions is one way to close the communication loop. On one mine site I was working at, there was a dual culture that existed in terms of safety. Employees were compliant with work practices and risk management systems, although feedback on any incidents that occurred or hazards that were reported was minimal. Of course, without accessible, clear communication, individuals would not be informed of what behaviours needed modification, which resulted in similar incidents occurring. Curtailing such a situation might have been prevented through all staff being regularly informed of the outcomes of any incident investigation that had occurred. Pathways for such forums could be through daily meetings or monthly toolbox talks or other such mediums where recognition of employee input can be provided and communicated to all.

The reinforcement of the learning organisation can be precipitated by any additional qualifications gained through training being used as an extension of a current job function. It has been shown that rewarding additional qualifications through the teaching or passing on of knowledge to others can lead to lower staff turnover and result in training being seen in a positive light (Williams, Schmollgruber & Alberto 2006). If applying newly acquired knowledge as a function of role extension, a level of maturity and individual readiness is needed. You can just imagine the outcome of a demure individual being tasked with teaching others their new skills when the mere thought of public speaking causes the person's hands to become dry and clammy. Their breathing may become shallow which then triggers the onset of a full-fledged panic attack. Prior to the acquisition of any new skills, the purpose, outcome and integration of the knowledge may need to be discussed prior to the person attending any workshop or seminar. Allowing the individual to exercise self-leadership can be linked to increased proficiency, adaptability and pro-activeness (Hauschildt & Konradt 2012), which may increase the chances of any new knowledge being passed on to others.

Increasing the inter-team transfer of knowledge may also be best suited if the prospective workshop has been designed in collaboration with the education providers and key members of the organisation. Through this collaboration, the relevance of the material can be vetted, as well as maximising the correct application of new skills and knowledge within the workplace (Meyer et al. 2007). A collaborative endeavour also shows an attempt by the organisation to invest time and energy in ensuring the content suits the culture and the target audience. In a constantly changing operating environment and in the midst of economic turmoil, these factors are pivotal and can put a plug in the gashing hole of money which can occur if training is not catered for the audience. Not being able to fulfil course numbers may create company pressure to fill course places, which may lead to inappropriate selection of participants where content does not match the job role.

The deep interaction of all key stakeholders into every aspect of the learning and transfer process with respect to roles and responsibilities has been shown to prove a holistic approach to learning transfer (Kawalilak 2012). Such contextualisation of content and course material with the organisation can give credence to the increasing number of internal consultants being employed by larger companies. Expanding learning and development teams may be a common choice for larger companies as a replacement for external consultants. The maturity of the company, expertise of employees and organisational culture may influence the choice of whether or not to use external consultants.

When developing safety leaders, be that through the use of internal capabilities or external providers, the following steps may assist in ensuring a successful transfer of knowledge:

- How is learning and development currently approached in your company? Are training courses seen as a nuisance or viewed favourably by leaders as a way to build new skills into the organisation? If a culture of learning is not valued by leaders, then any potential leadership programmes will be seen as a mandatory exercise or 'flavour of the month'.
- Within your company, is there current expertise that can be tapped into that can help facilitate and share core knowledge, or does that information need to be sought elsewhere? Such answers to these questions can dictate whether external consultants may be needed or internal consultants can be utilised.
- With any proposed leadership process or programme being implemented into a company, start with the outcomes and deliverables of such a process. Once the outcomes and desired behaviours have been articulated, then the development and contextualisation of the content can occur with key stakeholders. Without consultation or broader communication, the content may miss the mark and fuel resistance once an individual attends any coaching or training session.
- Leaders to support any learning process through their own active participation and involvement. By modelling such involvement it allows greater support to their team members to attend any training or coaching sessions. If individuals are not authorised to attend training due to operational requirements or more pressing work, this may speak volumes of what kind of learning organisation exists.
- Utilising technology and supporting structures can further embed core concepts. Examples of this may vary from webinars, blogs, case studies, integration of principles into work plans, podcasts or past participants sharing what they have learned from the leadership process to new participants.
- Measuring the change in the leadership initiative through agreed upon variables, which can include a pre-test and post-test self-leadership assessment or alternatively 360 feedback assessment. Other measurements may include retention rates, safety climate results, injury-incident rates, innovations within the company or visible change in behaviours as measured by third parties (coaches) or other impartial individual.

Coinciding with all of the above considerations is the minutia of detail that can also influence the success of the learning initiative. This includes the sourcing of the right coach, developing a training matrix, organising training rooms, tracking attendance and relevant statistics as well as ensuring a robust communication plan to all key stakeholders. Developing safety leaders is not a transactional approach as influencers can range from organisational factors to internal variables such as motivation or self-leadership. Many training initiatives become transactional due to a lack of supporting initiatives or absence of a long-term strategy.

Case study

An innovative safety leadership programme was being introduced by a consulting company into an organisation of over 1000 individuals. The composition of the workforce was roughly 80% craft workers and 20% technical experts or leaders. An organisational decision was made to roll out the safety programme to all employees, which constituted a two-day workshop with the quorum being 15 participants. The reasoning behind the company-wide roll-out was based upon safety being pivotal to all employees regardless of their job role or job position. Each workshop was costed at around $20,000 based upon full attendance of each workshop.

The embedding plan post-workshops was based upon key language being reinforced across site through posters and monthly emails expanding upon the content shared in the workshops. Leaders were asked to reinforce the language through their leadership meetings and call upon examples of how they have integrated the information into their work or personal lives. Prior to roll-out, a pilot group was run with both craft workers and the leadership team. Feedback was favourable and a schedule of training was created.

After two years, the majority of the organisation was trained and the obligatory posters were placed around the work site. The initial costings of the roll-out was exceeded by over $750,000 due to participants not being released to attend training or full numbers not being maximised during each workshop. After a period of time, questions were being raised by the board members such as 'what is the actual change in behaviour, besides this new language that has been created?' and 'why haven't we had full numbers on each course?' The answers to these questions were not easy to answer, and after further review any remaining training sessions were cancelled until a larger embedding strategy was implemented.

Questions

Q1. What could be some historical organisational factors that could be influencing the overall attendance rate of the scheduled workshops?

Q2. How could the consultants better gauge the organisational culture or contextualise the workshop content prior to commencing the training workshops?

Q3. If all of the workshops are run by consultants, what could be the business and fiscal risks of such an approach if internal resources are not being trained or coached?

Q4. How could the embedding strategy be better planned to ensure a successful roll-out of information and to ensure a culture of learning?

Epilogue

Once the consulting company were asked to cease any further training sessions, an internal review was undertaken within the company. From this review it was revealed that training was not seen as a priority compared to operational requirements, and in some instances the training was used for punitive measures if an employee had a 'bad attitude'. In such instances an employee might have been sent to the same training course twice. After a series of focus groups, the general consensus was that the workshops were well run and the information was deemed relevant for leaders but not as relevant for craft workers. Post-training, a lot of the core content taught was forgotten. The participation of key leaders was also absent which created a lack of consistency in language in certain sections of the workforce.

To enhance the embedding strategy, it was decided by the company that refresher courses would be needed to keep the information fresh. Further to this, discipline would be applied to any leader who did not allow their team members to attend the training. Content was also slightly varied to include more workplace examples as opposed to general examples shared in the workshop. With these amendments in place, the external consultants re-engaged the business and completed the remaining workshops and returned in 12 months to run refresher sessions to coincide with monthly toolbox talks and other forums. The consulting organisation did not realise this, but many attempts were previously made at establishing effective leadership behaviours within the company and failed miserably due to a lack of initial uptake or leadership buy-in.

What was missing from the embedding strategy was metrics to measure a change in behaviour as well as a plan to develop internal capability to minimise a dependency on the consulting company. Train the trainer sessions or other similar options were not discussed, and the success of the safety leadership process was measured by the attendance rates of participants. Coaching options to reinforce learnings from the leadership group were absent, and there was no additional support for leaders to share how content could be applied to the work front. In addition, the initial pilot group was made up of the more agreeable participants who exercise self-leadership and welcome any learning opportunities. The pilot group would have been better suited towards a random cross section of the leadership group and workforce. Finally, there was no measurement of safety culture or other measurement to ascertain the current state prior to the safety leadership implementation. It is challenging to measure changes in behaviour or impact upon the individual unless a baseline is established.

Organisational and personal application

The following suggestions can be integrated into your organisation or as part of your own personal safety leadership ethos. Comments are based upon the importance of the transfer of learning and chapter content.

Organisational application

- Is there a culture of learning present in the company? How is knowledge currently shared in the company and what is the usual response when leaders are asked to attend a workshop? If learning and development initiatives are seen as a chore as opposed to an investment, any leadership implementation may need to be put on hold until this issue is addressed.
- What could be some opportunities for employees to share back any key learnings that they have learned from any workshop or coaching process they have been through? Is there allocated time embedded into leadership meetings for fellow leaders to share some of their core learnings or to share what their commitment will be? If processes do not exist which allow a free sharing of information, then informal learning opportunities are wasted.
- Is there a formalised strategy that links any learning and development process to the broader company strategy and key outcomes? The absence of a broader strategy or articulated learning and development goals may equate to multiple workshops being run without any synergies or linkages between each programme or process. As a result, it becomes training for the sake of training.
- Are there clear pathways of development that have been clearly communicated within the organisation? Specific training programmes that have a clear selection criteria can be linked up well with an extension of responsibility and allowing individual growth in their current job role. Establishing clear selection criteria ensures that any learning programme is pitched towards the right audience and is relevant for their position.

Individual application

- What could be some helpful questions you can ask your team members when they return from any workshop or coaching session? What could be some questions that extend beyond the generic 'how did you go?' line of questioning. Such examples may include 'what will you do differently?' or 'how would I know there has been an effective change in behaviour?' or other specific questions that are catered for your team member.
- Reflect upon your own attitudes to growth and development. Do you actively seek out learning opportunities or only find yourself attending workshops when asked to by your company? A thirst for knowledge and development can create innovative ways of thinking and allow personal and organisational growth.

- How do you currently demonstrate self-leadership in terms of learning and development activities? Are you more of a self-directed learner or need to be motivated in order to grasp new ideas and concepts? Assessing your own level of self-leadership can help provide insight into specific actions that may need to be modified. As safety leaders, what one does can influence others through their direct actions.
- With all of the knowledge and information you possess, how do you currently share this knowledge with others? Is core information shared through general discussions or other informal ways, or is information passed on through a mentoring relationship? The informal sharing of knowledge contributes to a learning culture and minimises a dependency on one specific person.

Chapter summary

The mere attendance of any specific workshop or coaching session is not the panacea for a change in an individual's behaviour. To capitalise on any learning initiative, supporting measures are needed which extend beyond the person and relate back to organisational variables such as leadership support and supportive learning through structured processes. Translating leadership theory into practice can cause some slight discomfort for individuals, although the embedding of change can be assisted through self-reflection and conscious practice of new ideas or behaviours. Prior to any potential safety leadership roll-out, objectives should be clear and consideration of supporting processes need to be astutely thought out to maximise any potential return on investment. Learning is an ongoing process, and incorporating new knowledge into the organisation can have the dual benefit of increased competitive advantage for the business as well as personal growth for the individual.

References

Alavi, S, Wahab, DA, Muhamad, N & Shirani, BA 2014, 'Organic structure and organisational learning as the main antecedents of workforce agility', *International Journal of Production Research*, 52(21), 6273–6295.

Argyris, C & Schon, D 1978, *Organizational Learning: A Theory of Action Perspective*, Addison Wesley, Reading, MA.

Atwater, LE & Yammarino, FJ, 1996, 'Bases of power in relation to leader behaviour: A field investigation', *Journal of Business and Psychology*, 11(1), 3–22.

Blair, FE 1999, 'Does zero tolerance work?', *Principle*, 79(1), 36–37.

Cooke, DL & Rohleder, TR 2006, 'Learning from incidents: From normal accidents to high reliability', *System Dynamics Review*, 22(3), 213–239.

Dirnberger, G, Hesselmann, G, Roiser, JP & Preminger, S 2012, 'Give it time: Neural evidence for distorted time perception and enhanced memory encoding in emotional situations', *Neuroimage*, 63, 591–599.

Evans, KR & Lester, JN 2012, 'Zero tolerance: Moving the conversation forward', *Intervention in School and Clinic*, 48(2), 108–114.

Futris, TG, Schramm, DG, Richardson, EW & Lee, TK 2015, 'The impact of organisational support on the transfer of learning to practice', *Children and Youth Services Review*, 51, 36–43.

Geller, SE 2008, *Leading People-based Safety: Enriching Your Culture*, Coastal Training Technologies Corp., Virginia Beach.

Gerraty, RT, Davidow, JY, Wimmer, GE, Kahn, I & Shohamy, D 2014, 'Transfer of learning to intrinsic connectivity between hippocampus, ventromedial prefrontal cortex, and large scale networks', *The Journal of Neuroscience*, 34(34), 11297–11303.

Hauschildt, K & Konradt, U 2012, 'Self-leadership and team members' work role performance', *Journal of Managerial Psychology*, 27(5), 497–515.

Hogan, K 2003, *The Psychology of Persuasion: How to Persuade Others to Your Way of Thinking*, Pelican Publishing Company, Gretna.

Holton, EF III, Bates, RA, Bookter, AI & Yamkovenko, VB 2007, 'Convergent and divergent validity of the learning transfer system inventory', *Human Resource Development Quarterly*, 18(3), 385–419.

Hrybouski, S, Aghamohammadi-Sereshki, A, Madan, CR & Shafer, AT 2016, 'Amygdala subnuclei response and connectivity during emotional processing', *Neuroimage*, 133, 98–110.

Kawalilak, CA 2012, 'Successful transfer of learning', *The Canadian Journal for the Study of Adult Education*, 25(1), 75.

Kim, JH & Callahan, JL 2013, 'Finding the intersection of the learning organisation and learning transfer: The significance of leadership', *European Journal of Training and Development*, 37(2), 183–200.

Kirkpatrick, DL & Kirkpatrick, JD 2006, *Evaluating Training Programs: The Four Levels*, Berrett-Koehler Publishers, San Francisco.

Krause, TT 2005, *Leading with Safety*, John Wiley & Sons, Hoboken.

Long, R 2012, *For the Love of Zero: Human Fallibility and Risk*, Scotoma Press, Kambah.

Marsick, VJ & Watkins, KE 2003, 'Demonstrating the value of an organisation's learning culture: The dimensions of the learning organisation questionnaire', *Advances in Developing Human Resources*, 5(2), 132–151.

Meixner, C 2010, 'Reconciling self, servant leadership, and learning: The journey of the east as locus for reflection and transformation', *Journal of Leadership Studies*, 3(4), 81–85.

Meyer, E, Lees, A, Humphris, D & Connell, NAD 2007, 'Opportunities and barriers to successful learning transfer: Impact of critical care skills training', *Journal of Advanced Nursing*, 60(3), 308–316.

Napiersky, U & Woods, SA 2016, 'From the workplace to the classroom: Examining the impact of self-leadership learning strategies on higher educational attainment and success', *Innovations in Education and Teaching International*, doi:10.1080/14703297.2016.1263232

Neck, CP & Houghton, JD 2016, 'Two decades of self-leadership theory and research: Past developments, present trends and future possibilities', *Journal of Managerial Psychology*, 26, 463–480.

Renta-Davids, AI, Jimenez-Gonzalez, JMJ, Fandos-Garrido, M & Gonzalez-Soto, AP 2014, 'Transfer of learning: Motivation, training design and learning-conductive work effects', *European Journal of Training and Development*, 38(8), 728–744.

Shelton, JT, Lee, JH, Scullin, MK, Rose, NS, Rendell, PG & McDaniel, MA 2016, 'Improving prospective memory in healthy older adults and individuals with very mild Alzheimer's disease', *Journal of the American Geriatrics Society*, 64(6), 1307–1312.

Stewart, LJ & Palmer, S 2009, 'Capitalising on coaching investment: Enhancing coaching transfer', *Development and Learning in Organisations*, 23(3), 14–17.

Tait, A & Blinco, K 2014, 'Seeing a learning organisation', *The Australian Library Journal*, 63(2), 94–107.

Uleman, JS, Saribay, SA & Gonzalez, CM 2008, 'Spontaneous inferences, implicit impressions and implicit theories', *Annual Review of Psychology*, 59, 329–360.

Vecchio-Sadus, A 2012, 'The safety leadership challenge – Pathway to impact', The 2nd Annual Safety Psychology Conference October 29–31, Sydney, NSW, pp. 1–9.

Weick, KE & Sutcliffe, KM 2001, *Managing the Unexpected: Assured High Performance in an Age of Complexity*, Jossey-Bass, San Francisco.

Williams, G, Schmollgruber, S & Alberto, L 2006, 'Consensus forum: Worldwide guidelines on the critical care nursing workforce and education standards', *Critical Care Clinics*, 17, 237–241.

7   Journey forward

Continuing to challenge the status quo …

Safety leadership is a multi-faceted concept that goes well beyond the mantra of 'leading with safety'. The concepts discussed so far help provide context and suggestions for organisational application and more importantly leadership application across many industries. By understanding the definitions of what safety leadership entails and the variances of safety leadership across different job positions, consistency across multiple industries can be achieved. The unfounded definitions of safety leadership may lead to confusion and failed attempts at developing safety leaders. How one defines safety leadership may influence how one demonstrates safety leadership which then translates to tangible safety leadership behaviours.

Demonstrated actions speak volumes compared to good intent. Safety leaders who model safe behaviours start to set a foundation of expected behaviours for their team members. Each person is unique and has their own set of attitudes, skills and varied backgrounds. Adjusting your safety leadership style to the environment allows flexibility but also authenticity in demonstrating safety leadership behaviours. A conscious focus on transformational behaviours will extend beyond the safety compliance behaviours that are often expected from safety leaders. Through the RAVE model, a pathway was established to allow safety leaders to exercise safety leadership.

The tenets of relationships, authenticity, vision and engagement were shown as the core pillars to safety leadership. Further detail around each aspect provided guidance notes for organisational leaders. Change is constant and with this certainty in mind, it would be unwise to consider that any safety leadership paradigm will be set in stone. As organisations develop, so will leaders and their teams. Tweaks, amendments or further progressions to the RAVE model may start to emerge. Any additions are welcomed, as it would be naive and self-serving to believe that any set theory is permanent. It would be similar to saying that all leaders are unchangeable and cannot adjust their leadership style

Culture is the integral component of piecing all of the nuances of an organisation together which therefore becomes the unspoken blueprint of how employees should behave. Analysing culture can be undertaken through various means and effectively done when combined with new paradigms emerging with safety. Constant innovation may be the key to achieving the utopian goal of an engaged and safe workforce where well-being is the key to unlocking the intellectual potential of each employee through new and interactive methods. As one leader said to me many years ago, safety is similar to peddling a bike up hill. It is a constant effort and as soon as you stop peddling, that is when things start to go downhill. Through innovation, the means to get to the top of the hill may vary but the goal may remain the same. The archetypal safety dogma was challenged through the structure of the 5i's which pertain to intent, intelligence, instigate, implement and internalise. Through the 5i's methodology, a successful transference of knowledge and embedding of skills for safety leaders can be achieved within an organisation. An examination of the pitfalls of learning and development activities showed many reasons why such initiatives may fail in terms of achieving a successful transfer of knowledge. True safety leadership may encompass the establishment of supporting processes that allow any core information captured in a workshop or coaching session to be shared. Peer and group informal learning can sow the seeds of a learning organisation, where knowledge is valued, celebrated and promoted. Emerging from such a philosophy are the potential next stages and potential future pathways for safety leadership across the globe.

Imagine an organisation where authentic conversations are the norm and safety means more than just abiding by the policies and procedures. In this organisation relationships are the social collateral to get work done, and everyone is working towards a collective vision that is palatable to all. Leaders are seen and not just heard and there is no pretence to their interactions. Leaders are just as approachable as your trusted colleague and are not only open to feedback, but regularly request feedback. Safety and well-being go hand in hand and innovation is not only promoted, but justly rewarded. To transfer this vision of the possible to a reality, the generation of group learning and establishing a learning community may be warranted. Various platforms can act as the medium to allow such a sharing of information. Other traditional methods of sharing key lessons learned may be through organised forums, conferences, journal articles and of course through the power of the employees who share their experiences with others.

When exercised well, the merits of effective safety leadership can cross over to enhanced organisational culture and the moral and human justification of enhanced safety and well-being. Minimising workplace incidents can ensure the associated heartache and pain does not have to be felt by employees and their close friends and family members. For these benefits to be realised, the next evolution of safety leadership may be birthed through the fundamental and practical concepts shared thus far or perhaps the establishment of any new paradigms that emerge. Either way, the macro goal roughly remains the same, which is ensuring the well-being and health of others. Strong safety leadership also equates to effective leadership.

Empathy, authenticity, a powerful vision, rapport building skills and the engagement of others can allow safety leaders to leave a lasting legacy behind and allow one to be remembered in a way that inspires others to action. The legacy you leave behind will be echoed through the life of the company you work with. Create the vision and exercise the pillars of knowledge shared thus far. Ensure any success or failure is captured and shared with others, where others can benefit from your experiences. A community of one is isolating compared to a community of many. All the best in your safety leadership journey.

Index

Information in figures is indicated by page numbers in *italics,* information in tables is indicated by page numbers in **bold.**